THE MILITARIZATION OF CULTURE
IN THE DOMINICAN REPUBLIC,
FROM THE CAPTAINS GENERAL
TO GENERAL TRUJILLO

The Militarization
of Culture
in the Dominican Republic,
from the
Captains General
to General Trujillo

Valentina Peguero

University of Nebraska Press
Lincoln and London

Library of Congress
Cataloging-in-Publication Data
Peguero, Valentina.
The militarization of culture in the Dominican Republic, from the
captains general to General Trujillo / Valentina Peguero.
p. cm. – (Studies in war, society, and the military)
Includes bibliographical references and index.
ISBN 0-8032-3741-3 (cloth : alk. paper)
1. Civil-military relations – Dominican Republic – History.   2. Social
control – Dominican Republic – History.   3. Dominican Republic –
Social life and customs.   4. Dominican Republic – Politics and government – 1844–1930.   5. Dominican Republic – Politics and
government – 1930–1961.   6. Dominican Republic – Military policy.
I. Title.   II. Series.
F1938.4.P44 2004
972.93 – dc22
2004011874

To Eusebia, Angel Leoncio, and Rafael Ignacio Peguero Reyes
in loving memory of our parents,
Angel Peguero and Isabel María Reyes de Peguero.

CONTENTS

ILLUSTRATIONS

Photographs

Following page 90

Tables

ACKNOWLEDGMENTS

The generosity of many people who shared their knowledge and skills with me has made this study possible. Bernardo Vega in particular allowed me to review his valuable collection of documents from the U.S. National Archives, shared ideas, and kindly read and commented on the manuscript. The scholarly advice and suggestions of Roberto Cassá and Danilo de los Santos, as well as the insights of Rafael Vidal, helped me to better understand the intricacy of the Trujillo regime. I also appreciate the comments of William Skelton, who offered his expertise from the perspective of a military historian.

The voices of many gave life and substance to this work. Juan Bosch and Pedro Mir, despite many commitments, graciously took time to answer my questions and offer valuable insights and advice. Former generals Renato Hungría, José Joaquín Hungría, and Ramiro Matos Gonzalez, former colonel Luis Montes de Oca, General Clarence Charles Dunlop, Major General Luis Antonio Luna Paulino, former navy officer Alfredo Balcácer Vega, and others helped me to better grasp the complexities of military issues. Interviewees who did not require anonymity are gratefully acknowledged in the notes of each chapter. Thanks also to other interviewees who shared their insights but requested anonymity.

I am indebted to several professors and friends who, during the research for my dissertation, helped me deal with the core of this work, particularly Herbert Klein, Lambros Comitas, Rosario Espinal, Deborah Levenson, Carmen Durán, Francisco Henríquez, and Dato Pagán Perdomo.

My gratitude also goes to Carmen Iris Olivo and Andrea Merán Merán, who helped arrange many official and military contacts. I greatly appreciate the courtesy and facilities offered by Don Ramón Bernard and Vilma Benzo de Ferrer at the Archivo General de la Nación and

Museo de Historia y Geografía, respectively. María Nuñez de Taveras, Leovigildo Rodríguez, and the library staff of the Pontificia Universidad Católica Madre y Maestra facilitated the use of the collections in Santo Domingo and Santiago. Similarly, Carmen Iris Olivo and the staff of the library of the Universidad Nacional Pedro Henríquez Ureña helped in many ways. Antonio Báez, Enrique Campos, and Tom Reich provided valuable research support.

I appreciate the assistance of Anne Dyken, Richard Kopitzke, Henning Pape-Santos, Mary Nell Reif, and Arcadio Torres. Likewise, Colleen Angel, Christine Neidlein, Margaret Whalen, and other staff from the University of Wisconsin–Stevens Point Learning Resources Center kindly offered assistance and cooperation. Similarly, my gratitude goes to Luis Villar, Ibero-American bibliographer at the University of Wisconsin–Madison. My thanks also goes to Sandy Wanserski for her computer skills, humor, and for all those years of patience, to my sister Eusebia Peguero, who steadily provided assistance in various ways, and to Jan Swinford for her help and good will.

I would also like to express my appreciation for Juan Luis Abascal for his constructive suggestions, editing, and kindness. I am most grateful to the anonymous readers, and to Edward Paulino, whose criticism helped to make the book stronger. I regret I cannot name list the names of so many others who contributed to this book.

I was fortunate to work with the skilled editorial staff of University of Nebraska Press. For their advice, guidance, and support, I thank Gary H. Dunham, Elizabeth A. S. Demers and Terence Smyre. My thanks also go to Jennifer Backer for diligently putting together the final copy of the manuscript. Finally, my heartfelt gratitude goes to my husband, William Lawlor, who in addition to reading the manuscript in various forms, offered understanding, support, and patience, providing the tenacity required for the completion of this study. I could not have done this work without him.

INTRODUCTION
Historical Perspective

Libertad! Democracia! Libertad! Democracia! Democracia y Libertad! By the end of July 1961, Dominicans, for the first time in three decades, uttered these words with rage about the past, and with hope about the future. Early in June, my brothers, my sister, and I arose to the authoritative voice of our father, who, serious but expectant, told us, "Get up. Get dressed. Do not leave the house." Then he added, "I think it really happened."

Having said these words, he went out into the street. There he learned that the rumor that had been circulating for several days but many believed was a hoax was in fact true: Rafael Leonidas Trujillo Molina, the cruel dictator of the Dominican Republic for thirty years, had been killed by high-ranking civilian and military conspirators.

Our father returned to the house and shared the news, and we clearly understood. Ambushed and shot to death on the evening of May 30, Trujillo was no longer our nation's leader. What we did not fully understand at that time, however, was that Trujillo's military rule and militaristic values had left their imprint not only on the armed forces but also on Dominican society as a whole.

Before Trujillo came to power, a military culture, well embedded in Dominican society, had developed from a long tradition of armed struggles that allowed military leaders to move onto the political stage. In fact, of all the political, social, and economic forces that shaped modern Dominican history, none was more at the center of national life than the military.

A contemporary global development, the high level of participation of the armed forces in government has given rise to a wide range of theoretical approaches on militarism. According to Western liberal tradition, militarism is the domination of the military over civilians, emphasizing military thought in the life of the state; in Marxist theory, militarism is a social phenomenon "born with the split of society into classes."[1] The definition of militarism also varies from industrialized nations to Third World countries. Despite these differences, a number of scholars have conceptualized militarism as an influential force that permeates the political life of a nation by interfering in the political process for a short or long period of time.[2] Militarism, however, is not confined to the military and military activities. Militarism is also the "prevalence of military thinking and assumptions" in the day-to-day operations of society.[3]

Tracing the roots and development of this phenomenon, some specialists argue that militarism flourishes where democratic governments fail. Others argue that the division of power of the democratic system is "a perpetual invitation, if not an irresistible force, drawing military leaders into political conflicts."[4] Hypotheses of military political action also include theories about professional militarism or the "propensity and willingness to apply solutions based on a deeply traditional military ethos to national problems."[5] In broad terms, internal factors (economic crisis, political instability, alliance with specific groups) and external factors (influence and interference from outside forces or foreign countries) have contributed to military control of domestic politics.

The process of militarizing minds is intrinsically connected to militarization. Like militarism, militarization is a multifaceted term that implies numerous forms and different means for different segments of society. The terms are similar; there is not a clear-cut distinction between them. In fact, some understand the concept of militarization as fundamentally encapsulated in militarism. Nevertheless, militarization is customarily viewed in terms of the socioeconomic impact of the military on society and the preparation for war. Militarization is also regarded as the "encroachment of military forms, personnel and practices upon civilian institutions or social orders."[6]

Based on the premise that militarism and militarization engendered a military culture that permeated society, this book examines the evolution of Dominican military history and its impact on society from colonial times through the era of Trujillo. As the ultimate example of a Dominican officer who took control of the state, Trujillo and his militaristic regime are the primary focus of this book. The characteristics of the regime are in line with several indicators of militarism and militarization, such as deviation from democratic rule, chauvinism, discipline, glorification of power, high military expenditure, and others discussed by Marek Thee in his analysis of militarism and militarization.[7]

In this work *militarization* is mostly presented as a tangible, visible manifestation of the instruments of power, in terms of expenses, manpower, equipment, and civilian participation (for example, having citizens wear uniforms and receive military training). Militarism refers to the transcendence of military authority over civilian society and the military way of life. It also embodies militaristic attitudes—discipline, obedience, respect—imbued in the mind and psyche of the citizenry.

Salutations common among Dominican citizens, for example, reflect the means of communication in military culture. It is not unusual to hear Dominican men greet each other with expressions such as "Hola, General! Que tal jefe?" (Hello, General! How are you chief?) The expressions reflect the former military hierarchical command and the prolonged influence of the military in society. They also demonstrate how Dominicans' linguistic expressions call attention to power and military rank.

The genesis of this process goes back to the colonial period, when political positions and privileges granted to soldiers and officers tended to elevate the army above society. The prevalence of the military became evident by the early 1600s when the Spanish Crown named captains general as colonial governors of Santo Domingo. Based on hierarchy and subordination, their command and presence established an enduring trope in the Dominican imagination. With this figurative association at work, subsequent military figures transcended their authority to achieve domination over civilian society.

In this convergence of military and civilian power during the national period, soldiers like José María Cabral and Ulises Heureaux became politicians, mixing their military ability with charismatic qualities to exert power. As Dominican history shows, the involvement of the military in domestic politics was the government's primary concern, as politicians and military leaders used the armed forces to seize and retain power. Between 1844 and 1899, while struggling to establish an institutional framework for order and progress, the Dominican Republic had no fewer than fifty rulers, the majority of whom were military men. Similarly, in the twentieth century, military forces dominated the political affairs of the state. In fact, the period 1916–61 is the most compelling example of the military in power. In 1916 the United States intervened and installed a military government, which stayed in power until 1924. Just six years later, General Trujillo came to power and ruled for the next three decades, leaving his imprint on the development of the Dominican Republic.

Who was Trujillo? A stirring vision of determination and power, Trujillo, commander in chief of the Dominican military, was an ambitious thirty-nine-year-old general when he took control of the state in 1930. Once in command he developed a diverse and substantial military force, accumulated great power and influence, established singular authority over society, and glorified himself in the eyes of his countrymen. And he did all these things for thirty-one years. A product of Dominican culture and society, Trujillo lasted longer than any other Latin American dictator of his time.

How did he achieve such enduring status? Beyond the formative power of culture and history and beyond the authority achieved through military might, Trujillo's enduring authority involved a masterful combination of domestic and international politics. Nationally, the power of a strong military culture was on his side. Internationally, with the assistance of such countries as the United States, Spain, and Brazil, he built and equipped an army, navy, air force, and intelligence system that gave him domestic power that successfully set aside any challenges to his authority.

Furthermore, when Trujillo took control of the state, the Dominican National Guard, organized by the U.S. Marines, was a highly trained unit that had control over the country's arsenal. Trujillo controlled both men and weapons. In this respect, combining the instruments of power with military values, Trujillo used the armed forces to impose a new order in society that allowed soldiers to interact extensively with civilians.

Trujillo's use of the Dominican military to exert political leadership responded to a Latin American pattern of military interference in civilian affairs. Studies of the military have shown that during the first three-quarters of the twentieth century, most Latin American nations were under some type of military rule. From 1930 to 1960, strongmen became prevalent throughout the region. (Other dictators contemporaneous to Trujillo were Anastasio Somoza in Nicaragua, Getulio Vargas in Brazil, Domingo Perón in Argentina, Fulgencio Batista in Cuba, Marcos Pérez Jiménez in Venezuela, Carlos Castillo Armas in Guatemala, Gustavo Rojas Pinilla in Colombia, and Francois Duvalier in Haiti.) However, not all military regimes in the region were the same; they fell within a broad range of ideological identifications or political factions including military socialism (Bolivia, 1936–39), military-populism (Peru, 1962 and 1968), and military constitutionalism (the Dominican Republic, 1965). In each case, the leaders vied with other military groups for control of the government.

The overwhelming presence of the armed forces in the political life of these nations has provoked new analysis of the civilian-military relationship.[8] Social scientists have tried to understand how the military dominates or strongly influences the political system to the extent that for a period of ten years (1948–58) in Argentina, Brazil, and Chile, populist governments had "to adopt a moderate to conservative course as a requisite for survival" or collapse under the pressure of the armed forces.[9]

At the close of the twentieth century, there were fewer attempts by the military in Latin America to rule government directly. The heavy-handed military dictatorship fell out of favor politically after the fall of the repressive regime in Paraguay of Alfredo Stroessner in 1989. Having passed a decade (1989–99) without a single coup d'état, like a volcanic eruption, military political activism has reemerged in Latin America. The latest events are the rise to power of the former colonel Hugo Chávez in Venezuela in November 1999 and the military coup that toppled President Jamil Mahuad of Ecuador in January 2000. In the middle of April 2002 Chavez survived a botched coup attempt led by a group of high-ranking officers.

Before 1930 in the Dominican Republic, officers acting as politicians had a decisive role in changing governments and taking control of the state, as did Trujillo. During his reign Trujillo applied a traditional military ethos to solve national problems and strongly influenced the political, economic, and social fabric of the country. His idea of government may be extracted from his own writings, such as *Cartilla cívica para el pueblo dominicano*, *La nueva patria dominicana*, *Fundamentos y política de un régime*, and *El pensamiento político de un estadista*, and the military journal *La revista militar*. Aimed at demonstrating Trujillo's vision for the future, these works and other texts explain how many of Trujillo's political and military goals eventually became state policy.

The Trujillo era is complex. As Robert Crassweller states, Trujillo was "too important, too complex, and too colorful a man, and his influence on the life of the hemisphere was too great."[10] He devised a system aimed at developing and consolidating his political power by improving and strengthening the military apparatus, but Trujillo was incongruous.

Many of his actions were contradictory. At times he portrayed himself as a paternal figure; other times he was destructive. A U.S. official sarcastically interpreted the difficulties in dealing with Trujillo's changes, which invariably were reflected in the regime, as "feminine, as [in] Trujillo blows hot and blows cold."[11]

Owing to its complexity in both form and content, Trujillo's regime has generated considerable interdisciplinary study, ranging from historical to fictional accounts. Mario Vargas Llosa's novel *The Feast of the Goat* (2001) has captured the imagination and the attention of readers and has elevated interest in Trujillo and his time.[12] Nonfiction works focusing primarily on the military are *Todo por Trujillo* (1999) by Juan José Ayuso, *Las fuerzas militares en la República Dominicana* (1996) by José Miguel Soto Jiménez, and *Trujillo y las fuerzas armadas norteamericanas* (1992) by Bernardo Vega. In addition to a considerable number of articles, theses, and dissertations, in the last ten years alone many stimulating historical and political studies have generated significant interdisciplinary analysis.[13] The fascination with Trujillo stemmed, perhaps, from his supreme authority, which gave or took away power with a pen stroke.

These varied publications indicate that Trujillo's long rule resists simple political categorization. Trujillo's rule was repressive, authoritarian, paternalistic, personal, and totalitarian. By establishing no distinction between his personal wealth and the public treasury, by refusing to commit to any ideology, and by combining centralization of power with obedience to him, Trujillo ruled in a manner consistent with the sultanistic model described by Juan Linz.[14] But in terms of the military, Trujillo's rule requires other definitions. The presence of a broadly based national army, rather than a narrowly based regional or local army, allows Trujillo's regime to be compared with Caesarism, a form of dictatorship "in which a particular individual, often a military officer, exercises absolute power in the state by virtue of his control over the armed forces" and demands loyalty to his person rather than to the institution.[15] So it is not an accident or merely symbolic association that Ornes, publisher and editor of *El Caribe*, titles his book *Trujillo: Little Caesar of the Caribbean*. And Arturo Espaillat, the first Dominican to graduate from West Point and former chief of Trujillo's Military Intelligence Service (SIM), titled his biography *Trujillo: The Last Caesar*. For both Ornes and Espaillat, Trujillo's dictatorship was the embodiment of a Caesaristic regime. In this type of regime, the ruler uses the army to control and defeat his enemies; the ruler selectively and capriciously uses punishments for disobedience and rewards for obedience; and, framing authoritarian rule within a façade of constitutional rule, he creates conditions that place him above the law. Another distinctive feature of Caesarism is the adoption of modern economic programs.[16] Trujillo's regime exhibits every one of these characteristics.

The embodiment of order and discipline, Trujillo planned the operations of daily life in the Dominican Republic based on a military style that involved having armed soldiers all over the country, civilians dressing in clothing resembling uniforms, and military leaders appearing as distinguished personalities at social functions. Through intimidation, rewards, indoctrination, scare tactics, and manipulation of social customs, Trujillo dominated the hearts and minds of his countrymen, causing most Dominicans to obey his orders and feel respect for and loyalty to his regime.

Furthermore, while expanding his political power, Trujillo managed to keep the armed forces loyal and obedient. However, although Trujillo enjoyed the backing of the military, the institution was not monolithic, and Trujillo could not control all the members of the armed forces all the time. Internal military opposition toward and disaffection for the dictator and his regime surfaced on multiple occasions, but never enough to endanger Trujillo's position until 1961. Similarly, civilians supported Trujillo, but not all civilians accepted him. Thus, control and militarization of society took place, but not without resistance.

The reassessment presented in this book is necessary because previous analyses of the relationship between Trujillo's dictatorship and the armed forces have mostly centered on the systematic terror and torture used by the military to suppress opposition and keep Trujillo in power. Although this discourse neither denies the role of soldiers as instruments of terror nor diminishes the importance of the study of the violence and means and methods of control of the dictatorship, this study advocates moving beyond these already well-discussed topics. Terrorizing and torture were not the only functions of the armed forces. Indeed, during the first year of his tenure, Trujillo himself acknowledged that the function of the army was not only to maintain the public peace but also to fulfill different assignments.[17] What other functions did Trujillo assign the military? What was the military strength of the Dominican armed forces? What was the socioeconomic impact of the military? Were social class and color essential elements of recruitment and promotion? How different was Trujillo's army from previous military organizations?

Instead of engaging the theoretical approaches to the period, many of which have already been discussed by social scientists, the present study focuses on a thematic investigation and the analysis of empirical data and interviews. My aim is to provide a reasonably comprehensive account of the formation, socioeconomic foundations, and development of the military organization by interpreting data about its size and strength, functions and management, social and racial composition, and education and military training within a broad interpretive framework.

Even though the military consists of three main sectors—army, navy, and air force—this study deals primarily with the army because it had the longest and most significant role in imbuing the military spirit in society and in perpetuating Trujillo's regime. The following chapters trace the development of conditions that since colonial times have influenced the military ethos of the Dominican culture.

The focus of this book is the military, but the study goes beyond traditional military history to delineate several facets of Dominican society and the history of Dominican civil-military relations from the captains general to General Trujillo. It also traces the evolution of the military and the development of society from colonial times to independence, 1492–1844, and from independence to the U.S. occupation, 1844–1916. Central to the latter topic is the impact of the U.S. military forces in altering the Dominican social composition, particularly the structure of the officer corps. Trujillo's military career during the U.S. military occupation of 1916–24 and during the administration of Horacio Vásquez (1924–30), and his rise to power are part of the discourse on the Dominican political culture of the 1930s.

Based on the notion that by changing the military Trujillo altered society, this book looks at civil-military relations based on Trujillo's system of control, recruitment, and education of the military. One of the most important elements of Trujillo's plan to fuse military culture and Dominican culture was his proclamation of La Patria Nueva (New Fatherland). A flagrant misrepresentation of the democratic system, it attempted to promote a new order using the military as a model for society. Trujillo's plan for the Dominicanización of the Haitian-Dominican border and its military, nationalistic, and racist dimension also shed light on Trujillo's new order.

Trujillo's plan for operating a new military also included promotions, nepotism, and racism. The Haitian massacre of 1937 and the creation of the all-white presidential guard are studied as part of the racial ideology of the regime. Of utmost significance is the study of the growth of the armed forces and the expenditures of the armed forces from 1930 to 1961 and the national and international repercussions.

Trujillo attempted to reshape the nation by assigning civilian duties to the military, imposing military principles on civil society, and mixing military culture with popular culture. This work examines the impact of the abuses and extensive militarization, which in some cases caused uprisings in the forms of armed resistance and military conspiracies.

This study of the Trujillo regime is based not only on primary and secondary materials but also relies heavily on personal interviews. The information provided by a former president of the republic, by a former secretary of the armed forces, and by former and active officers and regular soldiers, intellectuals, and exiles helps validate and illuminate the analysis. The oral history offers information that cannot be extracted from documents and can come only from those who lived and survived the dictatorship. The book is organized more along topical lines than chronological ones so that political, social, economical, cultural, and intellectual elements can be woven together.

Since Trujillo's death, Dominican history has in large part focused on his dictatorship. Rich in multidisciplinary dimensions, this dictatorship attracts historians and political scientists as well as those interested in socioeconomic analysis, racial debates, and diplomatic and military studies. The rise of the Dominican population in the United States may also account for the increasing interest in Trujillo and his regime. Dominicans want to know more or are longing for those years when the republic had an "orderly society."

Extending military culture beyond the military and onto civilian society was one of Trujillo's main goals during his years as dictator. But instilling soldierly manners in the citizenry did not first surface during the Trujillo era. Before 1930, colonial, national, and foreign armies had already established a solid foundation for the society's military characteristics.

1. THE ORIGINS AND DEVELOPMENT OF THE DOMINICAN MILITARY AND ITS CULTURE, 1844–1916

In his celebrated canto "Hay un país en el mundo" (There is a country in the world) Pedro Mir, the National Poet of the Dominican Republic, makes a painful comparison of the suffering of his nation with "an adolescent girl kicked in the hip." On December 5, 1492, Christopher Columbus arrived at the island that later came to be known as Hispaniola or Santo Domingo, and Mir's nation became the first territory under Spanish domination in the New World.

Once the Spaniards arrived carrying crosses and swords, soldiers and priests worked in partnership to convert and control their new subjects: the Taíno Indians. In addition to weapons, the conquerors brought with them the Spanish military tradition of prestige and privilege and the military spirit of the *reconquista* (reconquest) after defeating the last Moorish stronghold in Spain. The fusion of military power and social prestige allowed the role of the military in society to be firmly established during the colonial period.

The Colonial Experience

Because of the violent nature of the conquest, the harsh conditions of forced labor, and disease, within the first three decades of the arrival of the Spaniards the Taíno Indians disappeared. African slaves replaced them as the labor force. In the meantime, the island became the center of Spanish power in the Americas. After Spain's conquest of Mexico in 1520, Peru in 1533, and other richer territories on the continent, however, Hispaniola fell into neglect.

Lacking protection because of this neglect, the *hacendados*, or owners of large farms, recruited their own militias and assumed the responsibility of defending their property. But without a regular outlet for the colony's products, settlers traded with French, Dutch, and British smugglers who had established their base of operation in the Antilles.

In response, Spain set up a colonial defense program in the area that included the reinforcement of military forces to protect ports and ships, and fortification of capital cities like Santo Domingo. Furthermore, responding to the development of the Thirty Years War (1618–1648), the Spanish Crown named captains general as presidents of the Royal Court of Appeals of Santo Domingo. They assumed both political and military leadership and became the highest authority in the colony.

The supremacy of the military weakened the power of the *hacendados* and altered the life of the colony. For example, Captain General Chávez de Osorio (1628–36) ordered the construction of fortifications and galleons in preparation for war. Although the ships were never completed, Chávez de Osorio and his assistants received large sums of money in granting licenses and permits to builders and merchants. For almost two hundred years afterward, the captains general monopolized all defense-related economic activities. In addition, they controlled the colonial elite, established a military oligarchy, and forced military culture on civilian life.

Despite the tensions between the military and the *hacendados*, French settlements advancing down the west coast of Hispaniola prompted the landed elite to unite forces with the military against foreign incursions. In addition, intercolonial wars strengthened the connection between the Catholic Church and the military. For example, in the Batalla de La Limonade, the Spaniards defeated the French on January 21, 1691. From then on January 21 was declared a holiday to honor the Virgen de la Altagracia. Every year hundreds of pilgrims travel to Higuey to visit the Basílica dedicated to the Virgen de la Altagracia. Thus a military victory became the foundation of one of the most important cultural traditions of the Dominican people, the devotion to the patron saint of the nation.

Her coronation took place on January 21, 1922, during the turning point in the U.S. occupation. In the spring the military government and the Dominicans reached an agreement for the departure of the Marines. Dominicans tied the announcement to the crowning of the Virgin of La Altagracia and claimed that the exit of the Marines was a miracle.

Mixing religious symbols with historical-military events can be traced to the time of Columbus. In 1495 during one of the bloodiest battles between the Taínos and the Spaniards in La Vega Real, a confederation of Taínos drove the Spaniards to desperation. In the midst of the fighting, the Spaniards claimed that they saw "a lady wearing a white dress with a baby in her arms" whom they believed helped them win the fight.[1] In remembrance of the event, on September 24, pilgrims set out to Santo Cerro, a hill close to La Vega, to pray to the Virgen de las Mercedes. Like January 21, September 24 is now a holiday. Both examples illustrate how deeply the military culture and traditions have been ingrained within the national character of the Dominican culture.

Haitian Domination

Despite the success of La Limonade, the colonial forces could not stop the French. By the Treaty of Ryswick in 1697, Spain ceded the western third of Hispaniola to France. During the French Revolution, the Treaty of Basel brought the entire island under French rule in 1795. By then in the French colony, the slaves had organized a rebellion, which turned into the Haitian Revolution. In 1804 the former slaves declared Haiti's independence.

The grand sweep of the Haitian revolution intensified the militarization of Santo Domingo. During the first half of the nineteenth century, a mélange of French (1802–8) and Spanish (1808–21) military rulers exercised control over the Spanish-speaking inhabitants of the east. Coinciding with the independence movement of colonial Latin America, the Dominicans, lead by José Núñez de Cáceres, declared their independence from Spain on December 1, 1821. Within weeks, with an army of 12,000 men, Haitian President Jean Pierre Boyer swept across the eastern part of Hispaniola, remaining in control for twenty-two years (1822–44). During this period Boyer enacted several measures that reinforced militarization in the eastern part of the island by combining administrative control with military values. Imposing a high level of military authority, Boyer appointed an army general, Maximilien Borgellá, to govern the new incorporated land. Borgellá established a military government and exercised power in a military fashion to rule the civilian population.

The Haitian military government created Battalion 32, which was made up of former slaves, and gave the command to Colonel Pablo Alí, who already was in charge of Battalion 31, made up of free blacks and known as Batallón de Morenos. These two battalions became the main line of defense of the Haitian government in the eastern part of the island. Boyer also enacted some revolutionary measures such as the complete abolition of slavery and land reform. These measures considerably reduced the power and land controlled by the traditional dominant groups (the landed proprietors, cattle ranchers, and the church), who together with other groups opposed Boyer's policies.[2] The governor confiscated properties and subdivided large farms, primarily those of the mostly white *hacendados*, into smallholdings and gave the plots to soldiers and other functionaries.

Boyer also introduced two other controversial measures: the Rural Code and obligatory military services. The purpose of the code was to increase agricultural production in the island by regulating labor and laborers and forcing the peasants to work on plantations under the threat of punishment. The code stipulated that except for government employees and professionals, all men, women, and children had to work in the fields. Proprietors and workers needed permission to move from their place of residency or to work on another plantation. Soldiers supervised workers' labor and movements. The general population resented these impositions, and the soldiers who owned their own plots did not stringently enforce the code's provisions.

The establishment of obligatory military service required that all men between sixteen and twenty-five years of age serve in the army. To tap the young male population to fill the ranks, administrators enlisted many students from the University of Santo Domingo. As a result, the university, an institution with a curriculum similar to a Catholic seminary and that functioned almost exclusively to serve the children of privileged groups, closed its doors. Originally this action became another source of resentment among the members of the elite and the Catholic Church, but in the long run the closing of the university provided opportunities for Dominicans to receive military instruction. Indeed, military leaders of the first republic (1844–61) acquired their military training in the Haitian army.

Meanwhile, Boyer's insistence on the implementation of the land tenure system led to a decline in production, and an unfavorable economic situation fueled the opposition. Hostility against Boyer grew among Dominicans and Haitians alike. In the east in 1838, Juan Pablo Duarte, a liberal, organized a secret society called La Trinitaria to separate the eastern part of the island from Haitian domination. The group organized cells made up of only three members, each of whom was to recruit three more participants. If the plan did not work, the majority of the conspirators would be protected by their lack of knowledge about other members.[3] In the west in 1842, General Charles Herard led a military revolt against Boyer. Haitians and Dominicans combined their efforts to overthrow Boyer, who, without military support, resigned and went into exile in Jamaica in March 1843. Afterward the Trinitarios continued to prepare the road for independence through a vast network of conspirators. Herard understood that the Dominicans wanted more than to get rid of Boyer and he tried to stop the separatist movement, but he was too late. Duarte's plan worked effectively, and on February 27, 1844, the Dominican people declared their independence from Haiti. Francisco del Rosario Sánchez and Ramón Matías Mella also played decisive roles in creating the new republic. Together with Duarte, Dominicans today honor them as Fathers of the Nation.

Militarization and Territorial Defense

Before Dominicans had time to organize military defense of the country, they faced the Haitians in the battlefield, and for the next twelve years successive Haitian invasions kept the nation at war and in a state of militarization. Dominicans forces suffered heavy casualties but also defeated the Haitian army in several battles (as happened on March 19, 1844, in Azua and March 30, 1844, in Santiago as well as on April 21, 1849, during a fierce battle near the Ocoa River in an area known as Las Carreras).

As the war wore on and weapons and manpower became scarcer, the national leaders debated over the nature of the new republic and its capability to defend its territorial integrity. Eventually the intensifying debate spawned civil war. Both the war for independence and the civil war contributed strongly to defining the role of the military in society and had far-reaching effects on the subsequent development of the nation, interrelating military ethos with national cultural values.

Some of the military patterns that developed during the nation-building process, such as military defiance and domination of civilian power, provide a broad basis for the understanding of Trujillo's experiments with new forms of military organization.

Military Leaders and the New Republic

A close look at the patterns and intricacies of the Dominican military before 1930 reveals that as independence was acquired, the military leaders interfered with the functioning of the government in three principal ways. They became protectionists, facilitators, or self-servers.

General Pedro Santana typifies the protectionist, vigilant leader, as he overturned governments for the self-proclaimed goal of protecting the nation. Santana, a conservative landowner, played a crucial role in defeating the Haitians and in organizing the army during the first period of nationhood (1844–61). His management style reestablished the connection between the elite and the military.

After the proclamation of independence, the liberals held power and soon clashed with Santana, who wanted to place the new republic under foreign protection, fearing future Haitian invasions. Just five months after independence was proclaimed, a military faction led by Santana defeated the liberals, and on November 13 he became the first Dominican president. To please Santana, the congress added Article 210 to the constitution, which allowed the president to make military decisions without being accountable to anyone.

The inclusion of Article 210 clearly indicates how military leaders began to inculcate martial values in society. During Santana's three administrations (1844–48, 1853–56, and 1858–61), he governed in a dictatorial manner. To compel citizens to obey orders, he appointed experienced officers as provincial governors. With sufficient military support to hold power, Santana concentrated his foreign policy on establishing a protectorate.

Santana was not alone in his protectionist pursuit. He shared the position with, among others, Buenaventura Báez, a five-time president (1849–53, 1856–57, 1865–66, 1868–73, and 1876–78). Báez unsuccessfully sought French and U.S. protection or even annexation.

Santana finally achieved his goal on March 18, 1861, when the Dominican Republic became a Spanish colony again. Consequently, a nationalistic movement known as the Restoration led to a four-year struggle against the annexation. The resistance movement proclaimed a second independence on August 16, 1863. Days later a provisional government directed a popular guerrilla war that effectively pursued the Spanish troops. Unable to maintain their hold on the colony, the Spaniards left in July 1865.

Leaders of the Second Republic

The subjugation under Spain had a double effect. It strengthened national identity and reinforced the tradition of military, not civilian, authority. In liberal quarters the leaders of the Restoration, while fighting for independence, were also competing for power among themselves.

In 1863 General José Antonio Salcedo became the first president of the Gobierno Restaurador. General Gaspar Polanco overthrew Salcedo's government in response, as he claimed, to a "unanimous petition from the army," which had lost its confidence in Salcedo's ability to manage national affairs.[4] Salcedo was tried, convicted of treason, sent to exile, and executed in 1864. Following Salcedo's fall, over the next eighteen years the executive power shifted hands sixteen times. The changes in rule and the precarious condition of the state became a major factor in the arrival of the facilitator.

General Pedro Guillermo is the prototype of the facilitator. In November 1865 he led a military insurrection that brought down the government of General José María Cabral. Cabral had been governing according to the liberal and democratic principles of the Constitution of 1865, sustained by the Partido Azul, or Blue Party. This document was in opposition to the "reactionary and repudiated" Constitution of 1854, the guide of the conservative Partido Rojo, or Red Party.[5]

Guillermo stayed in power for only twenty-three days, enough to ensure the installation of Báez, the leader of the Red Party, for the third time on December 8, 1865.

General Desiderio Arias is another example of a facilitator. In March 1913 Arias forced the head of state, Monseñor Adolfo Nouel, to resign. Arias did not assume the presidency but facilitated the transfer of power to José Bordas Valdez and later to Juan Isidro Jimenes.

Beginning in the late 1880s, a new type of ruler, the self-server, began to appear. The self-server managed the executive office as if it were his personal patrimony. General Ulises Heureaux, known popularly as Lilís, represents this type of ruler. Heureaux distinguished himself as a fighter during the Restoration wars and moved up through the ranks due to his military skills. His actions attracted the attention of General Gregorio Luperón, a leader of the Restoration movement and provisional president from 1879 to 1880. Heureaux became Luperón's chief of staff, and he rose from there to president of the republic in 1882.

When Heureaux's first two-year term ended in September 1884, he could not be reelected because of constitutional restrictions. With the acquiescence of high-ranking officers, Heureaux won the election of 1886 and held the presidency until his assassination in 1899. He retained power for so long because, among other things, he exercised effective control over the army. Trujillo would later be the ultimate self-serving ruler.

The three types of military rulers—protectionist, facilitator, and self-server—provide sufficient evidence of the varying political agendas of the military leaders and the invasive nature of the military into societal affairs. Understanding how the republican army formed, as well as the socioeconomic environment, is useful in analyzing Trujillo's eventual rise to power.

The Army of the Early Republic, 1844–61

Put together by local and regional leaders, the first army—known as Ejército Libertador or Ejército de Febrero—was an unorganized, temporary force. Its ranks were mutinous, desertions were high, and social class distinctions were evident. Members of the upper classes, who monopolized both government and army senior ranks, were part of the officer corps. Illiterate peasants staffed the infantry, often barefoot and/or without uniforms. An officer who could afford to wear a military uniform and "legging shoes" commanded them.[6]

Throughout the initial years of national development, a strong bond often existed between a leader and his troops. When Santana challenged the liberal leaders, for example, "his army" consisted of more than one thousand men, many of whom were his own workers, friends, and relatives who had abandoned their families and property to defend the fatherland.[7]

Meanwhile, the government enacted the first constitution in November 1844 and established the foundation of the regular army. Accordingly, the forces were to be divided into Ejército de Tierra, Armada Naval, and Guardia Cívica (land army, navy, and civil guard). Initially all Dominican men between fifteen and forty years of age were obligated to serve in the army, except married men with children, the sole children of poor widows, those who had elderly parents and were supporting them, and important businessmen.[8] The republic was in its infancy and had requested that citizens become soldiers. Dominicans responded to the call and a force of eight to ten thousand men formed the first regular army.[9]

La Guardia Cívica consisted of both Dominicans and foreigners. It was obligatory for all Dominicans between forty-six and sixty years of age and for foreigners who had resided in the country for more than three months to enroll in the Guardia Cívica. To expand manpower, the government established obligatory military service on July 15, 1845. Anyone not responding to the call was considered a traitor to the fatherland and was subject to trial under military law, which included the death penalty in certain cases.[10]

Ten years after independence, the influence of the military on civilians was readily apparent. General William L. Cazneau, an adventurer from Texas appointed by President Franklin Pierce to negotiate a lease on the Samaná peninsula, visited the country in 1854. During his visit Cazneau observed many activities associated with militarization. For example, once a week the male population had to report to their local military station for training. Some of these men replaced other reservists who had completed their required time of service.[11]

These procedures aimed at organizing the army had social and economic repercussions. The measures imposed heavy burdens on families. Since fathers were exempt from the draft, recruitment indirectly prompted an increase in the number of marriages and in the number of children. Furthermore, recruitment also contributed to an increase in the number of *compadrazgos*. Based on loyalty and respect, two principles greatly correlated with the military culture, the ritual of "coparenthood [linked] parents, child, and godparents in a close social or economic relationship."[12] Very often godparents were better off than the godchild's family. Local militia chiefs often became godfathers to a considerable number of children. These connections also benefited the militia chiefs. The bond established with the civilian population helped them overcome some of the recruitment problems.

Infused by military ethos, many people considered the military an integral part of government. As time passed both citizens and soldiers adopted the so-called attitude of warfare and showed enthusiasm for images of grandeur associated with the participants in a military conflict. Military leaders became prominent in the historical and public discourse. Provinces, towns, streets, and public buildings honored their names, and the government and the people celebrated historical events that had a military basis and exalted military values.

Because of the insular condition of the country, the creation of a naval force was also crucial for national defense. The first naval unit began to operate in 1844. By 1845 it had ten ships and a capable commander, General Juan Bautista Cambiaso, but not enough qualified sailors. Nevertheless, during Báez's first administration (1849–53), the government changed the course of the armed conflict with Haiti from a defensive to an offensive war; the navy was strong enough to attack several Haitian

ports. The offensive campaign prevented Haiti from invading the Dominican Republic for several years. Following those raids, Haiti and the
Dominican Republic were at peace until 1855.Civilians were proud of
their country's military might and admired those engaged in military
service.

The outburst of military unity was short-lived, and soon a struggle
for power led to an armed confrontation. As a result of political mis-
handling of state funds, as well as economic regional competition, in
July 1857 merchants, tobacco growers, and intellectuals from the Cibao
area organized local forces to fight against southern landowners, wood
exporters, and Báez's government. Santana, who was living in exile, returned to support the opposition against Báez. Santana's military ability
and charisma attracted men to serve under his command, and he forced
the departure of Báez and many of his followers from the country. Once
in control, the conservative leader turned against his liberal allies and
became president for the last time.

To attract potential officers, Santana's government established the
first military academy in 1860. Fifty cadets could enroll in the two-year
program of study.[13] Militarily, the creation of the academy was one of
the last and most important of Santana's decisions. His decision to annex
the republic to Spain, however, resulted in the temporary closing of the
school.

The Restoration Army

During the four years of Spanish control (1861–65), some Dominican
soldiers served with the Spanish colonial army, but many joined the resistance to reject the annexation. From 1861 to 1863, lacking leadership,
Dominicans fought irregularly against the Spaniards, but in 1863 the
Restoration government demanded that all sixteen-year-olds enlist to
help defend the fatherland. The call to fight the Spaniards had tremendous popular support in both urban and rural areas. Many peasants became soldiers. But by the time the Spanish troops left, the country's
agrarian-based economy was in disarray. In order to increase agricultural production, the government demobilized the forces, keeping only
a reduced number of men on active duty.[14]

The war against Spain had broken the control of the landed aristocracy, the traditional ruling class, and transferred power to the commercial
class.[15] The emergence of this new political force, together with other
socioeconomic determinants, increased the contention for power and

provoked the resurgence of civil war; people lived in a warfare state from 1865 to 1879.

Eugenio María de Hostos, a Puerto Rican sociologist and one of the first to analyze Dominican society, points out the economic burden of civil war on peasants. To avoid the draft, peasants abandoned the good arable lands near the villages and built their houses scattered throughout inaccessible areas.[16] In addition, the resulting disarray was reflected in the loss of military cohesion. Again no organized army existed.

In part the anarchy within the military reflected the wartime experience, which had a negative impact on the officer corps. A navy officer and journalist-diplomat, Manuel María Gautier, asserted that all those years of war led to the appointment of an excessive number of officers. Since the republic was "unable to give them any other reward, it granted them ranks."[17]

To remedy the situation, efforts to transform the military began shortly after the Blue Party took power in 1879 under the leadership of Luperón, who favored military reform and believed that one of the fundamental functions of the state was to prepare good soldiers. He envisioned a small army of well-trained men, having "elevated character and [the] pride of great men and celebrated captains" along with honor, valor, moderation, and firmness.[18]

In 1880 the government mandated three years of military service for men eighteen years of age and ordered the establishment of permanent schools and academies in the garrisons. The trend of military improvement continued during the administrations of other Blue Party leaders, such as Fernando Arturo de Meriño (1880–82), and Heureaux (1882–84, and 1887–99). Efforts to organize the military paid off, even if only temporarily. By Dominican standards of the time, the peaceful transference of power from Meriño to Heureaux in 1882 was impressive, and the two were the only presidents between 1865 and 1884 who ended their terms constitutionally.

Heureaux, a Model for Trujillo

During his first administration, Heureaux followed most of the political guidelines of the Blue Party. Soon after he took power for the second time, in 1887, he began to disconnect his government from the Blue Party leadership and principles, and for thirteen years a system of "co-option and coercion was in force throughout Heureaux's regime."[19] Although the country enjoyed peace and order and entered an era of modernization and national development, it would come at a heavy price.

By now the military had some of the characteristics of a standard army. The forces were adequately armed with modern equipment, appropriately instructed in tactical maneuvers, and regularly paid. As in Latin America, French and Spanish instructors taught in the military academy, and French and Spanish technicians trained and instructed Dominican soldiers and sailors. Thus, the military achieved a certain degree of professionalism as its members dedicated themselves to a long-term commitment to improve their knowledge and practice of the military profession.[20]

On July 10, 1887, Heureaux created the Policía Gubernativa or Guardia Civil, a military body organized to protect the agricultural fields, which he considered the base of the national economy and wealth.[21]

The navy also began to take institutional shape: naval regulations were formulated, and officers and sailors received professional training. Soon the navy acquired modern warships and naval equipment. Two large warships, the *Presidente* and the *Restauración*, acquired in 1886 and the 1896 respectively, were equipped with modern weapons and technology.

Although Heureaux transformed the armed forces into a better equipped, better-trained, and more professional organization, soldiers still depended on Heureaux's favoritism; the president did not intend for the military to operate on its own, and he established a number of paternalistic and personal relationships with officers and enlisted men. He gave out money, served champagne, and granted exemptions from import duties to friendly generals. Heureaux wanted to professionalize the army but at the same time wanted to use the forces to suppress his enemies, so he also rewarded loyalty with promotion.[22]

Heureaux concerned himself with the smallest military details, which sprang from his instinct to command and his need to be in control, but he also realized that this kind of involvement could be politically beneficial. To obtain support for his government, he appointed members of the opposition in high government posts. He also offered financial favors, such as tax exemptions, and facilities to investors and businessmen expecting that the beneficiaries would offer jobs, open commercial houses, create industrial factories, and activate the circulation of goods and money in return.

Because of his personal involvement in military affairs and his use of the military for political gains, Heureaux's power lasted for a longer continuous period of time than the rule of any other government during the nineteenth century. As we will see, Trujillo later used similar strategies, and scholars have indicated that when Trujillo became president, he had Ulises Heureaux as a model.[23]

Society and Cáceres's Military Reform

Despite the improvements Heureaux had made in the military, after he was assassinated in 1899 the organization of the military disintegrated and the fragmentation of political authority followed. Between July 1899 and January 1906, six different political chiefs tried to rule; all failed. Heading the turmoil, Juan Isidro Jimenes and Horacio Vásquez led two rival groups that embroiled the country in political upheaval from 1901 to 1903.[24]

In the ensuing chaos, the administration of General Carlos Morales (1903–6) created La Guardia Rural. This force was militarily organized but its functioning was essentially civil; its main responsibility was to patrol the roads, to assist judges in implementing the judicial system, and to prevent crime. A force of 940 men formed a regiment of four cavalry squadrons and four infantry companies.[25]

To suppress smuggling from Haiti and to enforce the collection of revenues, in 1905 the government organized a new force called the Dominican Frontier Customs Guard. The nature and function of this guard derived from the agreement known as Modus Vivendi, signed by the Morales government, which delegated control of financial receivership to U.S. customs officers. Under the control of the receivership, the guard consisted of approximately 125 men, including six American officers.[26]

The fragmentation and the organization-reorganization process of the Dominican armed forces continued during the administration of Ramón Cáceres, who became president in 1906. After he took power, Cáceres devised a plan to pacify the country and to disconnect the symbiotic relationship between the military and politicians. In trying to accomplish these goals, Cáceres named powerful local chiefs to work with his government in Santo Domingo, separating them from their areas of operation. Cáceres also used the army as a repressive machine; pacification turned into the devastation of human lives, animals, and property.

The worst carnage was in the area known as Línea Noroeste. Located in the northwestern part of the country, Línea Noroeste was a center of rebellions and resistance. The violent acts of Cáceres's army spawned broad resentment to the extent that even Cáceres's friends and collaborators openly disapproved of the severity of the measures. In "Lo que vi," Agustín Acevedo sharply criticized the repressive actions used by the government and argued that a better political environment could be achieved without brutal repression of the opposition.[27]

Nevertheless, Cáceres did not stop the persecution until he felt he had the population under control. Then he took a series of steps to convert the ragtag armies into organized forces. To improve military performance, a group of officers received special training and became instructors; new modern military equipment was introduced, and the battalions were reorganized.[28]

At the time of Cáceres's reforms, some divisions of the army were under the authority of the minister of war, while others were subject to the orders of provincial governors. To correct this perceived problem, on June 26, 1907, new legislation fused La Guardia Rural and La Policía Gubernativa into a new force, La Guardia Republicana. In its attempt to centralize the forces, the Cáceres government then also took control over the Frontier Customs Guard in 1908.[29]

In addition, Cáceres bought the political neutrality of some powerful military leaders, sent others to places where they did not have political influence, and appointed a friend, General Alfredo María Victoria, as commander of the army in Santo Domingo. Indirectly, the appointment of Victoria and the reorganization of the army became a double-edged sword that eventually led to Cáceres's death. General Luis Tejera, the son of Emiliano Tejera, who was the governor of Santo Domingo and one of the ministers in the Cáceres administration, had presidential ambitions. To consolidate his political plan, Tejera had asked Cáceres to appoint a friend of his, Colonel Anibal Roldán, as commander of Santo Domingo. The appointment of Victoria enraged Tejera, who in retaliation led a conspiracy against the president. Cáceres was ambushed and killed on November 19, 1911. Eladio Victoria, an uncle of Alfredo Victoria, succeeded him.

Soon after Cáceres's death the country returned to anarchy, leaving the nation in chaos from 1911 to 1916. For some, those years were the most unfortunate period in Dominican political history.[30] In the midst of military revolts, eight different governments ruled the nation in that five-year period.

The continuous political crises had a dramatic effect on Dominican history. In 1916 the United States invaded and occupied the Dominican

Republic, ushering in foreign economic, political, and ultimately military intervention.

Before the discussion of the U.S. occupation, let's take a brief look at the pre-1916 officer in a social-intellectual context. Báez, Cabral, and Santana, all rich landowners, acquired their fortunes before entering the military. Guillermo, Heureaux, and Luperón reached power through social mobility within the ranks, and all acquired considerable wealth. Some of the officers of the early Dominican armed forces were not only wealthy but also educated men. For example, during his tenure as U.S. chargé d'affaires for the Dominican Republic from 1889 to 1891, as Frederick Douglass commented that Heureaux proved to be "well versed in statesmanship." The president impressed Douglass with his literary and political knowledge, his fluency in Spanish, English, French, and Haitian Creole, and his collection of books.[31] Other distinguished officers had traveled throughout Europe and the United States and met with political and intellectual figures there. Luperón, for example, received the French Legion of Honor and was a guest of honor of Queen Victoria in England as well as of the king and queen of Denmark. He met well-known politicians and writers such as William Gladstone, Giuseppe Garibaldi, and Victor Hugo. Luperón also published three volumes of *Notas autobiográficas y apuntes históricos* in 1896 with the assistance of Manuel Rodríguez Objío.

Another example of the officer-intellectual was Gautier, who in 1861 published *La gran traición de Pedro Santana*, a booklet aimed at condemning Santana for the annexation to Spain. José Gabriel García, an artillery officer during the independence war, is better known as the father of Dominican historiography. He published, among other works, *Rasgos biográficos de dominicanos célebres* (1875), four volumes of *Compendio de historia de Santo Domingo* (1878) as well as *Memorias para la historia de Quisqueya* (1891). Benito Monción, a hero of the War of Restoration, published *De Capotillo a Santiago: Relación histórica concerniente a la restauración dominicana dictada en Turks Islands en 1887*. General Nemesio Casimiro de Moya, vice president of the republic from 1882 to 1884, prepared and published *Mapa de la isla de Santo Domingo* in 1905. He also published three volumes of *Bosquejo histórico del descubrimiento y conquista de la isla de Santo Domingo* (1913).

Considering the limited numbers of publications that were released in the Dominican Republic, these works had to influence the political thinking of their readers. As soldiers, these writers filtered real and imaginary images of *la patria* through their military eyes, deepening the military culture in society. As an illustration, in his article "Un recuerdo a los dominicanos" (A historical recollection for all Dominicans), Luperón praised the efficiency of his provisionary government, the harmony of the Restoration army, and the courage of the officers who motto was "Liberty! Equality!"[32]

In sum, the ongoing influence of the military over Dominican society developed during the colonial period. For defense purposes, the Spanish administration fused the authority of the military leader with the authority of the civilian governor and established the foundation of military hegemony over civilian authority. The prevalence of the military deepened during the Haitian domination. In the course of the nation-building process, struggle for power and foreign wars fragmented the authority of the central government. Although some (Luperón, Guillermo, Heureaux) reached power through social mobility within the ranks, social class distinctions were unmistakable. The officer corps became a domain of the elite. On the other hand, as the government imposed obligatory military service, warfare took on a novel aspect. Almost every family had to adjust to the requirements of the military service of male relatives. To a certain degree, the entire society became "militarized" because the extensive kinship in the service developed cohesive elements of the military subculture that shaped the life of the soldiers and of their relatives and their neighbors. Indeed, like a living organism, the military spread its influence all over the population connecting, like communicant cells, the different sectors of society.[33] The military fiber of Dominican society was subsequently strengthened by the intervention and occupation of the United States from 1916 to 1924.

2. THE MILITARY ASPECT OF
THE U.S. OCCUPATION OF
THE DOMINICAN REPUBLIC
The Marines and La Guardia

The United States and the Dominican Republic have a long history of interaction and confrontation, which began with U.S. expansion into the Caribbean in the Spanish-American War in 1898. Afterward, Spain lost Cuba and ceded Puerto Rico to the United States. Gradually other areas began to fold into the geopolitical domination of the "Colossus of the North." Between 1901 and 1916, the United States intervened in the affairs of Cuba, Panama, Nicaragua, Mexico, Haiti, and the Dominican Republic.

The United States saw opportunity for regional hegemony in Latin America and the Caribbean as the countries in this area struggled with financial mismanagement and political corruption. U.S. interventionists eyed the strategic location of the Panama Canal and were mindful of the development of World War I. The presence of unfriendly powers, especially Germany in Haiti and in the northeastern part of the Dominican Republic, deeply concerned the United States. Although U.S. policy forbid military interference in the political affairs of the region, the United States intervened anyway, forcing the resignation of Dominican President Francisco Henríquez y Carvajal. The United States added new elements to the military culture and reinforced the traditional Dominican pattern of military defiance of civilian government.

Dollars and Weapons
Dollar diplomacy was tested in the Dominican Republic early in the twentieth century. By 1905 political factionalism caused economic disruptions, and the Dominican government failed to pay European and U.S. creditors, who pressed for the payment of debts.

Confronting the crisis, President Theodore Roosevelt told the U.S. Senate that the United States had to intervene in the Dominican Republic or the European nations "would absorb all the Dominican revenues and it would be a virtual sacrifice of the American claims and interest in the island."[1]

Thus, on March 31, 1905, the Dominican Republic signed the Modus Vivendi agreement with the United States, under which the United States collected customs revenues and the Dominican government was obligated to use 45 percent for its expenses, while the remaining 55 percent was to be distributed among its creditors. In addition, the U.S. dollar became the standard currency of the Dominican Republic.[2] In 1907 the United States proposed to modify the Modus Vivendi agreement. The new version diminished the sovereignty of the Dominican Republic even more by prohibiting the Dominican government from increasing its public debt without U.S. consent. From this moment on, complete intervention was only a matter of time.

The Arrival of the Marines

The United States Marines Corps (USMC) first arrived in the Dominican Republic in 1905 to guard the internal revenue agents under the control of the receivership. But the presence of U.S. officers in the Dominican Republic did not deter domestic infighting, and political chaos made it difficult to enforce the terms of the customs agreement. Consequently, in 1916 the United States decided to not only restore order to the nation's finances but also create the conditions necessary for political stability. To achieve this goal, William W. Russell, minister to the Dominican Republic, requested from the government of President Juan Isidro Jimenes the dissolution of the Dominican armed forces and their transformation into a constabulary. The constabulary was to be organized and led by a U.S. citizen selected by the U.S. government, but appointed by the president of the Dominican Republic. The Dominican government would ratify and enforce the resolutions recommended by the director of the constabulary and would pay the personnel.[3]

Dominicans rejected the proposition and organized public protests. In the midst of all the pressure and debates, Jimenes accepted the appointment of Charles Johnston as a financial expert. This unpopular decision generated an uproar.

Desiderio Arias, the charismatic secretary of the army, headed the opposition. He adopted a strong nationalist position and became "anathema to Washington as the Zelaya of Santo Domingo."[4] (Juan José Santos Zelaya was president of Nicaragua from 1892 to 1905. He opposed the

U.S. plan of building a canal through Central America). Applying a two-pronged approach, Arias led the Congress to impeach the president and took control of the Santo Domingo Fortress. The United States offered to keep President Jimenes in power with the support of U.S. troops.

To keep President Jimenes in power, the Marines threatened to attack Santo Domingo if the "rebel forces [did] not disarm and turn over their arms and ammunition to the U.S. forces by six o'clock upon the morning of May 14th."[5] Faced with the reality of U.S. military superiority, Arias engaged in rear-guard sniping tactics, left the capital, and moved to Puerto Plata.

The presence of U.S. forces in the country put President Jimenes in a difficult position. He resigned on May 7, 1916, so as not "to enjoy power regained by foreign bullets."[6] His resignation was followed by the arrival of several U.S. warships transporting Marines to the ports of Santo Domingo, Puerto Plata, Macorís, and Sánchez. From then on, troops moved into the country in escalating numbers.

The Dominican Congress elected Henríquez to replace Jimenes. Henríquez sternly defended the right of the Dominican Republic to manage its own affairs and refused to appoint a U.S. financial advisor. Consequently, U.S. authorities did not turn over the Dominican government's portion of revenues collected.[7] This decision was a death sentence for Henríquez. His government could not survive the economic strangulation.

To alleviate the financial crunch, on September 12, 1916, the executive office abolished all army commands and demobilized the First and Second Battalions, also known as the Ozama and the Yaque, respectively. Only the Guardia Republicana, or police force, remained in charge of maintaining public order.[8] The economic and military vacuum, combined with the quarrels among political parties, facilitated the occupation.

Captain Harry Knapp, navy commander of the Atlantic Cruiser Force (and military governor from 1916 to 1918), proclaimed military occupation on November 29, 1916. The Second Brigade was deployed "as an army of occupation" to enforce the decree of Commander Knapp and maintain public order.[9] In effect, in assuming responsibility for the maintenance of law and order, the military government tried "to remake Dominican society," designing and implementing programs intended to change the republic's political, economic, and social life.[10] In effect, during eight years in the day-to-day management of the country, the

Marines restructured the military and injected a new military subculture into Dominican society.

Peasant or Rural Resistance to the Occupation

In military terms, by occupying the country the United States granted itself the opportunity to achieve its ultimate goal of organizing the Dominican armed forces. Yet the first military action after the occupation was not organization but disarmament and combat.

In disarming the population the Marines collected two thousand shotguns, twenty-nine thousand revolvers, nine thousand rifles, and several thousand other small arms.[11] Nonetheless, resistance sprang up in the country. At first the armed resistance lacked organization. There was some sporadic fighting when the Marines landed, but their "vastly superior weapons made the fighting, and the casualties, very unequal."[12]

One of the most important skirmishes took place in La Barranquita, where "forty-five Dominican soldiers [fought] against 600 marines."[13] As in other initial battles, the rebels were defeated, and for a while the Marines immobilized the guerrillas. With their superior weapons, the invaders controlled the most important military headquarters and imposed their military power on nearly the entire country. Only in the eastern provinces—El Seibo and San Pedro de Macorís—did the Marines fail to quell guerrilla activities. In assessing the potential damage the guerrillas might cause, the military government mockingly predicted that the rebels "will start out full of patriotism and Dominican rum, and in the first fight [would] fight well."[14]

From 1917 to 1922, the guerrillas, headed by a variety of competent leaders including ex-soldiers Vicentico Evangelista and Chachá Goicochea, history teacher Fidel Ferrer, and peasants Ramon Natera and Martin Peguero, were not easy to defeat. Like most civilian men, the rebels had military experience and consequently knew how to handle arms and to fight the enemy. This particular situation may explain why despite the inequality in military strength, the effectiveness of their tactics caused "considerable anxiety to the Military Government," according to Knapp.[15]

Four years after the armed confrontation had begun, the militarization of the country became a priority of the military government, which requested additional personnel to combat the insurrection. On July 2, 1920, Rear Admiral Thomas Snowden, military governor from 1918 to 1921, asked the U.S. Chief of Naval Operations to increase, at once, the number of Marines stationed in the Dominican Republic from 1,998 to 2,900 men. Based on a report from one of his officers, Snowden argued that guerrilla raids were frequent, that hostility in the cities was evident, that lives of U.S. officers, including the governor himself, had been directly threatened, and that as a result of the shortage of soldiers a large part of the country was not covered by troops.[16] To reinforce the Second Brigade, the Fifteenth regiment, numbering 50 officers and 1,041 men, was sent from the United States to San Pedro de Macorís.[17]

After almost six years of successful warfare, a combination of factors led to the guerrillas' surrender in 1922. One crucial element had been the arrival of the new military governor Rear Admiral Samuel S. Robison in June 1921, who implemented an aggressive anti-guerrilla program.

Robison's new approach to the peasant rebellion included amnesty for all insurgents, building new roads, and developing an effective communication system. Consequently, the armed resistance began to disintegrate. By the middle of June 1922, many guerrillas had returned to their peasant lives, while others, convicted of various crimes, were serving jail sentences.[18]

Militarization, Women, and Urban Resistance

Peasant resistance was not the only opposition the military government confronted. When the guerrilla movement was at its height, a wave of nationalist discontent spread all over the country, primarily in urban areas. Restlessness erupted during the unforgettable Semana Patriótica (patriotic week) of June 12 to June 19, 1920, when collective protests sparked broad resistance against the occupation. Protesters called for a campaign of civil resistance against the military government, the immediate withdrawal of the occupation forces, and the collection of funds for an international propaganda campaign.

Important to the campaign was the active participation of the Junta Patriótica de Damas, a women's organization created on March 15, 1920, to protest the presence of the military government. Leaders of the movement included Abigail Mejía, Luisa Ozema Pellerano, and Ercilia Pepín. Adopting a militant attitude, the women collected money to send delegates abroad to protest the occupation and gave speeches that galvanized audiences. They also made hundreds of Dominican flags to be used during Semana Patriótica.

The flag became a symbol of their activism, the weapon of their struggle. Considering that the flag flying in front of the invaders would elevate

the spirit of the people, the women distributed flags among the population to be raised when Marines walked through the streets. Furthermore,
hundreds of women signed a letter prepared by Pepín, demanding the
withdrawal of the U.S. forces of occupation, and sent it to the U.S. Senate
Committee studying the Dominican situation.[19]

A woman of courage and determination, Pepín symbolized women's
resistance to the occupation. In November 1921 the military government invited her to represent the Dominican Republic at the international conference organized by the National American Women's Suf-
frage Association in the United States. She rejected the invitation. How
was she going to represent her country with credentials signed by the
head of the occupation forces?[20] Pepín's attitude and the actions of the
Junta Patriótica de Damas showed how women actively participated in
the struggle for national liberation. Their involvement in the nationalist struggle invigorated the Dominican resistance and reinforced the
international support against the occupation.

In the meantime, inspired by the results of Semana Patriótica, the
Dominican people adopted a more defiant attitude to restore national
sovereignty. They organized meetings, rallies, and protests. The public
meetings brought together Dominicans from different social strata to
organize *juntas nacionalistas* across the country and to support the leaders
of the movement.

Not surprisingly, the political mobilization of the urban masses
alarmed the military government. In his request for an increase in Marine
forces, Snowden stated that after the public meetings, the strength of the
"political agitators," as he called the leaders of the resistance movement,
had increased.[21]

Among the leaders Governor Snowden considered political agitators
were Américo Lugo and Fabio Fiallo, two well-known intellectuals who
belonged to the radical wing of the nationalist movement, the Unión
Nacional Dominicana (UND). Lugo wrote an article titled "La semana
patriótica" (The patriotic week) that accused the United States of de-
stroying Dominican institutions and freedom. Fiallo denounced the occupation and described it as "cruel civilization" that came through the
back door during the night to attack with bayonets and machine guns.
In newspapers and rallies, they demanded the immediate and unconditional withdrawal of U.S. troops. For their attitude, they, along with
other UND members, writers, journalists, public speakers, and protesters,

became targets of military repression and served as justification for the expansion of U.S. military personnel in the Dominican Republic.[22]

The censorship and limited freedom imposed by the military government did not quell the nationalist outburst. With the money collected by the women and from other sources, former president Henríquez and other nationalists traveled throughout Latin America, denouncing and protesting the occupation. Dominicans in Latin America, Europe, and the United States employed every possible channel to denounce the abuses, the repression, and the presence of U.S. Marines on Dominican territory. All these efforts paid off, and the international community responded with massive solidarity for the Dominican cause. Confronting national repudiation and international pressure, the USMC proceeded to organize the Dominican army.

Recruitment and Reorganization of the Dominican Military by the U.S. Government

Although running down the rebels and disarming the population became priorities for the military government, its most important military task was the reorganization of the Dominican armed forces. Executive Order No. 47 of April 7, 1917, created the Dominican Constabulary Guard, which appropriated $500,000 for equipping, training, and maintaining the new organization. Realizing that the word *constabulary* did not appeal to the Dominican people and reasoning that from the former Guardia Republicana, the people were more familiar with the word "Guardia," Knapp subsequently renamed the force Guardia Nacional Dominicana.[23] The search for the proper name continued and Executive Order No. 631 of June 2, 1921, changed the name to Policía Nacional Dominicana.

Before establishing a detailed program for the training of the Dominican constabulary, however, the United States initiated the recruitment and improvised training of Dominican soldiers. Former members of the Dominican navy and the Guardia Republicana could join the constabulary provided the military government approved their records and qualifications. The incentives of a steady salary and free room, board, clothing, and medical assistance, were enticing, but there were still obstacles to overcome in recruitment.[24]

For example, few Dominicans wanted to serve with an invading force, and of those willing to serve, even fewer had the required military background. Traditionally the officer corps was made up of members of the

Dominican elite, and at first most members of this group vigorously rejected the occupation. The elite's hostility toward the military government resulted from a combination of two main factors: patriotic anti-occupation attitude, and rejection and resentment because the presence of the military government provoked the elite's removal from political power. In his 1917 annual report to the U.S. government, Knapp recorded that upon taking possession, the president and all of the members of the Cabinet "had cleaned out their desks, and had not since appeared in the Government Palace." He lamented that it was not possible to get Dominicans of the "proper caliber" who would accept high administrative offices, and since Knapp could not force Dominicans into office, he filled the posts with U.S. officers.[25]

Although at first the elite's attitude was a great disappointment to Knapp, ultimately he was grateful for it. In the same report, he regarded "the action, taken by force of circumstances, as the most fortunate thing that could have happened" because he was able to work with military personnel over which he had control. But the appointment of military personnel in civilian positions proved consistent with the Dominican tradition that allowed the military to manage the operational functioning of the country.

Knapp ran the country through his staff, but lacking guidance from Washington, he "assembled a committee of North Americans in Santo Domingo to formulate a detailed plan for a constabulary."[26] The ultimate goal in creating La Guardia was to reshape the military institution, to forge a new soldier, who, disengaged from politics, would be capable of bringing stability and peace to the nation. It was not a simple task. To begin with, three U.S. departments were dealing with the Dominican situation: the Department of War, the State Department, and the Department of the Navy. Eventually the Department of the Navy—which "had no internal organization for administering a foreign government"—took control of Dominican affairs.[27]

The struggle for power between the Department of the Navy and the State Department lasted for several years, leaving men on the ground to their own devices as observed by Carl Kelsey, a scholar who visited the Dominican Republic during the early 1920s.[28] In addition, U.S. participation in World War I diverted time, energy, and attention to Europe, granting the military government almost complete autonomy from Washington.

These and other reasons account for the ambiguously defined functions of La Guardia. Was it a police force with an army function, or an army with a police function? In fact, it was a hybrid, "never large enough to discharge the military functions incumbent on the national army and too military to devote itself, except spasmodically, to its police duties," according to one of the Marine officers.[29]

This issue contributed to a defining disagreement between the two leading commanders, Chief of the Military Government Knapp and Commander of the Second Provisional Marine Brigade Joseph H. Pendleton. Knapp was in favor of a police force; Pendleton wanted an army. In defending his view, Knapp said, "I believe that Dominicans are capable of producing a body of excellent trained police, and in my opinion police are what are needed in this country, not an army."[30] Knapp's point of view prevailed, but the ambiguity and difficulties continued nonetheless. Washington had ordered the navy to assume full control, but it had not specified a policy to be carried out.[31]

Initially the military government divided the country into two districts. The Southern District, which had its headquarters at Santo Domingo City, was the responsibility of the Third Regiment. The Northern District, garrisoned by the Fourth Regiment, had its headquarters at Santiago. The Eastern District, composed of the provinces of El Seibo and Macorís, was created in 1919. All three districts were under the control of the brigade commander and general staff stationed in Santo Domingo.

The tenure of Brigade Commander Pendleton was short—he left Santo Domingo in October 1918. After his departure, Brigadier Generals Ben Hebard Fuller, Logan Feland, Charles G. Long, and Harry Lee commanded the Second Brigade, each serving for about a year. In addition, the Marines experienced a significant number of changes, varying from unexpected promotions to being posted in isolated rural areas.

Another major problem was the diversity of functions assigned to the new organization. In addition to its military duties, La Guardia was also assigned civilian tasks. Soldiers built highways, bridges, hospitals, and schools and took on varied public works projects that had been started by the Marines.

Thus, La Guardia was at work several months after the invasion, but the military government had not yet decided on uniforms, arms, or a salary scale for the different ranks of the "new" Dominican soldiers. Moreover, because "the organization was not complete yet, the ranks were not yet decided" and many noncommissioned officers of the Marine

Corps serving with La Guardia had to cover some of their own military expenses.[32] This particular situation placed the Marines stationed in the Dominican Republic at the level of the U.S. army of the early nineteenth century when it was mandatory for officers to buy their uniforms from their pay packet.[33] Nevertheless, for Dominicans an arbitrary salary scale was established. The monthly salary of a captain, for example, was $125.00; a private earned $15.00.[34]

In 1917 the military government issued several ordinances suitable for the professionalization of La Guardia. Order General No. 1 of May 14 established regulations regarding standardization of equipment and dress code specifications. Order General No. 2 of September 26 specified the rule of conduct expected from members of La Guardia and the punishments for violations. Hence, together with a set of values and attitudes, the Marines instilled—at least for a time—new patterns of order and discipline in the Dominican military. The Dominican officer corps benefited greatly from these regulations, and the application of basic administrative rules changed the image and perception of the military profession.

Furthermore, since almost no upper-class Dominicans joined La Guardia, the military government enlisted men from the middle and lower class. Having a different skeleton in the officer corps produced significant change in the composition of the military and in society in general by allowing for social mobility.

Being a soldier meant having a stable job with some social prestige, but even these incentives did not always attract recruits. Like the elite, members of the middle and lower classes refused to serve in La Guardia or under the forces of occupation. Most Dominicans, regardless of class, loathed the U.S. occupation. For example, Fellito Guerra, a member of the lower class and a baseball pitcher, received an offer from a Major League team to play in the United States. He refused the proposition in protest of the U.S. occupation of his homeland. Henceforth, Dominicans "adored him not only for his athletic skills, but his patriotic attitude."[35]

By September 1917 the total number of recruits was only 729; a year later it reached 1,161 men. In 1919 the organization had 1,186 men, little more than one-third of the ultimate goal of 3,000 men.[36]

In the meantime, Brigadier General Logan Feland reported that animosity from local governments and the general population greatly frustrated the Marines. Logan suggested that the success of the guerrillas not only undermined the prestige of the military government, but it also had social and racial connotations. For the commander, each raid meant a "victory over the hated whites," which was very appealing to the "ignorant" mass that had no empathy for the Marines.[37]

Cultural, Racial, and Social Tensions

Life in the Dominican Republic was not easy for the Marines. Moving in a hostile environment, U.S. soldiers were regularly attacked and harassed by Dominicans who resented their presence. Those "posted in the villages and smaller towns lived primitively in tent camps or native huts" without fresh supplies of food.[38] Far away from relatives and friends, overworked and sleep deprived, and facing near constant insurgency, some Marines violated military rules in carrying out their duties and provoked negative sentiments against the military government. To make things worse, when the United States entered World War I in 1917, "many of the 2nd Brigade's best officers left [the Dominican Republic] for the battlefront in France," and those who remained were not happy about their fate. As Commander Pendleton expressed, it was difficult, "when the first real war of one's service came, to be shelved down here."[39] Those stationed in the eastern region had to be on constant alert for guerrilla attacks.

After the displacement of Marines from the Dominican Republic to the battlefields of Europe in 1917, the military government opted to promote U.S. corporals and sergeants to the rank of captain to assist in the development of the organization. In June at least eight sergeants and six corporals were recommended for such promotion. Such promotion meant contempt and disrespect for La Guardia, and Dominican soldiers were infuriated and felt humiliated.[40] A Dominican lieutenant could be under the command of a U.S. corporal.

The behavior of the Marines and the enforcement of certain laws made matters worse. Many Marines obeyed military rules, but some of them began to engage in profiteering, unlawfully obtained liquor, exceeded authority, assaulted civilians, and committed manslaughter and other criminal offenses. Captain Charles Merkel, for example, tortured and killed several Dominican citizens in the eastern region, among other crimes. Merkel committed atrocities so grave that instead of facing the charges he opted for suicide. The Marines' high command attributed Merkel's harsh treatment of Dominicans to his German origin, but records indicate that other Marines committed similar barbaric crimes: civilians were put to death for minor infractions, incarcerated without having their day in court, and deprived of most basic civil liberties.[41] These were not isolated incidents: Marine violence was widespread. Under the occupation, Haitian citizens also suffered at the hands of the U.S. Marines.[42] In November and December 1921, in Haiti and the Dominican Republic, respectively, the members of the U.S. Senate Committee on the Occupation of Haiti and Santo Domingo listened to witnesses testify about the abuse, cruelty, and murder committed by the Marines. Some of the atrocities were heinous that they were considered crimes against humanity.

Controversy also erupted over the implementation and enforcement of certain laws that violated the customs and traditions of the country. For example, while fighting the guerrillas, the military government began the process of disarming the population by demanding that Dominicans surrender all arms.[43] The policy certainly reduced the number of weapons in circulation—and the number of homicides—but it also had psychological and cultural ramifications. Dominican fathers traditionally gave a revolver to each of their sons to recognize that they had reached manhood. In some cases, the teenagers would buy their own weapons to prove they were no longer boys but men. For someone to surrender his weapon was, to some extent, to surrender his adulthood and to break his bond with his father. Many resisted and were accused of concealing arms.[44]

In 1918 the military government tried to suppress another Dominican tradition: the cockfight. Cockfighting had a political connotation: it was said that if a Dominican government wanted to be overthrown, it only had to prohibit cockfights. Complicating matters was the fact that the guards in charge of enforcing the law were also cockfighters. Failure to enforce the law led to charge of disobedience; therefore, a guard who neglected this duty was subject to punishment according to U.S. military regulations.[45]

Furthermore, it appears that the military government underestimated the patriotic roots of the Dominican army. For a Dominican soldier, the suppression of the army born in February 1844 represented "the elimination of the most visible symbol of . . . sovereignty and . . . glories."[46] Although the United States restructured the military institution, Dominican soldiers continued to feel strong nationalistic sentiments.

The friction between the U.S. Marines and the Dominican soldiers had not only a nationalistic character but a racial one as well. The Marines arrived with a heavy cargo of prejudice and an anti-black attitude that likely set back the U.S. goal of professionalization of the Dominican military. It appears that racial discrimination became part of the recruitment process. As noted by Robison, he had "been given unofficial instructions to 'lighten' the Guardia a little," particularly at the officer level.[47] At the time of the occupation, about 85 percent of the Dominican population was either mulatto or black, but all were considered black by U.S. standards. The Marines viewed the Dominican Republic as a conquered land inhabited by inferior black people, which to abuses and confrontation. In describing the problem, Calder points out that race became a "potential irritant" in any encounter between Dominicans and Marines. When a writer accused Marine officers of using racist terms, "Military Governor Knapp came to their defense, questioned whether officers would do so," and denied that the U.S. enlisted men denigrated the Dominicans.[48] In the meantime, a combination of factors prompted the United States to devise a plan for the evacuation of its forces from the Dominican Republic.

La Guardia, the Marines, and the End of the Occupation

The Dominican resistance to the occupation, international pressure, and the election of Warren G. Harding to the presidency of the United States in November 1920, among other factors, all prompted the early departure of the U.S. Marines. After he took office, Harding, who criticized Wilson's intervention in Latin America, proposed a gradual withdrawal of the Marines, from the Dominican Republic, general elections supervised by the military government, recognition of all the acts of the military government (to maintain the efficiency of La Guardia), and a prolonged presence of U.S. officers after the departure of the Marines. The conditions of the withdrawal under Harding's plan caused a nationalistic uproar, particularly among members of the radical Unión Nacional Dominicana, who advocated the *pura y simple* position of unconditional withdrawal. While the nationalist resistance showed its strength through numerous demonstrations, those willing to negotiate began to reconsider their options.[49] In the interim it was time to question, again, whether the Dominican soldiers were capable of replacing the marines.

Franklin Delano Roosevelt, acting secretary of the navy, had expressed his concern about this issue in 1919 in a memorandum to the military government of Santo Domingo. He wanted to know how well prepared the national forces were to replace the Marines, and "what was going to be done" if the replacements were not ready.[50]

La Guardia was not prepared to take over in 1919, and it was not ready in 1921 either. To solve the problem, Brigadier General Harry Lee, head of the Marine Brigade, directed attention to the reorganization of La Guardia and the Dominicanization of the officer corps. The reorganization had to be accomplished in a relatively short time. Among the tasks to be completed were: restructuring the operational system; providing technical knowledge and military training; and centralizing the command to remove partisan politics from the barracks. Lee developed an aggressive recruitment program, created a training school, established a hierarchical structure, and began the implementation of an adequate administrative policy.

To train native officers and troops, the military academy began to function in August 1921. The educational center located on the premises of the Agricultural School of Haina had accommodations for about 25 officers and 130 enlisted men. The curriculum featured several disciplines, such as administration, law, sanitation, military topography, and basic principles of engineering and military tactics. The academy was the first Dominican military school to offer continuous graduation of cadets, and from it emerged a bureaucracy with a high level of preparedness and a close-knit military spirit.

In the meantime Francisco Peynado, an experienced lawyer familiar with Washington political culture, together with Harding's Secretary of State Charles E. Hughes and Sumner Welles, influential U.S. commissioner for negotiation with the Dominicans, prepared a new plan for withdrawal.

On September 23, 1922, Dominican newspapers announced the Hughes-Peynado Plan. Among other things, the plan called for the validation of the customs tariffs established by the military government and the installation of a provisional government. This plan was greeted unenthusiastically by Dominicans. Lee and Robison didn't like it either, especially the provisions for the complete withdrawal of the forces of occupation and the diminished role of the military government. Lee and Robison argued that La Guardia was not ready for the transition according to the plan and requested that U.S. officers be left in positions of power. Like the Dominicans, Welles strongly disagreed with the military leaders and no changes were made to the agreement. On October 21, 1922, Juan Bautista Vicini Burgos became provisional president, and he would stay in power until July 12, 1924. On the same day, Military Governor Robison left the country. Lee, as the ranking officer of the U.S. Marine Corps in the Dominican Republic, replaced him. With the installation of the provisional government, a number of restrictions limited the activities of the Marines. They could not carry arms outside the perimeter of their barracks. Movements of the regular troops throughout the country needed to be approved by the Dominican Government. Commander Lee had military duties only and was responsible for completing the training of La Guardia.

With a more passive role, Lee had more time to concentrate on the execution of his mission. Considering that the primary goal of the military government had been to reorganize the military, it was imperative to accomplish that goal before the U.S. forces left the Dominican Republic. After the provisional government assumed control, La Guardia expanded and, with accelerated promotions, the number of officers doubled. Under the direction of Colonels Richard M. Cutts and Presley M. Rixey, the Marines expedited the training of Dominican officers. Between March 1923 and July 1924, more than 400 men received advanced training. By the time Dominicans elected Horacio Vásquez as president on July 12, 1924, approximately 1,300 men had received general training. Thus, in a relatively short period of time, the Marines transformed the military from disorganized, divided units into a unified, centralized institution with standardized training, modern weapons, and a hierarchical command.[51]

The United States had finally achieved its goal of transforming the Dominican military. When the Marines left, their reorganization of the Dominican armed forces had changed not only the military institution itself but also the structure of Dominican society. By reshaping the armed forces, the occupation engendered a new paradigm of military-civilian relations that forever changed the course of Dominican history. On the domestic front, the era of strong local and regional political leaders came to an end, as well as the domination of the officer corps by the elite. Despite many problems, the military government achieved its goal of organizing and modernizing the Dominican forces along professional lines. The occupation was instrumental in transforming the social structure of the power-holding group as the officer corps became more socioeconomically diverse. In this respect, considering that "military socialization most readily transmits culture," especially in less industrialized countries,[52] one may argue that La Guardia reflected the cultural values of society and transmitted the cultural ethos of the military into society.

Cultural Interactions and Artistic Expressions

The eight years of U.S. military occupation left Dominican society with some cultural ties to the United States. By and large, the upper classes gradually shifted their taste from European to American products. U.S. music, dances, and language also permeated Hispanic cultural traditions of the urban elite.

Many Dominicans, however, rejected all things American. The merengue, a dance full of African rhythm and melodies that began to develop in the mid-1880s, evolved into an instrument of resistance in the Cibao region and established a link to patriotism during the occupation.[53] In addition, a distinguished group of artists and writers used their creative talent to denounce the occupation. Abelardo Rodríguez Urdaneta, for example, created an image in which the Dominican fatherland was tied to the claws of the eagle. Lincoln, awakened by the cry of freedom from the Dominican people, arose ashamed from his coffin. Américo Lugo published a newspaper article titled "La semana patriótica" in which he accused the United States of demolishing Dominican institutions such as the Dominican army, as well as Dominican cultural heritage.[54] Other writers, such as Fabio Fiallo, Félix Evaristo Mejía, Ercilia Pepín, Max Henríquez Ureña, and newspaper editors, contributed to the nationalist literary campaign against the military government. In the end, as most people refused allegiance to any U.S. customs, the presence of the Marines reinforced Dominican nationalistic and militaristic values.

There were a few positive outcomes of the occupation. One was the development of baseball, which Cubans had introduced to the Dominicans at the end of 1891. Amateur baseball flourished in Santiago, Santo Domingo, San Pedro de Macorís, and other major cities; professional teams were already established by the time of the occupation. The Marines joined local baseball clubs and sponsored games and competition for recreation and to engender good will. Competitions between the Marines and Dominican baseball players increased interest in the sport among segments of the general population.[55] Today, baseball is a national pastime, and many Dominicans play in the U.S. Major Leagues and earn large salaries.

Educational reform, improvement of health and sanitation, and implementation of the first Dominican census in 1920 created social legislation concerning women and children. These and other significant reforms meant to improve the administrative system and to deliver better services to society.

Since the Marines occupied Haiti and the Dominican Republic at the same time and reorganized both countries' militaries, the reorganization changed the balance of forces between the two armies. After the withdrawal of U.S. forces, the Haitian army realized that it had lost its dominance over the Dominican army. Although the Haitian army had more men (2,817 officers and soldiers, compared with 2,743 Dominican officers and soldiers), it did not have the military equipment to invade her neighbor: the occupation forces left 3,000 Springfield rifles and some machine guns but destroyed "all the military equipment and armament of the Haitian government."[56] Thus, the occupation "settled once and for all the inability of Haiti to invade the Dominican Republic."[57]

Like the Dominican Republic, Haiti—as well as Nicaragua—was influenced by the U.S. occupation. Military power was centralized, the forces received professional training, and the nations increased their military strength with modern U.S. equipment. The idea of organizing constabularies as apolitical forces and using soldiers as teachers of democracy, however, was a failure. In Haiti, where the Marines kept figurehead presidents during the entire occupation period, Stenio Vincent, elected in 1930, had no control over the army. The USMC directed all the operations of the Haitian army. In the Dominican Republic and Nicaragua, respectively, soon after the Marines left, two strongmen trained by the Marines, Trujillo and Anastasio Somoza, assumed power not by democratic procedures but by violent means. Both used the military as an instrument to achieve political goals.

3. FROM SOLDIER TO COMMANDER IN CHIEF

Trujillo's Military Career

The origin and development of the military explain why the history of the Dominican Republic, for the most part, may be written based on a men-at-arms story. Long years of fighting had contributed to the spread of militarism and enhanced the image and power of the army's leaders. Society saw them as builders of the nation and offered them respect and reverence. As a result, commanding generals like Trujillo seized opportunities to become political leaders. To understand Trujillo as a political figure one needs to study Trujillo's military career. It reveals not only the man's persona and multiple facets of his personality, as well as his skills as an astute political maneuverer, but it provides insight into the military culture, especially its penetration of the political system and the social divisions of the Dominican Republic in the early twentieth century.

Trujillo's Formative Years

Described by an American diplomat as a "handsome man in uniform, with an erect bearing and the aura of an emperor,"[1] Trujillo was born into a lower-middle-class family of *gente de segunda* (second-class people) of mixed Dominican, Spanish, and Haitian ancestry. Trujillo's parents, José Trujillo Valdés and Julia Molina, had eleven children, seven boys and four girls. Trujillo, the third child, was born in San Cristóbal on October 24, 1891. Like many other children of his time, Trujillo attended school irregularly, but his schooling continued at home under the guidance of his maternal grandmother, Luisa Ercina Chevalier, and her second husband, Juan Pablo Pina, who owned a printing press and was one of the few cultured individuals of San Cristóbal.

Some of Trujillo's biographers accuse him of being a delinquent, a cattle thief, and a convicted check forger. Another accusation characterizes him as a member of La 44, a gang known for terrorism and robberies in the eastern region.[2] He is said to have engaged in blackmail, forceful persuasion, and graft.

His first job was as a telegraph operator. He later worked in the American-owned sugar mill San Isidro and in the Puerto Rican–owned mill Boca Chica where he became a security guard. Those who worked with him admired his physical and mental capabilities and tireless dedication to work. Trujillo became fascinated by soldierly life early. In 1910 during his service as a telegraphist in San Cristóbal, Trujillo tried to show that he was a person with a special calling for military life. When one of his fellow workers, Eudoro Canó, was sending a message from the local chief of police to General Alfredo Victoria, commander of the Santo Domingo fortress, Trujillo, expressing his desire for power, remarked that he had "the feeling and the conviction" that one day he would have more power in the army than General Victoria had.[3] He aspired to the highest military post even before he applied to La Guardia. For years he had been signing his letters to friends and relatives as "General Trujillo," "Chief of the Army," or other imaginary ranks.

Trujillo and the U.S. Marine Corps

The landing of the U.S. Marines offered Trujillo the opportunity to become a soldier; for this reason most of the studies about Trujillo highlight the close connection between Trujillo's dictatorship and the occupation. In his study *The Military and the State in Latin America*, Alan Rouquie considers Trujillo's rise to power as "a poison fruit of the Yankee occupation."[4] In Howard Wiarda's analysis of the dictatorship, Trujillo "carried the work of the Marines forward" in the process of modernizing and equipping the armed forces.[5] Indeed, the Marines paved the way for Trujillo's agenda. From La Guardia he emerged as a politician and managed to obtain the highest position of power: president of the republic.

On January 11, 1919, Trujillo joined La Guardia as a provisional second lieutenant. In his application Trujillo described himself as a white married man who did not drink or smoke. He also indicated that he had no criminal record. La Guardia honored Trujillo's request for admission to the military, and he was sent to San Pedro de Macoris, where he developed a reputation for fighting against the rural armed resistance. There, he learned how to eliminate the opposition violently.

The pressure on the U.S. military government to create the military academy in 1921 allowed Trujillo to become an officer in La Guardia. He was among the first twenty-five officers to enroll in the academy, where he pursued his training "under the wise guidance of the American instructors."[6] But other factors—including his employment record, letters of recommendation from his former employers at Boca Chica, and a lack of nationalistic scruples against joining the U.S. military forces—also aided him in his career. His daughter Flor de Oro admitted, "[U]nlike many Dominicans, who refused to collaborate with the Yankees, [Trujillo] joined the native police force recruited by the Marines to help keep order."[7]

The military uniform appealed to Trujillo tremendously. Even after becoming president, he would frequently attend public events wearing his military uniform. The one he liked the most, his uniform of Generalissimo, was a "symphony of gold." A combination of "a white-plumed hat thickly crusted with gold braid, gold brocaded swallow-tailed coat with hefty epaulets, [and a] tricolored sash and gold-striped blue trousers"[8] had some features of Trujillo's other uniforms. Jesús de la Rosa, a scholar and former navy officer, believes Trujillo's preference for military uniforms reflected his admiration for Heureaux, and indeed Trujillo's uniforms were almost identical to those of Heureaux.[9]

Personal appearance was important to Trujillo, and he had a passion for nice clothes and cleanliness. Admiring the manners of the rich and famous, Trujillo carried himself as if he were one of them. Nevertheless, his ancestry and background barred him from the upper class. Trujillo also loved medals. He had an extensive and valuable collection of medals awarded to him by the Dominican Republic, by foreign countries, and by international organizations, but the decoration he was the proudest of, according to Arturo Espaillat, was "his faded threadbare medal attesting to his service to the Marines."[10]

Trujillo assimilated the Marines' military culture well and rose to the top of his military career in less than ten years. A combination of political and military factors as well as social maneuvers and historical circumstances contributed to his speedy rise.

The Military Government and Trujillo's Records

Trujillo's accelerated advancement rested partially on the withdrawal of the Marines. Fortunately for him, as the Marines prepared to leave the Dominican Republic, all first lieutenants were promoted to captain, but

Trujillo was the only officer to be promoted to captain without first serving as a first lieutenant.[11] He also fulfilled the Marines' expectations of a good officer. In the military academy he distinguished himself as a good student. Several of his proficiency reports indicate a grade average of 3.5, and Captain Thomas Watson, recruiting officer of the USMC and Trujillo's instructor and mentor, characterized Trujillo's performance as one of the best in the service.[12] Apparently young Trujillo's cooperative attitude toward the occupation forces paid off for him in many ways.

Despite Trujillo's academic success, however, court papers give evidence of his less than stellar behavior. A year before he went to the military academy, on January 23, 1920, Lieutenant Trujillo stood trial for having "engaged in improper and illicit sexual relations" with a seventeen-year-old Dominican girl. Isabel Guzmán testified that Trujillo raped her on several occasions over three days. In the same court-martial proceedings, José Núñez, Carlos Alduey, and Estevan Alduey accused him of extortion and bribery. The trial lasted from January 23 to March 4, 1920. Eleven witnesses testified for the prosecution, but Trujillo denied all accusations and was acquitted of all charges.[13] According to the prosecution, a conviction would have been a "scandal and disgrace of the 'Guardia Nacional Dominicana' and of the Military Government of the United States in the Dominican Republic."[14] Scholars Richard Millett and Marvin Soloman conclude that Trujillo may have been acquitted for two reasons: a conviction may have encouraged the denunciation of other crimes committed by members of La Guardia and the Marines at a time when they were busy fighting anti-occupation guerrillas; and "accusations of abuses against the civil population seem to have had little influence upon the American evaluation of an officer's potential value to the Guardia."[15]

The trial did not hamper Trujillo's future. Ironically, his military career progressed at ever-increasing speed after the hearing, and on December 22, 1921, he advanced to the rank of second lieutenant. Other accusations and even more controversial developments also failed to impede his professional advancement. Among the incidents, the February 23, 1924, murder of Major Julio César Lora, commander of the Northern Department, by Lieutenant Pedro Pablo Sanabia became "a source for Trujillo's advancement and ammunition for his enemies."[16] The motive for the crime arose not from a military confrontation or a political disagreement but from a love affair: Sanabia's wife was Lora's mistress.[17]

How did the husband find out about the affair? Public opinion pointed to Trujillo, who was very much aware of Sanabia's explosive temperament and knew Lora's death would be beneficial to him. A mere ten days after the crime was committed, Trujillo became the acting commander of the Northern Department, even though he was ninth in line for the promotion. The officers ahead of him in seniority were outraged and protested this violation of the military code. Promotion, however, was based on both seniority and a good military record. Because Ramón Saviñón bested Trujillo in that regard, Trujillo saw to it that Saviñón would not prevail. According to some witnesses, Trujillo organized a party ostensibly to celebrate the impending promotion of his colleague. Trujillo somehow managed to get Saviñón drunk and left him in Santo Domingo's Plaza Central, and he did not receive the promotion.[18] Although Trujillo's direct involvement could not be proven, this type of episode, with some variation, repeated itself time and again during his thirty-one years as dictator. Those familiar with Trujillo knew that no obstacle, moral or otherwise, was too great for him. As a former colonel said, "Trujillo would eat an elephant without belching."[19]

Trujillo and Society

When Trujillo applied for a commission in La Guardia in December 1918, the population of the republic was about 800,000, about 85 percent of whom lived in rural areas.[20] More than two-thirds of the working class were employed in agricultural production and cattle farming, and this group, together with small landholders, landless peasants, and impoverished individuals without job classification, made up the lower class. The middle class, including professionals, intellectuals, and commercial groups with less than major investment (like retailers of domestic products and foreign merchandise), was just beginning to form. The sharply delineated upper class comprised wealthy farmers and landowners, large commercial investors, exporters and importers, and also rich or well-paid lawyers, physicians, and engineers. Otto Schoenrich, a U.S. judge who visited the Dominican Republic in 1917, observed that many members of the wealthier class spoke one or more foreign languages and had studied or traveled in Europe or the United States.[21] The gap separating the rich from the poor, and the urban from rural population, was well-defined.

In his search for power, glory, and prestige, Trujillo may had forgotten how deeply social class distinctions could run in Dominican society of the 1920s. Social stratification was both extended and complicated. Power and wealth alone were insufficient for crossing the line separating the elite from the rest of the population. In 1927 Brigadier General Trujillo became chief of the army, but this prestigious position did not insulate him from public humiliation when the aristocratic Club Unión, "the sanctum of the well-born of Santo Domingo," rejected his membership application.[22] Indeed, the club's rejection could not have been due to his lack of wealth, for he had already accumulated a considerable fortune; his social origins disqualified him. Trujillo did not belong to the *gente de primera*, the white or almost white aristocratic elite.[23]

Trujillo's Women and Marriages

Before the humiliating experience of Club Unión, other social clubs rejected Trujillo's applications. Determined to change his social position for the better, in 1925 Trujillo divorced his wife, Aminta Ledesma, a woman of humble origins, and then married Bienvenida Ricart, a member of the aristocracy, in 1927. With Bienvenida's support, he gained admission to the club that had shunned him. When he was elected club president in 1932, he enacted his revenge by allowing the organization to languish.

In 1929 during his second marriage, he fathered a son, Rafael, known as Ramfis, by María Martínez, "a woman of Spanish descent who was then a great beauty. What was perhaps more important, she had great talents for acquiring, organizing and managing many types of business."[24] Astute and audacious, she matched Trujillo "in all the nuances of personality and character."[25] In 1935 Trujillo sent Bienvenida on a trip to Paris. During her absence the Congress passed a new divorce law allowing divorce if the wife did not bear a child after five years of marriage. Trujillo divorced Bienvenida, then married María later that same year. Ironically, after the divorce Bienvenida became Trujillo's mistress and had a child, Odette, by him.

The three-times-married, twice-divorced Trujillo had a long list of extramarital affairs. One of his biographers justified such behavior in noting that women elated him and feminine beauty "genuinely impressed" him. In addition, "handsome and of striking bearing, it hardly need be added that his enormous popularity with the fair sex stems from something other than politics."[26] Considering himself a macho, he needed to show his sexual prowess by having as many women as he could. Stories about his sexual appetites were plentiful, and parents tried to keep their unmarried daughters out of the public eye. They knew that Trujillo had a group of men in charge of "collecting beautiful women" for his harem.[27] Virginal girls were especially appealing to him. To "repair" their honor, Trujillo often selected military men to marry them. Not all women were reluctant to satisfy Trujillo's sexual requests; for some, to be chosen as an "object of Trujillo's desire elicited a certain forbidden pride, even among the highly sheltered but rebellious adolescent daughters of the elite who snuck off to official functions."[28] On the other hand, many refused to please the dictator, as did Graciela Fermín, a beauty of high moral standards who resisted all types of pressure to become another of Trujillo's sexual objects.[29] Similarly, Minerva Mirabal, who detested Trujillo and his regime, rejected Trujillo's personal interest in her and, as we shall see, paid the consequences. Nevertheless, because his power and personality appealed to many, he had numerous concubines. Some of them were secretly kept, but others were well-known, as was Lina Lovatón, "a tall and beautiful young woman whose family was one of the most exclusive in Ciudad Trujillo."[30] At first Trujillo seduced her; later she fell in love with him and had a daughter and a son by him. Under the threat of Trujillo's wife, María, Lina moved to Miami to live comfortably in a mansion that the dictator bought for her.

Trujillo's romantic and sexual relationships were occasionally interconnected with his political manipulation. He used his mistresses not only for personal gratification but for political purposes as well. Trujillo seduced and used women to punish enemies, to humiliate functionaries, and to test and reward loyalty.[31]

Projecting his macho image beyond the romantic realm, early in the dictatorship, Lieutenant Teófilo Mercado informed the dictator about anti-Trujillista activities, apparently organized by exiles in Cuba. Trujillo told Mercado not to worry because a government "headed by an *hombre macho*" and ready to face any event will not be overthrown by "little notes or by lies."[32] This posture revealed a profile of the man who sought control the nation in a military fashion.

Trujillo's USMC Friends

Trujillo knew the value of maintaining a good relationship with his former instructors and other U.S. officers, and he nourished those connections for more than four decades. After 1930, when he took control of the state, he invited those friends to the Dominican Republic and entertained them lavishly.

Colonel Richard M. Cutts, one of Trujillo's Marine commanders, was among his best friends in the USMC. At the beginning of Trujillo's political career, Cutts acted as a protector. During the hostile political campaign of 1930, the U.S government became suspicious of the army's participation in political disturbances, and questions surfaced about Trujillo's involvement. Cutts, however, believed Trujillo had the political cleverness and capability to deal with the Dominican political climate because he was "more Americanized" than any other Dominican. Cutts also trusted that Trujillo could carry forward the work of the Marines, tightening central control and improving the state's military strength to maintain stability.[33]

Colonel James McLean, a former employee of the customs receivership who became an officer of La Guardia, was also Trujillo's friend. McLean knew well Trujillo's uncle, Teódulo Pina Chevalier, with whom he coauthored a pamphlet on the Haitian-Dominican border. *Datos históricos sobre la frontera dominico-haitiana* delineates many of the policies Trujillo later implemented in his program for the "Dominicanization" of the border.

Upon completion of his military training, Trujillo maintained a particularly close connection with Watson. Apparently young Trujillo's cooperative attitude toward the occupation forces paid off for him in many ways. The U.S. officer, who rose to the rank of lieutenant colonel in La Guardia, later served as instructor of the military academy established by Trujillo. Watson also worked as Trujillo's liaison to the U.S. government for the purchase of arms, to acquire loans, and to pass along praiseworthy publicity. Personnel of the U.S. Legation in the Dominican Republic expressed its concern about Watson's working for Trujillo, because the president behaved as though he could obtain whatever he wanted from the United States.[34]

According to reports from the legation, Trujillo was "greatly attached to Major Watson," especially after a hurricane devastated the capital city in September 1930. At Trujillo's request, Major Watson came back to the Dominican Republic, this time with a double role as naval attaché and director of food distribution and hospital services. He also helped strengthen the intelligence service. Watson and Trujillo's friendship eventually extended beyond military affairs. Occasionally the Watson family, at Trujillo's invitation, spent their vacations in the Dominican Republic, and the major's children addressed Trujillo as "Uncle Rafael."[35]

Praising himself as the guarantor of the U.S. military legacy in the Dominican Republic, in his correspondence with his former instructors Trujillo assured them that he had maintained the organizational structure of La Guardia. He explained that to maintain the Marines' discipline inside the quarters had required great effort and energy on his part, to the extent that his hair had prematurely turned gray.[36]

Good relationships with USMC officers played an important role in Trujillo's military career, but during his dictatorship they became particularly significant. From a political point of view, Trujillo established a relationship that made some of the USMC officers Trujillo's clients. This relationship stressed personal rather than institutional connections, in which "the patron [acted] as a broker for clients seeking material rewards."[37] In some instances Trujillo was the patron; in others he was the client. Clearly, after his consolidation of power, having a lot to offer to his U.S. friends, the dictator acted more as a broker.

In any case, Trujillo exploited and manipulated U.S. military officers, as well as government officials and businessmen. With flair, affection, decorations, and ceremonies, Trujillo maintained a close connection with important figures of the USMC. During Trujillo's first visit to the United States in 1939, U.S. officers welcomed the dictator enthusiastically, lobbied and obtained a meeting with President Roosevelt during a tea reception, invited their former pupil to visit military installations, and entertained him with several receptions and parties.[38] The relationship between Trujillo and his U.S. military friends was so firmly cemented that even against the Department of State guidelines, Trujillo's friends in the USMC assisted the dictator in acquiring war material and in dealing with complex diplomatic issues, as well as obtaining political support from the White House and from influential politicians, even until the final days of his dictatorship.

Domestic Politics

Domestic politics also played an important role in Trujillo's speedy rise to the top. His promotions reaffirmed the dynamic interplay between militarism and politics that characterized Dominican political history. Trujillo's promotions succeeded each other at an astonishingly rapid pace from 1924 to 1930. On September 11, 1924, at age thirty-three, Trujillo received a promotion from captain to major and assigned temporarily to head the Northern Command, an influential position with high political visibility. Barely three months after this promotion, on December 6, he advanced to lieutenant colonel and was appointed chief of staff and assistant commander of the Dominican National Police, the new name of La Guardia. Six months later on June 22, 1925, President Vásquez appointed him Colonel Commandant of the Dominican National Police, replacing Buenaventura Cabral. Cabral, a colonel commandant of La Guardia in August 1922, replaced the U.S. commander when the Marines left the country. The appointment pleased Welles, because he considered Cabral a professional soldier "without political affiliations or aspirations" who would keep the military institutions free of political factionalism.[39] But soon after the occupation forces left the country, Cabral lost his position after he was accused of inefficiency and lacking commanding ability. The real reason Cabral was ousted had nothing to do with his abilities.

Vásquez, an experienced politician, knew the importance of having the military chief politically identified with the party in power.[40] Trujillo was considered a loyal "horacista" and became Vásquez's protégé.

The return to political-military appointments frustrated the U.S. government; the U.S. legation expressed its concern about the Dominican National Police's involvement in politics "failing to fulfill entirely the functions originally assigned to it by the American authorities."[41] The U.S. officials expected that promotions would be made on the basis of merit only. Their disappointment was, perhaps, particularly acute because Cabral's command had close ties to the military government.

Others also benefited from promotions based on politics. Simón Díaz, an old friend of the president, received an appointment to captain of the Dominican National Police without ever attending the military school, a requirement the United States had instituted. The old trend of political appointments persisted, exerting a corrosive effect on an officer corps that continued to dabble in politics.

William Russell, minister to the Dominican Republic, confronted the fact that eight years of efforts to separate political factionalism from the military were having little effect. He expressed his anger in several memos to the U.S. secretary of state and blamed the politicians for undermining the professionalization of the soldiers. By distracting the army from its main function and redirecting the institution along political lines, Russell pointed out, the Vásquez administration was developing the conditions for self-destruction.[42]

Russell was right. If one accepts the theory that "as the officer corps becomes more professional over time, military coups against the government will decline and the armed forces will tend thereafter to seek their goals as a pressure group,"[43] then Vásquez undermined the efforts to professionalize the military. He provided Trujillo with a framework with which to raise the military above the legal foundation of civilian government.

Changing La Guardia

When Trujillo became chief of the military he assumed control of an organization that to some extent was disconnected from the traditional power structure. But it did not take him long to bridge the nascent gap between military and politics. The military soon "was a one-man operation with all power centralized in the hands of Trujillo."[44]

Converting the military into the primary source of his authority began shortly after his appointment as chief of staff. Trujillo, showing self-reliance and organizational skills, sent a report to Luis Pelletier, secretary of the interior, police, war, and navy. Trujillo reported on the state of the armed forces and suggested an extensive top-to-bottom revision of the military structure to heighten effectiveness and professionalism of the forces. Trujillo's suggestions focused on four major areas—equipment, military code, military training, and intelligence—but he also mentioned other aspects demanding immediate attention: the reorganization of the medical corps and the revision of the accounting system.[45] These reforms set Trujillo's military project in motion.

The activation of covert operations was crucial to Trujillo's military and political plans. Thus, he also proposed the reorganization of the secret police as "an independent entity organized on a scientific basis, giving it the importance it deserves." To implement this plan, Trujillo requested the appointment of a Committee of Experts, whose membership included himself.[46]

After the government approved the request at the end of December 1924, Trujillo dedicated the next six years to promoting the necessity of improving and expanding the military and to advancing his political goals. With literary elegance, his public relations team created polished images of his military achievements, particularly after June 23, 1927, when the Dominican National Police was converted into a brigade with two regiments and reduced its name to two words, National Police.

Trujillo received a promotion to brigadier general on August 13. From then on, Trujillo's political career took off in earnest. More substantive changes began to take place after Trujillo's promotion, as he grasped the opportunity to further restructure the military. On August 17 he issued a military ordinance and introduced a new structure in line with his plans for military expansion.[47] Emphasizing strength and national pride, this new structure included a more fundamental restructuring of the forces: converting the National Police into an army. Planning to reshape the military institution with the help of civilian journalists such as Roberto Despradel and Rafael Vidal, Brigadier General Trujillo informed the public about the transformation and effective reorganization the forces had undergone since he was in charge. Yet, he said, more needed to be done. The forces needed to be strengthened, and the two thousand men under his command needed better equipment.[48]

The annual report of 1928 of the secretary of the interior, police, war, and navy indicated that in 1927 the military had an infantry corps, but it lacked artillery and the cavalry unit was very small. The organization had thirty-nine trucks, fifteen cars, and ten buses but used freight cars to transport military equipment. Directing the media campaign, Vidal, who met Trujillo while serving a sentence for a murder, emphatically opposed the U.S. notion of using the police only as a security force, and argued that the Dominican Republic of 1927 needed to have an army in addition to a well-organized and well-trained security force. He believed a correlation between the army, as the guarantor of the institutional system, and the state, as the guarantor of progress, demanded imperative action. Vidal proposed expanding the military from 2,000 to 5,000 men, subdividing the military into infantry and cavalry, and modernizing equipment and transportation infrastructure, which would include airplanes. To establish the superiority of the army, Vidal called for continuing improvement in training, better living conditions in the barracks, and the recruitment of specialists, including military health experts.

Patriotism and resentment against the U.S. military intervention compelled him to support the reorganization and modernization of the armed forces. Vidal pointed out that "the recent military occupation of the country by the United States, unfair and painful, was marked by the absence of a Dominican army, and this reason justifies our need to create a small army."[49] Vidal's recollection of the occupation and the diminished military status of the armed forces it brought remained unfavorable even sixty years later. During a series of interviews with me in 1978 and 1979, Vidal, well in his eighties, eloquent and clearly argumentative, expressed more than once his anger against the "foreign yoke." He did not deny having met Trujillo in prison or that he served Trujillo well and received material rewards for his service. He did, however, deny that he was an assassin, claiming that he killed another man in act of self-defense. He also emphasized that he fell out of favor with Trujillo. But, militarily speaking, more important was his work as editor of *La revista militar*. Vidal used the editorials to advocate the transformation of the police into an army. The journal, simply known as *La revista*, was created in January 1926.

La Revista and Homage to Trujillo

Trujillo was a master at using propaganda to his advantage. The published objectives of *La Revista* were to defend the interests of the Dominican National Police, to disseminate information relevant to its members, and to relate educational and cultural topics to the forces. As an analysis of the material published in the journal indicates, however, the true objectives were quite different. In fact, *La Revista*'s main goals were to project a positive image of the military and to praise Trujillo's accomplishments. Both editorials and articles usually included adulation for Trujillo, the transformer of the military organization, which was on par with other armies around the world in efficiency, discipline, equipment, and hygiene.

The editorials argued that the force organized by the United States was, to some extent, alienated from its mission of protecting the national integrity of the country. Indeed, the Dominican people had come to view the Dominican National Police as a force imposed by a foreign government. Congressmen strongly debated to change the name of the National Police to National Army. Congressman Tácito Cordero argued vigorously against the name and functions of the National Police, because, in his opinion, the force was nothing more than a "colonial replica" of the Marine Corps.[50] In addition to stirring patriotic feelings, Cordero may have enraged the elite against the foreign forces that had provoked their eviction from political power. Independent of the elite's motivations, the mere idea of a nonpolitical military establishment, imposed by the foreign government that occupied the country for eight years, could not work in the Dominican Republic of the 1920s; Dominicans had by then developed a fierce nationalism.

The editorials of *La Revista* of May 1928, for example, headlined strong criticism of the U.S. creation of the Dominican National Police as the only armed institution in the country. According to the editor, the military government created the police force to help exert U.S. guardianship "over the small nations along the Panama route" and to produce changes that altered the "special relationship" of these nations with the

Department of State because these changes regulated "unfortunate economic dependence on Wall Street bankers."[51] On May 17, 1928, the Dominican National Police changed its name to the National Army. At first the transformation appeared to be nothing more than a name change aimed at reinforcing control, albeit one that signified nationalism and a rejection of the U.S. notion of a Dominican security force. But there was more.

La Revista clearly indicated the political direction in which Trujillo was headed with the name change: experimenting with and imposing a new form of military organization based on indoctrination and control. With consummate ability, he managed to get the enlisted men and officers to subsidize their own brainwashing. It was mandatory for all soldiers, regardless of rank, to buy the magazine.

La Revista also served as a means of psychological intimidation. A December 1928 editorial, for example, outlines ten years of Trujillo's military career, praising his intelligence, capacity for effective control, and understanding of all the parts of the military machine. It then concluded with the warning that any military person who visited Trujillo's office, regardless of rank, should understand beforehand that Trujillo's eyes would penetrate him to the deepest part of his body and soul; Trujillo would know the truth.[52] No one should be foolish enough to lie to El Jefe.

After 1930 Trujillo further stressed the supremacy of subjective intimidation. Psychological power became psychological terror, institutionalized by the state as a mechanism of control. People were to stop thinking and just obey in order to survive. Dato Pagán Perdomo, a university professor and radical opponent of the regime, described the people's fears. The psychological terror, he explained, penetrated people's minds and bodies to the extent that those who during the night dared to think of the dictator's downfall were sick the following day with fever and a nervous breakdown. Pagán's words illustrate the state of mind of the people, and reflect the fear of Dominican society during the dictatorship.[53] The process was gradual, but its effect was profound.

Politics and Corruption
Other journals also magnified Trujillo's work. For example, in 1926 the *Revista Carnaval* dedicated a special edition to describing "Trujillo's brilliant job" as commander. In an effort to highlight Trujillo's achievement, the magazine minimized the importance of the Marines in organizing

and training the National Police. The magazine pointed out Trujillo's efficiency in reshaping the National Police into a self-sustaining army, capable of protecting the nation from internal and external attacks.[54]

One of Trujillo's apologists described the members of the armed forces before Trujillo became commander as men with very elementary notions about militarism. After Trujillo took the reins, however, soldiers received military training that placed them above Caribbean and Latin American military personnel.[55] No one could deny that the military improved significantly during Trujillo's tenure as commander. However, the improvement served the future dictator, not the Dominican people.

Signaling the direction of his militarization plan, Trujillo argued that there was a need for more up-to-date weaponry. For example, he reported that the army was using "ordinary 'Lee Enfield' rifles" and that it immediately needed sufficient cannons and machine guns in order to create an artillery unit.[56] Thus, the government approved expenditure for special military needs, including the purchase of Springfield and Browning rifles and the acquisition of military vehicles. Early in 1927 the government paid $500,000 to a number of military suppliers for vehicles, gasoline, arms, and other goods, but Trujillo could never demonstrate how the funds were spent.[57]

In 1928 a scandal broke out in the army. The government wanted to purchase two thousand rifles from a British arms dealer but initially ordered only five hundred rifles and one thousand bullets per rifle. The Dominican government paid seventy-seven dollars per rifle, but it was later discovered that the rifles cost only twenty-five dollars in London. Subsequently the government annulled the rest of the order, but Trujillo, and perhaps high-ranking Dominican officials involved in the deal, benefited handily either through illegal commissions or under-the-table payments.

Furthermore, it came to light that the weapons, made in 1893 and refurbished in 1910, did not meet the army's needs. Thus, the government needed to buy more modern weapons soon thereafter, and Trujillo would continue to profit from the lack of governmental financial control.[58] In other words, "behind the facade of reformer and modernizer, Trujillo was undermining his superiors" and profiting at the expense of the state and the Dominican taxpayers.[59]

While Trujillo worked on consolidating his position as the supreme military authority, he was also strengthening his political position, acting with significant autonomy from the central government. A group of congressmen concerned with the signals of self-government in the military requested an investigation of the Dominican National Police. According to them, the institution was functioning with such independence from the central government that indeed it acted as "a government within the government."[60]

There is no way to assess all the motivations behind Trujillo's political maneuvers, but there is solid evidence that when he reached the highest rank in the army, he realized he was in a position to reorganize the military in the way he wanted.

As a young man Trujillo dreamed of being a soldier, and he had the skills, talent, and will to accomplish this goal. The presence of the Marines facilitated Trujillo's military career, and La Guardia was an ideal for Trujillo to develop his political ambitions. Once in control of the military, Trujillo actively sought the transformation of the security forces left by the Marines. But he never forgot his Marine Corps training and instructors. He honored both the organization and instructors by naming the east side of Avenida George Washington "U.S. Marine Corps." But if Trujillo was indebted to anyone for his meteoric rise both militarily and politically, it was to Horacio Vásquez. When Vásquez came to power in July 1924, Trujillo was a captain, but when Vásquez left the presidency in February 1930, Trujillo replaced him. By elevating Trujillo to the highest military position, President Vásquez indirectly offered Trujillo the opportunity to demonstrate shrewdness and pragmatism. Indeed, by accelerating Trujillo's military promotions, President Vásquez contributed significantly to Trujillo's rise to the presidency. With the president on his side, as we shall see, General Trujillo became, ironically, his mentor's strongest opponent. The general changed the relationship between the military and government by developing a new civilian-military bond through which he rewarded and compensated civilians, who in turn built alliances and supported Trujillo's political program. Studies about Trujillo indicate how his skill at combining national pride with paternalism and ruthlessness caused him to be loved, feared, and hated by the Dominicans. Some accounts detail how he was brutal, cynical, and progressively maniacal. Others describe him as a hard worker and a good organizer with a strict sense of authority.[61] Competence, organization, and discipline were inherent in Trujillo's military persona, and he demanded the same from his subordinates.

4. THE ROAD TO THE PRESIDENCY
FOR THE ARMY'S COMMANDER
Society, State, and Soldiers

Under accelerated militarization from 1916 to 1924, a generation of Dominicans grew to political maturity struggling against the U.S. military occupation. While fighting the military government, the people hoped that the country would improve state-society relations through democratic election of a civilian government. At first the administration of Horacio Vásquez generated some optimism with its marked respect for civil liberties and its offer of various degrees of material prosperity. Unfortunately, in 1929 a combination of economic and political problems disrupted Vásquez's democratic experiment and crushed the fragile economic recovery, and Ureña took over as provisional president. In the middle of May 1930 Trujillo, the army's commander, took control of the state. With military support, Trujillo lost no time in building an oppressive dictatorship, using the armed forces as an instrument of politics to militarize society.

Society and Culture in 1930
Trujillo's accession to power cannot be isolated from the context of Dominican history and culture. Without disregarding Trujillo's determination and shrewdness and his role in shaping the events that led to his election as president, not all of what happened was solely the work of the army's commander. Nor was the army entirely responsible for the establishment of the dictatorship. Indeed, the widespread military culture and social and political conditions merged with world events to sweep Trujillo to the presidency.

Trujillo sought the presidency when the Dominican economy went into a serious decline and the populace had little confidence in its leaders. These negative factors and the lack of a well-structured political system and effective leadership led to despair. Liberal intellectuals, such as Américo Lugo, believed that to solve the problem, the country needed a strong government, even if it was a despotic one.[1]

Dominican society in the 1930s was not much different from that of the 1920s. Certainly, the U.S. occupation had broadened the base of the officer corps and introduced other social changes, but these modifications did not transform society drastically. For example, illiterate and poor peasants remained outside the mainstream of society. Census data of 1935 disclose that of 1,479,417 inhabitants, about 82 percent lived in rural areas and worked in agricultural production.[2] According to Juan Linz's analysis of sultanistic regimes, the "isolation of the rural masses, their lack of education, and their poverty are probably necessary to assure their passive submission" and cooperation with a regime. Such regimes are compatible with societies dependent on an agrarian economy with commercial and some industrial enterprises.[3] Arguably, the description fits the socioeconomic conditions of the Dominican Republic in 1930.

The majority of the middle class lived in urban areas and were employed as professionals, in business and commercial enterprises, and in the military. As the transitional stage of the middle class, military service became desirable for members of the lower strata searching for social mobility. Racially, mulattoes made up nearly 70 percent of the nation's population, as well as a sizable portion of the middle class.

Constituting about 13 percent of the population, blacks, together with poor mulattoes and poor whites, formed the bottom layer of the Dominican social structure. Residing primarily in agrarian communities, the lower class survived by exchanging goods and services for provisions or money. Composing about 16 percent of the population, whites were over-represented at the top of the social hierarchy. They controlled the most profitable sectors of the economy and held the top positions in government, including the presidency. The majority of the elite resided primarily in the urban centers of the Cibao region, San Pedro de Macorís, and in Santo Domingo.

The press raised questions concerning the estimated cost of operating the military and the social origins of soldiers. In early February *La Opinión* tried to establish a correlation between enlisted men and salary incentives. Its editorials suggested a good soldier was impossible to get for seventeen dollars, the monthly salary of a recruit. The paper demanded an explanation for the low salaries of enlisted men at a time when the army was running a large deficit even though almost one million dollars had been assigned to the military.

Echoing *La Opinión*'s concerns, *Listín Diario* asked who would want to be a soldier for seventeen dollars a month. Answering its own question, the paper responded that only people from the bottom of the socioeconomic scale aspired to become soldiers. Most of them were illiterate, landless peasants. The paper also argued that because of their lack of education, many of those accepted into the military perhaps were not the most qualified for the job and failed to understand their mission. Their socioeconomic background probably explained their military behavior, which *Listín Diario* criticized, because the soldiers thought "they [were] armed to confront the citizens, with reason or without reason, and not to serve and to defend them."[4] Therefore, the newspaper claimed, the government should establish higher standards for entrance into the military.

Certainly, the majority of the military came from the lower class, but the middle and upper classes had substantial representation as well. Officers had close contact with the civilian elite; their acquaintance reinforced the traditional pattern of close and direct relations between the upper class and military leadership.

At the national level, however, all social classes remained politically weak. In a moment of political crisis generated by a confrontation between military commander and president, the elite was unable to stay in power. Neither of the other two classes was able to take control and stop Trujillo from becoming president.[5]

The State and the Economy

The Vásquez administration may be viewed in the context of the "affluent years of liberal pause," which corresponded with a period of economic prosperity in Latin America at the end of World War I.[6] This period, boosted by flourishing export economies and abundant foreign investments, is known as the "Dance of the Millions," and this prosperity temporarily increased Dominican trade and the state revenues. However, after the war the prices of staple crops fell on the world market. By 1926, however, auspicious world prices led to another period of economic growth.[7]

Vásquez's government took advantage of the new economic bonanza to finance public works projects such as highways, aqueducts, schools, railroads, and telephone lines. The boom in public construction encouraged further developments. Agriculture, commerce, and industry flourished. Luis Mejía, a congressman during the Vásquez administration, believed the unprecedented favorable living conditions in the Dominican Republic from 1924 to 1930 put the revolutionary tradition on hold. As a result, the nation enjoyed peace, and the apparently favorable economic situation was instrumental in bringing about more material progress.

New public buildings changed the contours of the largest cities. Wealthy individuals built elegant houses, imported expensive furniture, and consumed a variety of imported goods from Europe and the United States. For a great majority of Dominicans, however, this was not a period of prosperity. Furthermore, together with foreign capital, the United States had considerable control over the economy and over the Dominican government. Soon the president began to lose popularity. General discontent coincided with the world economic crisis of 1929. As in other Latin American countries, under the catastrophe of the Great Depression, in the Dominican Republic trade plummeted and the economy collapsed.[8] Political demoralization and the economic crisis caused many to be willing to accept a strong man in exchange for an upturn in the economic fortunes of the country.

In a speech reflecting the ideas and concerns of the upper and middle classes, Federico Álvarez, a well-known lawyer from Santiago, described the state of affairs at the Ateneo Amantes de la Luz on July 19, 1929. He claimed that the government did not have an economic policy; employees were incompetent, businesses were dishonest, the national treasury had been pilfered, and economic growth had ceased. Álvarez believed that to correct these problems, profound reforms were necessary. However, he criticized the slogans for change and reform chanted by the authorities. The reforms, he observed, were not conceived along the lines of institutional structures but were being sought in the providential personification of someone, a savior, a demigod, destined to "attain the miracle of social and political transformation" without a careful examination of the country's best interests.[9] Businessmen afraid of social and political disruption had adopted a pessimistic attitude, Álvarez said, and to them, authoritarian control appeared necessary to restore economic progress. Álvarez's speech suggested that without realizing the consequences, the upper class developed the political conditions that facilitated the rise of Trujillo.

Wrapped in high political rhetoric, Álvarez's discourse had its effect on intellectual circles. Poets, writers, and a group of friends published Álvarez's speech as a contribution to the national debate that they thought would influence the democratic thinking of the Dominican people. Ironically, among Álvarez's friends who published the speech was Joaquín Balaguer, who later became one of Trujillo's right-hand men and a figurehead president in 1960. Álvarez himself served as a judge during Trujillo's regime.

The Erosion of Vásquez's Presidency

Political tension began to increase in the middle of 1927. By then the ailing, sixty-eight-year-old Vásquez had managed to amend the constitution to extend the presidential term from four to six years. As Vásquez tried to succeed himself, his vice president, Federico Velásquez Hernández, resigned in protest of Vásquez's manipulation of the constitution. José Dolores Alfonseca, a powerful and controversial member of the executive committee of Vásquez's Partido Nacional, replaced him. After Alfonseca was sworn in as vice president, a web of intrigue and political maneuvers eroded public support for Vásquez's administration even more.

Facing accusations and attempting to weather the political challenges, Vásquez hired a group of U.S. financial experts in April 1929 to study the economic situation of the country and make recommendations to the government. The commission, headed by Charles G. Dawes, former vice president of the United States, found serious deficits in the administration of the national treasury. The group recommended, among other measures, a cut in the budget of several departments, including the army.[10]

To reduce the expenses of the army, the president asked Minister of Defense Alfredo Ricart Oliva and General Trujillo, separately, to present their suggestions to him. Ricart's proposal cut expenditures deeper than Trujillo's. Without reducing military services, Ricart's proposal decreased the budget by $300,000; Trujillo's proposal featured a reduction of only $182,000. Nonetheless, Vásquez chose Trujillo's proposal, as he was afraid to hurt the general's feelings and felt secure under the protection of his soldiers.[11]

In the end the Dawes Commission had a negative impact on the Vásquez administration. The opposition strongly criticized the president's decision to allow foreigners to investigate internal economic problems. In addition, the reelection bid splintered Vásquez's Partido Nacional, but Vásquez continued to campaign for another presidential term.

Taking advantage of the situation, Trujillo moved into the political scenario. When leaders of the Partido Nacional questioned Trujillo's political aspirations, Vásquez laughed and affirmed that after the death of Juan Isidro Jimenes, no one could challenge his presidency.[12] Later, when evidence of Trujillo's disloyalty to the president came to light and Vásquez had the opportunity to fire the general, the president failed to act. Instead, he offered Trujillo the defense secretariat, an offer that Trujillo rejected.

Apparently social class distinction and elite arrogance blinded Vásquez's perception of reality. To him, Trujillo was a social newcomer, an *advenedizo*. He was convinced that the general would not get the political support from the elite that he needed to gain the presidency, and Vásquez also knew that only parts of the officer corps supported Trujillo. In the president's judgment, those two factors would keep Trujillo from realizing his political ambitions. Confident, Vásquez expressed that Trujillo had no choice but to support his administration.[13] Time proved him very wrong.

Soldiers' Political Actions

At the military level, Trujillo's political project was making headway. Since May 1928 the army was no longer in charge of law enforcement tasks, at least officially. Its new function was to serve as the guardian of sovereignty and independence. The new role was a reflection of the militarism-guardian thesis, which numerous Latin American military institutions had practiced at one time or another. The thesis maintains that "the proper political role of the armed forces is to defend the nation's constitutional system from violation by civilian governments or from usurpation by revolutionary groups." Relying on this argument, "the military keeps a watchful eye on governments and applies pressure, issues warnings, and, if necessary, deposes governments and rules for a brief period of time when it believes that the constitution is being violated."[14]

In 1930 the Dominican military put the theory to work, actively participating in a scheme against President Vásquez. Commander in Chief Trujillo denied any military involvement in the plot, but in a conversation with one of his former instructors he "justified his duplicity" on the grounds that Vásquez had violated the spirit of the constitution by extending his term from four years to six.[15]

To enhance the political image that Trujillo was already projecting through the media, Lieutenant Rafael Espaillat and Colonel Ernesto Vega Pagán worked at "polishing" Trujillo's image.[16] Trujillo's sense of timing, willpower in pursuing his goals, and efforts to enhance his leadership paid off. The records of the secretary of the interior, police, war, and navy describe the outstanding job Trujillo did as commander of the army. According to these files, the structure of the new organization followed the U.S. prescription; that is, forces were divided into two departments, and clear lines divided the officer corps into three categories: headquarters, officers, and cadets. More evenly distributed across the land, soldiers lived in clean and comfortable garrisons.[17]

U.S. legation records concur that Trujillo's ability as a commander was superb; his organizational competence had turned the army into an instrument for the preservation of order. High-ranking diplomats pointed out that Trujillo was successful "in preventing the Army from being filled with political appointments."[18] In short, to U.S. officials, Trujillo had assimilated well the lessons he learned from the Marines at the Haina military academy. He had accomplished their goal of producing a nonpolitical and efficient Dominican army.

If it is true that Trujillo had disengaged the army from partisan politics, he brought political participation back to the military as he ascended toward political power. When soldiers dressed as civilians shot at opposition candidates and the Army took control of the town councils and replaced them with pro-Trujillo men, it became obvious in early 1930 that soldiers throughout the country were exerting their influence in favor of the not yet publicly announced candidacy of Trujillo.

By then, Vásquez was coping with a medical condition that weakened him politically. Suffering from serious nephritis, the president was admitted to Johns Hopkins Hospital in Baltimore on October 31, 1929. Some of Trujillo's enemies, including Virgilio Martínez Reyna and Vice President Alfonseca, decided to take advantage of Vásquez's absence to dismiss Trujillo. Planning to charge the army chief with disloyalty to the president and send him to jail, Alfonseca summoned Trujillo to the presidential offices. Informed of the plans against him, Trujillo initially refused to appear. Later, in a gesture of confidence and defiance, he put to work a Machiavellian tactic: he presented himself at the meeting accompanied by fourteen of his loyal officers. Surprised by his entourage, the group at the presidential office was unable to act against him. Cleverly and with calculated precision, Trujillo played the game in reverse. He took the offensive and became the accuser.[19] The verbal confrontation between the acting president and the chief commander of the army turned fierce. An infuriated Trujillo stormed out of the presidential offices, leaving many with the impression that he would prepare his forces for military action. To prevent bloodshed, the United States intervened. Minister Evan Young assumed the role of mediator "and won assurances from both sides that they would not initiate any action that might lead to trouble."[20] The assurances Young accepted were little more than lip service, given only to fulfill a diplomatic request, not a serious commitment to order and tranquility.

The United States

The controversial participation of the United States in the course of events that eventually led Trujillo to the presidency influenced the direction of the political campaign. On the one hand, the United States opposed Trujillo, as his rise to power would discredit the efforts of the United States to set up a nonpolitical military institution. On the other hand, U.S. diplomats struggled to ensure their influence over Trujillo without jeopardizing the nonintervention principles of the Good Neighbor policy. Two U.S. ministers to the Dominican Republic, Young and Charles Curtis, apparently received orders to discourage Trujillo from pursuing his political ambitions. Young, who saw nothing wrong with Vásquez's plan to extend his executive mandate, met with Trujillo on several occasions to remind him of his military duties and U.S. expectations of a depoliticized army, but this counseling did not work.[21] Trujillo simply was not interested; he knew he would be able to go forward without encountering any serious obstacles.

Young then tried to convince Trujillo to preserve the political stability of the country by respecting the constitution, or to go back to civilian life and compete with the rest of the candidates on an equal level. At this crucial juncture, Curtis replaced Young on January 28, 1930. Curtis's lack of familiarity with the acumen of the actors in the political drama was much to Trujillo's benefit. For some, the replacement signified that someone in the State Department was supporting Trujillo's political interests.[22]

Nevertheless, the records seem to support the view that Curtis tried to foster Trujillo's loyalty to Vásquez, but the general engaged in a game of duplicity. Trujillo's political maneuvers were so evident that Curtis suggested the removal of Trujillo and Colonel Díaz from the army. In Curtis's own words, "Unless we can eliminate [Trujillo], a revolution by or against Trujillo is certain."[23] When tension mounted and Vásquez asked for political asylum for him, his wife, and members of the cabinet, Curtis requested the presence of a U.S. warship to support the Vásquez government. But State Department officials dealing with the Dominican situation rejected the petition because the presence of a warship would contradict the Good Neighbor policy, which precluded the use of force as a tool for negotiation. The diplomats believed that the only chance they had to prevent Trujillo's candidacy was a personal appeal, and they further believed that any public recrimination would work against the department's plan.[24]

In all of this, "the United States considered [Trujillo] a better option than his enemies from within and from without" during the entire time the dictator governed "except for a two-year period after the end of the Second World War."[25] During the crisis of 1930, however, by adopting a middle-of-the-road position, at first the State Department wanted to keep Trujillo out of politics and tried to convince him that he would serve his country better by using his power to guarantee order and peace. Later, the State Department changed its initial position and expressed its willingness to recognize Trujillo as president of the republic. The following excerpt from a letter to Curtis illustrates this contradictory position: "[W]hile the Department hopes that you will be able to persuade Trujillo not to be a candidate, it realizes the great difficulty of bringing it about and should you not succeed and Trujillo be elected it is most important that you should not impair in any way your relationship with him. Therefore the Department cannot emphasize too strongly the necessity of making your appeal in a most friendly spirit."[26]

Meanwhile, Trujillo undauntedly continued his maneuvering to replace Vásquez and organized his own political coalition, the Confederación de Partidos. Joseph Cotton, acting secretary of state, recommended to Curtis the services of Trujillo's former commander, Colonel Cutts, who had great influence over Trujillo, to convince the general to abandon his inappropriate military behavior. It was not appropriate for the head of the army to be a presidential candidate.[27] Colonel Cutts, now stationed in Haiti, drove over to see Trujillo and subsequently reported that he had spoken to Trujillo with "the utmost frankness" and felt that, without minimizing the general's aspirations, Trujillo was the best choice.[28] For Cutts, Trujillo not only possessed the ability to manage the country's affairs, but he enjoyed even more popular support than the legation realized.

Cutts' support had significant political weight for the future dictator. Trujillo knew well that with Cutts as a mediator, as long as he was able to maintain stability by controlling the army, sooner or later the United States would support his political ambitions. After the meeting with Cutts, understanding that time and circumstances were on his side, the army commander took advantage of every possibility to orchestrate his move from the military headquarters to the National Palace.

The End of the Democratic Experiment

Early in 1930 political leaders opposed to Vásquez, led by Rafael Estrella Ureña, made a pact and formed a civic movement that rapidly gained strength. By then, with the political atmosphere heating up, Trujillo knew that the upper classes were in no position to antagonize him; on the contrary, he used soldiers to intimidate them. Officers and men in uniform conducted illegal searches of houses and individuals and disarmed many citizens, including those who were entitled to bear arms. For example, a group of soldiers seized the vehicles of the president of the senate and of the president of the chamber of deputies, and confiscated their chauffeurs' revolvers.[29] These were not acts of soldiers out of control, but under orders.

Miguel Angel Paulino, who had been discharged from La Guardia for disciplinary reasons and had been readmitted as an army captain by Trujillo, headed La 42, a band of thugs that systematically intimidated Trujillo's adversaries with acts of violence. They burnt houses and properties, destroyed vehicles, and assaulted people during the political campaign.

Trujillo used the military to defy a civilian government, but he also illustrated the weakness of the political system. Realizing that Trujillo had betrayed him, Vásquez took refuge in the U.S. legation in Santo Domingo. During a conversation with Curtis, Vásquez acknowledged that "with the Army unfaithful to him, he could not hope to accomplish anything."[30] At this juncture of affairs, Alfonseca resigned on February 26, 1930; Vásquez followed on March 2. Both went to exile in Puerto Rico. The Congress swore in Estrella Ureña, a lawyer and Vásquez's former secretary of foreign relations, as acting president. In retrospect, from 1924 to 1930, despite political stability and some material prosperity, the government showed its inability to articulate a political project capable of solving one of the most important national problems: preventing the military from controlling the state. On the contrary, Vásquez's old political patterns of friendship and spoils generated the desire for change and helped Trujillo materialize his political ambitions. With Estrella Ureña as the vice presidential candidate, Trujillo formally declared his intention to run for the presidency on March 17, 1930.

On May 16, 1930, after a controversial and violent campaign, Trujillo became president of the republic. Surprisingly, the chief of the army did not have to revert to the traditional military coup d'état to rise to power. He turned instead to a more accepted way of gaining office—an election. He had played the game so skillfully that he, a military man, had emerged as a political leader from a civic movement. At the end, the "revolution" against Vásquez that began "as a revolt of the liberal spirit"[31] ended up as a dictatorship. Perhaps Trujillo's enemies underestimated his will and tenacity and failed to act in time. No one would stop him until 1961.

In considering social class responses to Trujillo's rise to power in 1930, Juan Isidro Jimenes Grullón, a physician and social scientist who strongly opposed Trujillo, indicates that at first, with the exception of some members of the elite, the population repudiated him for various reasons. Large parts of the elite rejected Trujillo because he was not one of them. The middle class scorned him because he lacked "outstanding intellectual qualifications" and because of his tainted past and anti-nationalist behavior during the occupation. The majority of the lower class did not know who Trujillo was or were plainly indifferent to him.[32] Reinforcing Jimenes Grullón's view, Curtis, the U.S. minister to the Dominican Republic, noticed that Trujillo's social background caused the members of the upper class to "turn up their noses" and that his "cattle thieving and similar offenses alienated many peasants, and his love affairs caused many to thirst for vengeance."[33]

If he was repudiated by all social sectors, why was Trujillo elected? In addition to the socioeconomic conditions and the political environment, during the election campaign Trujillo presented himself as the savior: "There is no danger in following me," he claimed. He had promised that if the people favored him with their votes, he would never use his power to tyrannize the population. He also gave assurances that he would bring political stability and lead the country toward properity.[34] These statements featured the political touches the people, particularly the ruling class, were looking for. Although he ordered reprisals, Trujillo charmed people with promises of peace and progress.

Even when Trujillo was not accepted "as one of them," once he had risen to power, he received support from almost all sectors of the population. Intellectuals, especially, offered their talents and ideas to develop the philosophy and policies of the regime. Among them, Joaquín Balaguer, Ramón Emilio Jiménez, Arturo Logroño, Julio Ortega Frier, and

Manuel Arturo Peña Battle became ghostwriters or front men for Trujillo's policy. Similarly, nationalist leaders such as Max Henríquez Ureña, Francisco Henríquez y Carvajal, Rafael Estrella Ureña, and many more participated in the rituals of Trujillo's self-glorification and aggrandizement.[35] Others, like Juan Bosch, Angel Miolán, Pedro Mir, and Juan Isidro Jimenes Grullón, took stances against Trujillo and lived in exile or social ostracism. |

The Outset of the Era of Trujillo

Trujillo selected one of the two most important national holidays, Restoration Day, to celebrate the beginning of his megalomaniacal administration. He turned the national celebration into *una fiesta en grande* to commemorate his ascendance to "the throne." On August 16, 1930, wearing a military uniform with golden trimmings and a hat that resembled those of Ulises Heureaux, surrounded by officers, bureaucrats, and diplomats, Trujillo took his oath as president of the republic. The next day *Listín Diario* reported that twenty thousand Dominican flags adorned the capital. Music and fireworks in plazas and parks entertained the people; money was distributed to poor adults and candy to children. Military parades were also part of the festivities, which continued for several days.[36] On August 16 of each following year, Trujillo and the nation reenacted August 16, 1930, with parades, speeches, ceremonies, and other festivities to please Trujillo's penchant for flattery. Greedy for adulation, Trujillo made sure that his name was all over the country. Cities, towns, buildings, statues, streets, rivers, and parks were renamed in his honor or in honor of a family member. Santo Domingo, the capital, was renamed Ciudad Trujillo.

On September 3, just a few weeks after the inauguration, the San Zenón hurricane swept the country, killing thousands of people and causing extensive damage. *Listín Diario*, *La Información*, and other newspapers reported a death toll of four and six thousand. The damage estimates ran between $20 million and $40 million.

The natural disaster provided Trujillo with an opportunity to demonstrate his organizational skills, and he initiated an impressive effort toward the reconstruction of public buildings, highways, and housing. The hurricane also provided him with an excuse to suspend constitutional rights and to disguise the disappearance of some of his political enemies as hurricane victims. After the hurricane, Trujillo ordered

Paulino "to secure large quantities of gasoline," and days later "the dead bodies of those killed by La 42" as well as "the victims of the hurricane were drenched with the fluid and burned."[37]

Ironically, the hurricane was profitable for Trujillo on many fronts. The dictator "availed himself of the opportunity to seize by governmental decree all funds held by Dominicans in the banks in Santo Domingo."[38] And although the republic received massive international assistance to help rebuild the country, there was never any public accounting of the use of the funds. In contradiction to Trujillo's election campaign promise, the state acquired excessive might, controlling the nation and its economy with a despotic grip.

The Resources of the State and the Military

In financial terms, the first period of Trujillo's administration, 1930–34, was critical. Confronted with the effect of the economic depression of 1929 and the devastation of the hurricane of 1930, the government faced a deepening balance-of-payments crisis. National income dropped from fifteen million pesos in 1929 to seven million pesos in 1931.[39]

The deterioration of the economy threatened the stability of the regime. In order to prevent popular unrest, the government declared a state of emergency, as well as the temporary suspension of payments on Dominican foreign bonds. Trujillo disliked the idea of asking for a moratorium, but he had no other choice but to negotiate a settlement with the United States. With the approval of the U.S. government, on October 23, 1931, the government enacted the Emergency Law and suspended external debt payments on capital for two years but continued to pay the interest. This measure, which allowed the government to divert funds from customs revenues, increased national income by 33 percent.[40] In the meantime, Trujillo used sweeping emergency powers to impose despotic legislation, to constrain wages, and to strengthen the military. The ten government departments were reduced to seven. The reduction of the bureaucracy caused social despair, distress, and endangered public health, as expressed by Roberto Despradel, Trujillo's secretary of state at the time, in a communication to the U.S. secretary of state. Trujillo himself admitted that the departments of health, social welfare, schools, sanitation, and public transportation suffered the most.[41]

The army, however, did not suffer at all. On the contrary, its allotment of funds increased from 10.1 percent to 13.6 percent of the national budget.[42] How much more Trujillo spent directly or indirectly for military purposes is unknown. Both the executive power and the secretaries had *fondos especiales*, specific amounts of money to be diverted from one government unit to another. For example, in the 1930s the government allowed funds to be diverted from the education budget to the army, causing the temporary closing of several reformatory and regular schools. The increase of military expenses at the cost of education caught the attention of the international press. In mid-February 1931, the *Baltimore Sun* published several articles on the closing of schools, criticizing Trujillo's economic policy.[43]

Such policies stemmed from Trujillo's political plan. He had to keep the soldiers happy in order to maintain their support. In addition, Trujillo was after all, an army man. When he became a presidential candidate he promised that from the highest position of power he would always take care of the soldiers.[44] True to his word, Trujillo did not see any discrepancy between the reduction of public services and the budgetary increase for the army. He called these measures the "perfect essential correlation" in a moment of economic crisis.[45] With laws created to his advantage, the "perfect correlation" of the crisis served Trujillo's purpose of accumulation of wealth.

He set out to redirect the economy by exploiting the natural resources, by limiting control over the economy by foreigners, and by imposing a series of state monopolies. In forging his policy of economic nationalism, Trujillo also sought to end U.S. control of Dominican customhouses. After lengthy negotiations, the Dominican Republic reestablished financial control over customs in 1940 with the signing of the Trujillo-Hull Treaty.

Combining monopolistic policy with the regime's commitment to economic development produced favorable results by the beginning of War World II. During the war, both exports of Dominican products and import substitution through domestic manufacturing stimulated economic production. The economic gains allowed the government to balance the budget, to pay off all external and internal debts, and to maintain the value of the Dominican peso at a par with the U.S. dollar. The government entrusted the Central Bank, created in 1947, to replace U.S. dollars with Dominican peso bills and coins. However, Trujillo's greed and encroachment upon the most profitable businesses overshadowed these achievements. Many state enterprises became part of his economic empire as he fused his personal finances with those of the nation. In the past, strong presidents with military backgrounds, such as Pedro Santana and Ulises Heureaux, had emerged as builders of the nation. With the assistance of intellectuals and members of the traditional ruling class, Trujillo merged Santana's militaristic practices with Heureaux's political and military pragmatism and appeals of order and progress. To achieve his goals, the dictator carefully prioritized the steps for success. First on the list was the reorganization of the army.

5. CHANGING THE MILITARY, ALTERING SOCIETY
Control, Recruitment, and Education of the Armed Forces

Reorganizing the military, a work in progress since Trujillo became brigadier general in 1927, acquired a new tone after Trujillo took control of the state. Management was the distinctive characteristic of Trujillo's system. Thus, when General Trujillo became President Trujillo, he personalized and dictated the terms of his relationship with the forces. The system had little room for individual initiative. Within this framework Trujillo maintained his authority, but resistance did occur within the military. However, Trujillo dealt with opposition swiftly and efficiently. On the other hand, the system created a social space for the military as the regime sought to make military service a key opportunity for Dominicans to find employment and advance economically and socially. Subsequently, as Trujillo professionalized and modernized the military, he altered society and changed civil-military relations significantly.

Trujillo's Military Style and Leadership
Analyzing the link between the military and the political arrangements of Trujillo's regime and its activities, some writers, as mentioned in chapters 3 and 4, have forcefully articulated how Trujillo's reorganization of the Dominican armed forces solidified his relationship with the United States and entitled the dictator to receive preferential treatment no matter who was the executive at the White House.[1] From this perspective, making a "left-handed compliment" to the U.S. officers who trained Trujillo, Arturo Espaillat states in *Trujillo: The Last Caesar* that the Generalissimo always considered himself a Marine Corps officer, and even during moments of strong disagreement between the two governments, Trujillo's love for the Marines "was responsible for his unwavering loyalty to the United States."[2]

By expanding and modernizing the armed forces in close association with his former Marine instructors, Trujillo's devotion to the United States symbolized, in many ways, the legacy of the USMC establishment in the Dominican Republic. The influence showed ostensibly in centralization, discipline, ranks, uniforms, training, the arsenal, and in other relevant features. Like most modern military organizations, the USMC had a military bureaucracy, which for efficiency depended on training, permanent and periodic evaluations, and attendance at military school. Under Trujillo's command many of these elements were integrated with some Dominican features and evolved into Trujillo's system.

Underlying Trujillo's military project was a new approach to the meaning of professionalization. For the Marines directing La Guardia, being a professional soldier meant full-time service to the organization and being apolitical. Trujillo's new approach meant to guarantee political stability by using soldiers to paralyze the opposition. He perceived the military as a well-disciplined, loyal institution and dominant building force of society. Soldiers had a civic duty to lead citizens "out of the shadow of the past" to the "light of the future" under the guidance of the state.[3] For Trujillo, the National Army was the "North Star" of the regime's political ideas and a "force of social equilibrium" upon which the government counted to guarantee the prosperity of the country and the administrative reorganization of public services, as he indicated in his first speech addressed to the Dominican Congress on August 16, 1930.

Trujillo's discourse pointed out that strengthening the army was necessary "to raise the level of the Republic in all respects." Trujillo also stated that the military had an important role in developing the nation and in order to accomplish that goal, Trujillo had to restructure the military organization.[4] In pursuing that goal, Trujillo made sure he stayed close to the direct command of the army at all times. Consequently, on May 26, 1933, he became Generalissimo of the army; in 1952 he also became commander in chief of the armed forces of the republic.

According to the Constitution, the president was the commander in chief of the armed forces, but none of the presidents that nominally ruled when Trujillo was not officially the president of the republic—Jacinto Peynado, 1938–40; Manuel de Jesús Troncoso de la Concha, 1940–42; Héctor Trujillo, 1952–60; and Joaquín Balaguer, 1960–61—dared to make any significant changes to the military organization unless Trujillo approved. This compliance with military authority was not unique to the Dominican Republic. As in many Latin American countries, the Constitution has been ineffective in limiting military intrusions. Often the system of fundamental laws and principles of government had little more than symbolic value.

To prevent anyone from becoming too powerful and to keep the military leadership at all times, Trujillo took three basic steps. First on the agenda was an internal purge to impose subordination throughout the army. The second move was politicization. In reorganizing the armed forces, Trujillo made no effort to present the army as a depoliticized institution or to represent his administration as a demilitarized government. On the contrary, the political system was highly militarized, and the military openly participated in political activism. Third, to guarantee submission to the regime, the dictator established a system of rewards that corresponded to the interaction between the leader and his subordinates. The leader "is not merely a 'stimulator'—he is also being 'stimulated' by those who are close to him, mainly during the process of the transference of goals," especially when performance leading to the achievement of such goals seems appropriate.[5] Hence, Trujillo's military developed its own system of stimulus-response patterns of rewards and punishments. He began with punishment.

Internal Purge

Soon after Trujillo took power, armed revolt broke out in several parts of the country. A political leader, José Paredes, and a military commander, General Alberto Larancuent, led armed resistance against the regime in separate revolts. After several weeks of confrontation, the army defeated the rebels. To punish them for their actions and to intimidate the opposition, Paredes and Larancuent were shot in the public squares of San Francisco de Macorís and Santo Domingo, respectively.

Next, the government directed military action against all real or potential troublemakers who might have access to arms or enough political influence to turn the military against the regime. Martínez Reyna was among the earliest victims of Trujillo's destruction of political figures. During the election campaign of 1930, Reyna, a leader of Partido Nacional and a friend of Alfonseca, opposed Trujillo's presidential aspirations. Two weeks after the election, Reyna and his pregnant wife were shot to death in their own home. Also on the target list were local or regional caudillos and traditional military chiefs, among them Cipriano Bencosme, a member of the Horacista party and regional leader in the province of Moca, who organized a rebellion against Trujillo. To neutralize the resistance, the dictator himself went to the combat zone in the area of Puerto Plata. The army used infantry and cavalry units as well as motorized armored troops and airplanes to track down the insurgents. Realizing the weakness of their position, the rebels disbanded and tried to escape, but on November 19, 1930, Bencosme, betrayed by one of his former supporters, was handed over to the army. He died in custody, but the government reported his death as the result of military confrontation.[6]

From a military standpoint, the rebellion of Bencosme has historical significance. During the occupation the U.S. Marines had used airplanes to combat the guerrillas in the east, but the 1930 rebellion saw Dominican forces employ airplanes for the first time against other Dominicans. Trujillo's agenda for destruction of the opposition included the legendary caudillo Desiderio Arias. Familiar with Arias's power and charisma, Trujillo at first adopted a conciliatory attitude and tried to negotiate a compromise: Arias was to lay down his arms in exchange for personal security. During a meeting with Trujillo on May 2, 1931, Arias rejected the offer and instead demanded personal security for him as well as respect for his party and for the opposition in general.

Arias's defiance infuriated Trujillo. The dictator accused the aging caudillo and two of his associates, Francisco Morillo and Victoriano Almánzar, of having murdered a peasant and asked them to surrender. Arias, whom one of Trujillo's apologists described as being "as cunning as a fox, as agile as a cat and swift as a greyhound,"[7] refused to give up and continued to challenge the army for several weeks. Government troops killed him along with some of his followers on June 20, 1931. The next day the *Listín Diario* published a long article on Arias's political life. The paper pointed out that even Arias's enemies acknowledged his leadership and admitted that his death was "lamented as if he had been a hero." Arias was a regional leader at the time of his violent death, but he later became a national hero.

Following the elimination of Arias, Trujillo continued to destroy or intimidate the opposition. Albert Hicks's account of Trujillo's murders, *Blood in the Streets: The Life and Rule of Trujillo*, reveals that between May 1930 and November 1931 more than one thousand Dominicans fell victim to Trujillo's vicious crimes. Headed by General José Estrella, death squads systematically eliminated hundreds of people. Many were victims of clandestine assassinations, "attempting to escape" while being taken to prison, or they "hanged themselves" in their cells. Under Trujillo's harsh treatment for enemies of his regime, most of the "turbulent" political leaders and many of their supporters were exiled, jailed, or perished inside or outside prison; otherwise they gave up and cooperated with Trujillo.[8]

The dictator expected loyalty not only from an officer himself but also from his extended family. Sergeant Enrique Blanco, who challenged Trujillo's army with what was called a one-man revolution, kept hundreds of soldiers on a war footing for several months in the Cibao region. Instead of giving up, he killed himself when he realized that he had no way to escape the army's persecution.[9] In reprisal hundreds of Blanco's relatives and friends were killed.

Military Deployment and Civilian Support

Reinforcing militarism and his authority, from April to July 1931, beginning in the Cibao region, Trujillo deployed about fifteen hundred soldiers throughout the country. They were accompanied by eloquent speakers, writers, and poets, such as Joaquín Balaguer, Osvaldo Bazil, Tomás Hernández Franco, and Jacinto Peynado, who used their oratorical skills to praise Trujillo in towns and cities. The military deployment went to the east region, stopping at San Pedro de Macorís, La Romana, and Sánchez; to the south to Barahona, and Azua; and to the north in Puerto Plata and Monte Cristi. Wearing new uniforms and headed by a musical band, the well-armed troops marched in military formation, organized in cavalry, artillery, and infantry units. With glossy images and pictures, the press describes the soldiers carrying machine guns, bearing explosives and gas bombs, and riding military motorcycles.[10] These displays showed the army's military strength and readiness, and there was only one chief, Trujillo. In Trujillo's own words, he wanted to show the nation that his regime could stop any subversive action against the government and was ready to punish anyone who threatened insurrection.[11] During the demonstrations Trujillo, riding a horse, received the applause and adulation of thousands of spectators. As the soldiers entered cities and towns, people from the surrounding areas enthusiastically joined them. As an illustration, early in April in the city of Santiago over seven thousand mounted horsemen and others on foot paid respect to Trujillo. Similarly in Dajabón at the end of the month three thousand men on horseback welcomed a delighted Trujillo.[12] The commander in chief loved this type of theatricality. More important, these performances served to spread military culture, values, and attitude, to all sectors of the population.

Providing opportunities for military-civilian interaction, these gatherings, called *revistas cívicas*, appealed to the population in general, but they were especially attractive to the peasantry. Such a demonstration of force was not only appealing but it had a psychological impact. The spectacle astonished people. Dominicans had never seen anything like these spectacles. Knowing that the show embodied the political significance of the system during the three decades of the regime, mainly during the first ten years, Trujillo repeated these demonstrations across the country periodically. The pervasiveness of such displays in the public sphere also served to promote the military, to spread fear among the population, and to impress the unsympathetic. Consequently, military leaders who survived the first step of the purge, realizing the hopelessness of any armed uprising, like the politicians quietly retired to their homes or joined the system.

Meanwhile, the dictator expanded the internal purge even further. His next move was to eliminate from the roster of officers the "undesirable elements, so that the force would respond to the purposes for which it was created."[13] This included all those who had shown their disaffection with the new order. The purge acted as a preventive measure to stop any potential insubordination among the forces, as well as a device aimed at alienating anti-Trujillo personnel from the military. Facing intimidation, propaganda, and death, regional chiefs succumbed. In 1937 in the National Palace, about four hundred of them offered a lunch to Trujillo to express their admiration, loyalty, and appreciation for the political stability that the dictator had brought to the country.[14] Such stability demonstrated Trujillo's increasing control over the military.

Recruitment and Loyalty

Personality and patriotism had influenced military appointments in the early national periods. Trujillo merged these elements and new ones in his redesigning of the recruitment process. Enlistment was voluntary, but there were legal provisions for compulsory military service (for example, in a state of emergency such as an invasion). Voluntary service began with a four-year appointment, which could be extended indefinitely. To qualify for admission to the armed forces, a man had to have Dominican citizenship, be eighteen to twenty-five years old, be at least five feet six inches tall, be in good physical and mental health, and have no criminal record. Because Trujillo considered peasants to be more loyal than men from the cities, recruitment of enlisted men took place mostly in the countryside.[15] The procedures of recruitment emphasized two of the formal elements of military culture: discipline and loyalty.

To fit Trujillo's design, the recruitment pattern had other distinctive features. First, admission into the military was to some degree a political appointment and a family matter. The requirement for a clean criminal record meant, among other things, that relatives involved in anti-Trujillista activities made the candidate ineligible. Second, Trujillo transformed the enlistment of new military personnel from an ordinary process of selection to an act of reward. Third, to be accepted as a soldier meant becoming a member of a privileged caste, but achieving this privilege was not easy. Fourth, the personal and psychological degradation the soldiers had to endure, sometimes in the form of physical punishment, wore down any emotional or mental resistance to the regime.

Let us look at the story of Ignacio Gómez Núñez, a teenager from the town of Tamboril, who wanted to be a soldier. The young man became a private on July 6, 1950, a few days before his eighteenth birthday. His first disappointment came soon. One week after being admitted to the army, he learned that from then on Trujillo was the most important person in his life. Everybody and everything else became secondary, including his mother, his father, and the fatherland. "My mother was sick," he recalled later, "and my father [had] abandoned us when I was eight years old. I wanted to be a soldier to help my mother." Gómez Núñez explained that during the training the instructor told him that between Trujillo and his mother, "the 'Jefe' was first." The young man "felt helpless and cried out loud almost every night." With sadness he mentioned that "my superior, angry, humiliated me and some of my training mates called me names. Two months later, after I started my military training, I was discharged as unfit for the army. Although it may appear foolish, I was happy as I had never been before."[16]

Gómez Núñez's experience and the methods the Trujillo regime employed were not unique. As Peter Barnes explains, they fit a pattern used in other authoritarian regimes, by which soldiers were (and are) conditioned to obey and to respond positively to even the most trivial or irrational rules and commands.[17]

Throughout his dictatorship, Trujillo overemphasized obedience. José Miguel Soto Jiménez, a Dominican officer and historian, and secretary of the armed forces of the government of President Hipólito Mejía, indicates that loyalty was the center of gravity of the system.[18] It increasingly focused on Trujillo, to the extent that the fatherland, the national heroes, the national symbols, and the military institution were relegated to a position of relative inferiority in comparison to the tributes rendered to the dictator.

Raymundo Cuevas Sena, former air force sergeant, wrote about experiences similar to those of Gómez, but he blamed not only El Jefe but the Trujillista officers for creating an atmosphere of fear. The officers taught the soldiers that Trujillo was like a god and that they must obey Trujillo at all costs. "I was told," Cuevas Sena said, "that as a soldier I should understand that all civilians, including my parents and my brothers and sisters, were my enemies and that I have to follow orders even if the order was to kill them."[19] Sena later expressed his resentment against such indoctrination by conspiring against Trujillo in 1958.

Héctor Trujillo, Trujillo's youngest brother, secretary of war and the navy in 1948, described the other side of the coin by citing the fundamental distinction between military recruitment in the era of Trujillo and in the years before 1930. In the past, said the secretary, men were dragged into the army to serve and defend the political interest of different factions. After 1930 they had to beg to be accepted.[20]

Like Héctor Trujillo, Abelardo Nanita, an intellectual who devoted his literary gifts to elevate Trujillo, magnified the importance of being a soldier in the era of Trujillo. In the past, he explained, being a soldier was like having the plague. At the time of conscription, young men abandoned their area of residence. But after 1930 it was enough to place an advertisement in the newspaper, and immediately hundreds of young men presented themselves as candidates.[21] Trujillo and Nanita's statements were not just congratulatory and mere propaganda. The pronouncements were based on facts. Despite the humiliation and indoctrination, many Dominican men wanted to serve in the army. But why?

The desire of many of these young men was grounded in the socioeconomic conditions prevalent in the country. Certainly, "Trujillo's grip on the army had made it a good place to make a living."[22] Many were looking for stable employment and economic advancement. A volunteer had the opportunity to gain social status by changing his position from a poor, landless, jobless peasant to a salaried soldier. When the former peasant returned home with shiny shoes, a neat uniform, and money in his pocket, he commanded respect. Eugene M. Hinckle, a U.S. diplomat who prepared a report about the state of the Dominican military in 1938, indicated that the monthly salary of a colonel was $275.00, a captain $125.00, and a first lieutenant $90.00. First sergeants, corporals, and privates earned $28.50, $18.00, and $15.00, respectively. He indicated that these numbers represented only basic pay and considered members of the army a privileged class who were paid relatively well compared to other government employees.[23] In addition, the regime frequently assigned land to soldiers in one of the agricultural colonies; many were drawn by the opportunity to become landowners.

A retired private said he became a member of the army because at the time it "was the escalator of the poor man."[24] But this avenue for upward mobility was not restricted to the poor. As long as they complied with the requirements, members of any class were eligible for recruitment and promotion. Within this framework an important socioeconomic variable emerged. Searching for power and prestige, the upper and middle classes were well represented in the military academies.

Military Culture, Machismo, and Masculinity

Directing the male population to embrace military life, Trujillo's system incorporated informal elements of Dominican society into military life. Traditionally military life exemplified masculinity and machismo, whereby a man displayed courage, strength, and sexual prowess. To some extent, being a man also meant being a soldier. The gun, the uniform, and the horse, all associated with male power, excited the minds of young men who viewed the military as an opportunity to gain respect and prestige. As mentioned in chapter 2, when a young man became an adult, the father customarily gave him a gun, which symbolized that the period of adolescence had ended. They also took sons to prostitutes for sexual initiation.

Although the issue of prostitution may be considered marginal within the modus operandi of the military, one has to keep in mind that Trujillo, in pursuit of political objectives, manipulated the enlisted men with self-gratification and aggrandizement. Understanding that as a symbol of power the possession of women elevated the macho image of the soldiers, the regime used women to foment the traditional cultural value of masculinity.

Conversations and interviews with former officers and enlisted men have revealed that fiestas to dance merengue, to drink rum, and to meet women were organized to entertain the troops. Since many Dominican men define their masculinity by the number of their amorous or sexual conquests, women who attended these parties also became part of the incentives to reinforce soldiers' *machista* behavior and to inflate their conceptualization of maleness. Some of these women were already pre-selected "as gifts" or future wives for the officers and enlisted men. Women were also used to keep soldiers in undesirable military posts. Under condition of anonymity, a former officer told me that Father Antonio López de Santa Anna, arguing that prostitution was against the moral principles preached by the Catholic Church, asked Trujillo to eliminate a house of prostitution in Dajabón known as El Cabaret de Julia. Trujillo responded that he would give an order to close the place if Santa Anna promised that priests would patrol the border with Haiti. The answer implied that in order to handle dissension or discontent, Trujillo used prostitution to keep soldiers happy in isolated posts. In addition, brothels served as places to collect information for intelligence purposes. Over a friendly glass of beer or rum, men talked and women listened and passed information to those working for the Military Intelligence Service (SIM) or other agents. Thus, another reason for Trujillo to keep brothels like El Cabaret de Julia as a place of recreation for soldiers was to establish a controlled political environment. While introducing his recruitment procedures and reinforcing cultural traditions, Trujillo also introduced administrative changes in the organization.

Administrative Changes

The period between 1930 and 1945 saw significant changes in central command. One of the first steps in restructuring the military occurred on February 20, 1931, when company headquarters were established in the capital of each province. The military territorial organization, however, continued with its division into two departments—North and South—as established by the U.S. military government in 1917. The provinces of Santo Domingo, Azua, Barahona, San Pedro de Macorís, Seybo, and the southwest border constituted the Department of the South. Santiago, La Vega, Moca, Duarte, Montecristi, Samaná, Puerto Plata, and the northwest border made up the Department of the North.[25]

To check and balance the country's political and military forces at once, in 1933 Trujillo realigned the territorial division of the military along administrative territorial boundaries.[26] By establishing geographical boundaries simultaneously under the jurisdiction of military and civilian authorities, Trujillo made his military organization more efficient. The government not only brought the provincial authorities under more direct control but also placed the people under both political and military control.

During those first fifteen years, the central command introduced other modifications in the military territorial division. In 1937 the battalions located in Ciudad Trujillo were divided into two regiments: Generalissimo Trujillo and Ramfis. In December 1942 a military order created the Department of the Border. Under the leadership of a lieutenant colonel, this department's main mission was to supervise military activities along the Haitian border. The military and geographic jurisdiction included the provinces of Barahona, Benefactor, Libertador, and San Rafael.[27]

In 1943 the general command and the military territory faced yet another reorganization. First, surprisingly, the government suppressed the recently created Department of the Border, as well as the Department of the South and the Ramfis Regiment. The Department of the South became the South Intendancy and two new departments surfaced: Southwest and Northwest. Two years later in 1945, another change took place. The army distributed forces into two regiments, the Generalissimo Trujillo and the 18th of December, and into four Departments, the Northwest, North, Southwest and a new one, the Department of the East.[28]

The Generalissimo then introduced other modifications in central command that increased uniformity and enhanced the strength of the army. The frequent changes and reorganizations continued until Trujillo's death, but it is an arduous job—and perhaps not very useful for the goals of this study—to keep track of all the new departments and units that appeared and disappeared very often after 1945. It seems that these changes resulted from a variety of factors, such as Trujillo's unpredictable moods and the fear that his actions might cause his subordinates to turn against him. Thus, most of these changes simply reconfirmed the structure designed for the army between 1930 and 1945. For instance, from the start to the end of his regime, Trujillo sought to supervise the army's central bureaucracy. Thus, the bulk of the armed forces were concentrated in the capital and all decisions originated from the central command in Ciudad Trujillo, where Trujillo easily deployed forces at any given time. To minimize the likelihood of plots against him, he periodically named civilians, rather than military personnel, to the position of secretary of the war and navy. In this way Trujillo not only imposed military culture on society but also imposed civilian participation on the military. Between 1931 and 1942, for example, Jacinto Bienvenido Peynado, Plinio R. Pina Chevalier, Francisco Penso, and Teódulo Pina

Chevalier served as secretary. But it did not matter who received the appointment; Trujillo never relinquished his control of the military. Pivotal to the existence of the regime, loyalty was reinforced through Trujillo's direct management and retention of the army's leadership. In September 1952, a month after his brother Héctor Trujillo became president of the republic, Trujillo traveled extensively, visiting and inspecting military installations across the country. At each military post he gave orders relative to the "well being, security and discipline of the military body." Such orders ranged from kitchen provisions to the reorganization of the military command.[29] During each visit, in line with the Caesaristic model of exercising absolute control over the armed forces, he demonstrated that he, not his brother, was the commander in chief. Showing himself to be an energetic commander, in some places, such as Santiago, for example, he arrived at midnight at the San Luis Fortress and immediately began to inspect the barracks and to give orders. He visited La Vega on September 29 and returned there the next day to verify that officers had followed the instructions he had given them the day before. Establishing himself as the supreme commander, Trujillo altered the civil-military relations by mixing military activities with politics. During his trip, each town he visited turned his arrival into a festival. In Villa Isabel, for example, a multitude including representatives of all social classes went to the streets to chant, "Viva Trujillo!"

Party and Army

Trujillo's military organization developed cohesion and redirected civil-military relations through a mass political organization. Trujillo merged all pluralistic political organizations into a monolithic institution, the Partido del General Trujillo. It became the institutional apparatus to represent Trujillo's ideology, which, theoretically, corresponded to the liberal doctrines of the Enlightenment, but in reality it was the embodiment of Trujillo's political scheme. In 1932 the organization officially adopted the name Partido Dominicano. A mass organization party, it replaced the other seven parties that exited the country when Trujillo took over. For almost ten years thereafter, afraid of Trujillo's reprisals, no one dared to form or be the leader of an opposition party.

Under its motto of "rectitud, libertad, trabajo y moralidad" (righteousness, freedom, work, and morality, which corresponded to the initials of Trujillo's name: Rafael Leónidas Trujillo Molina), Trujillo's party expanded its function and supervised and controlled government employees. In 1935 for example, the Partido Dominicano, acting as a quasi-governmental agency, conducted the national census.

The creation of the Partido Dominicano represented a sharp break with political tradition. It had legal and judicial authority to act as the controller of individual and collective actions. To some extent, the party's buildings symbolized barracks for civilians, particularly for government employees. Like soldiers, they had to participate in myriad activities in the military style of discipline and order. Membership in the party, which was obligatory for all public employees and members of the armed forces, included a 10 percent deduction from the monthly paycheck to finance party programs and activities and to offer social assistance to different sectors of the Dominican population. Foreign employees, who did not have to be members of the political organization, had the same percentage deducted from their checks, too. By subsidizing political activities, citizens and soldiers were forced to share ideological identification with the regime. The fragmented and factional military participation in politics of the past now became coercive and cohesive. Trujillo carved out a political outlet for military men but at a price.

The military organized by Trujillo combined strict discipline and unconditional loyalty with continuous indoctrination of its members. By blending coercion with persuasion, these tactics fit the pattern of most modern armies that "seek to minimize reliance on coercion by subjecting [the] soldier to indoctrination."[30] In this particular case, however, the regime framed the indoctrination of soldiers in a broad body of activities endorsed by the Partido Dominicano, including attendance at political meetings and cultural activities that were continuously offered at one of the party's many locations. Reciprocally, government officials visited the barracks to address fundamental issues of Trujillista doctrine.[31] After 1932 the army and the party were the two main instruments of political power upon which the regime relied.

In explaining the symbiotic relationship of the two organizations, Trujillo viewed the army as an "apparatus of coercion to prevent overflowing of the turbulent waters of the party"; the party was the channel and the school for the education of the citizens.[32] Moving toward greater control over groups, party leaders in all villages, towns, and cities had to report to the higher party level twice a week. The report addressed political activities; economic, social, and financial conditions; agricultural progress and problems; and behaviors and attitudes of the population.[33] Public employees, in particular, were under constant scrutiny. Any behavior considered inappropriate was referred to the army for further action. A triangular connection between party, military, and regime was thus established. Local leaders, civilians and military, acted as political agents in the service of Trujillo, the party served as an agency of denunciation, and the army became an agency of intimidation and repression to guarantee political loyalty to the regime. With these centrifugal elements in his hands, the dictator gradually instilled his own character into the military organization. Yet despite the purge, and despite administrative and political control, from time to time disaffection surfaced within the military.

Military Conspiracies in the 1930s

Military revolts and conspiracies against Trujillo began early in the 1930s; the intelligence service detected at least ten plots between 1930 and 1934. The most serious of these plots, organized by members in the high command of the armed forces, took place in 1933. Former army chief General Ramón Vásquez Rivera, Colonel Leoncio Blanco, commanding officer of the Department of the South (with headquarters in Barahona Province), and air force chief Major Aníbal Vallejo led the conspiracy. Betrayed by a detractor, they and other participants were arrested and received sentences on charges of sedition. Most of the conspirators suffered greatly in jail, but wardens inflicted one of the most barbaric methods of torture on Blanco by pulling out his fingernails.[34]

Blanco's problems stemmed from his position in the southern provinces, where, by way of graft and corruption, the military post yielded a side income and Blanco became rich and popular. To his misfortune, however, wealth and prominence worked against him. Some believed he had political ambitions, and with his popular appeal, he challenged the Jefe's megalomania.[35]

To complicate matters, an incident arose in 1933 over land under Blanco's territorial jurisdiction, land occupied by Haitians but claimed by Dominicans. With mediation by the United States, the solution to the problem favored the Haitians, whereupon Trujillo, believing that Blanco had handled the affair inappropriately, publicly reprimanded the officer and incarcerated him for seven months. Consequently Blanco turned against Trujillo and organized the uprising that landed him in jail again. In prison, Blanco had the courage to spit at Trujillo when the dictator went to his cell to insult him. He was tortured and hanged for his actions.[36]

Vallejo's involvement in the conspiracy might have stemmed from his national sensibilities or resentment against Trujillo. Studying aviation in Cuba and traveling to the United States afforded him a new perspective on Dominican reality. Abroad he learned more about Trujillo's repressive system than he had known while living at home. Convinced of the need for political change, he joined Blanco's plot.

Discharged from the military and sentenced to twenty years in jail, Vallejo received a presidential pardon in 1937 and was later appointed highway inspector. What appeared to be a stroke of good fortune turned out to be a trap; Trujillo set him up to be killed. In 1938, while assessing road conditions at the southern border, the government announced that Vallejo had been murdered in Haitian territory.[37]

A breach in professional conduct on Trujillo's part appears to have been the primary reason for Vásquez Rivera's participation in the plot. A Puerto Rican by birth but a naturalized Dominican, Vásquez Rivera could never be president and therefore did not have political aspirations. His irritation originated when the dictator reorganized the military in January 1933 without even consulting Rivera, who was the commanding general of the army.[38] Humiliated and angry, Rivera joined the conspiracy. After sentencing him to prison, Trujillo pardoned Rivera and then appointed him to a diplomatic position in France. Years later Rivera "made the mistake [of coming] back to Santo Domingo" and was accused of conspiracy again. This time, he was arrested for plotting to murder Chief of Staff Héctor Trujillo.[39] In January 1940 Vásquez Rivera and about thirty other implicated individuals, both civilian and military, were killed in prison or on the streets.

Escalating repression and violence drove military men and their relatives to adopt a defiant attitude similar to that of the Saviñón brothers. Clemente Saviñón had plotted against Trujillo in 1938. When his plan failed, he sought refuge in Haiti, where Trujillo's men later killed him. Embittered by Clemente's death, his brother Tancredo, a retired army general, convinced several officers and enlisted men to join forces to overthrow Trujillo, but the conspirators died under the fire of Trujillo's guns. Crassweller suggests that more than a real conspiracy, Tancredo's plan was imaginary, macabre, and more like a movie plot than a plan based on reality. Metaphorically, like "Irma Pavolin, who gave her body and her life for France in the Franco-Prussian war by deliberately spreading syphilis among the enemy," Saviñón, who had been diagnosed with terminal cancer, spread animosity against Trujillo and sacrificed his life and the lives of others to discredit the dictator.[40] For both Pavolin and Saviñón illness was not a deterrent to fight for their cause.

Whenever disloyalty or even the suspicion of disloyalty surfaced, Trujillo's relatives replaced officers accused or suspected of conspiracy. Ironically, three of his brothers, Aníbal, Virgilio, and José Arismendi, even conspired against Trujillo in the early 1930s. Antagonizing Trujillo, they sought to establish their own source of power within the military institution. Aníbal, chief of staff of the army, challenged his brother's supremacy by acting with some degree of autonomy against orders and by acquiring lands and properties, which antagonized his brother. To avoid a confrontation, Trujillo dismissed Aníbal on the grounds that he lacked proper military disposition and character.[41]

Virgilio, Trujillo's older brother, wanted to exercise tutelage over Trujillo and had political aspirations. This caused friction between them and developed into confrontations. Stationed in Santiago, Virgilio tested the area for political purposes by contacting potential supporters. Informed of his brother's activities, Trujillo sent a colonel to escort Virgilio to Ciudad Trujillo. "If he refuses," Trujillo instructed the colonel, "you should act as a soldier."[42] Aware of his difficult position, the colonel sent a message to Trujillo's mother, informing her about Virgilio's situation. Virgilio sought refuge in her house. Later Virgilio went into exile as ambassador to Spain, but the resentment between him and Trujillo lasted forever.[43]

Because Virgilio had had a business association with Luís Amiama Tió, one of Trujillo's assassins, he did not return from abroad when his brother was assassinated in May 1961. In 1962, when Amiama Tió became a member of the council of state, which took on the task of rebuilding the government, Virgilio "sent to the man who had helped to kill his brother a cable" reminding him that his birthday "had come and gone" without receiving a traditional birthday card from Amiama.[44]

José Arismendi ("Petán") had as much desire for power and glory as his brother Rafael. Trying to compete with Trujillo, Petán led a conspiracy in the military garrison of Bonao, a town that had become his feudal estate. When Trujillo learned of the plot, he sent Petán to Europe as a military attaché. After his return, counting on the loyalty of officers and soldiers from the garrison, Petán organized another rebellion. This time, so "successful had Petán's efforts at seduction of the military been that there were a few instances of bloodshed when new units replaced those who had listened to Petán."[45] To restore his authority and to isolate Petán

Inauguration
portrait of
Trujillo, 1930.
Courtesy Museo de
Historia y Geografía.

Trujillo in dress
uniform. Courtesy
Colección de los Santos.

Ramfis Trujillo at age five wearing his military uniform of army colonel in 1933. Courtesy Archivo General de la Nación.

Rhadamés Trujillo at age fourteen wearing his military uniform. Courtesy Museo de Historia y Geografía.

Ramfis Trujillo in his air force uniform. Courtesy Colección de los Santos.

Trujillo and his brother, Héctor, accompanied by military officers during the inauguration of the Cattle National Fair in 1955. Courtesy Colección de los Santos.

Women wearing white representing arms factory personnel in a parade for Trujillo. Courtesy Colección de los Santos.

Wives of members of the National Police carrying a banner during the parade on August 16, 1958. Courtesy Museo de Historia y Geografía.

Thirty women holding a flag honoring Trujillo as Benefactor of the Fatherland during the national parade on August 16, 1958. Courtesy Museo de Historia y Geografía.

"Coronation" of Angelita Trujillo as Queen of the Fair of Peace and Confraternity of the Free World, 1955. Courtesy Colección de los Santos.

Women wearing white lace dresses with red hearts symbolizing love for Trujillo. Queen Angelita is in the front row, third from right. Men who participated in the Corso Florido event also had a heart printed on their shirts. Courtesy Colección de los Santos.

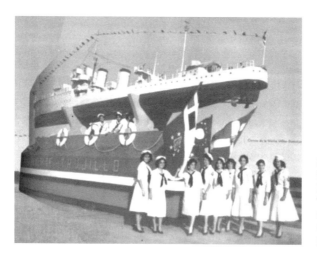

Navy wives in a parade honoring Trujillo, 1955. Courtesy Colección de los Santos.

Schoolboys in
military-style uni-
forms. Courtesy
Colección de los
Santos.

Baton twirlers (Batón
Ballet) in the parade
during the celebration
of Trujillo's twenty-
five years in power.
Courtesy Colección
de los Santos.

María Teresa Mirabal.
Courtesy Museo de
Historia y Geografía.

Minerva Mirabal.
Courtesy Museo de
Historia y Geografía.

Patria Mirabal.
Courtesy Museo de
Historia y Geografía.

from his local power basis, Trujillo again sent his rebellious brother to Europe as a military attaché.

To protect himself from military rebellion, Trujillo amassed an enormous amount of weapons that he kept under strict control. The soldiers, however, found themselves ill-equipped. Those stationed in outposts had no "more than a round or two of ammunition."[46] Instead of bullets, soldiers received continuous reminders about where their loyalty lay. A large placard in the barracks asserted: "Soldiers—always remember that your motto is eternal loyalty and unconditional adherence to Generalissimo Trujillo."

Culture of Kinship and the Military

Stressing the civil-military nexus to militarize society, Trujillo used kinship to link political objectives with military actions. Ideologically, the regime designed training to further policies of repression by presenting Trujillo's enemies as the army's enemies. In this way, repression of the people would not be repulsive to the soldiers.[47] It was understood as a matter of survival. In this sense the army and Trujillo, "intimately linked" as they were, "formed a closely bound whole, inseparable and indestructible,"[48] similar to by kinship relations.

In this respect, the close connection of kinship served Trujillo's dual purpose of enforcing loyalty and exercising discipline within the ranks. Kinship also played an important role in establishing interdependent cultural relations as it linked people of all social classes to the dictatorial regime through the paternalistic figure Trujillo projected. He was the best man at thousands of marriages, civilian and military, and the godfather of thousands of children. With the blessing of the Catholic Church, Trujillo developed a taste for *padrinazgos* and *compadrazgos*, a co-parenthood system he used for populist appeal. The system raised parents and their children to some degree of intimacy with the "Jefe" and to a close social or economic relationship. To begin with, the parents of each child received a hundred dollar bill.[49] For many poor families, this was a considerable sum. Moreover, acting as a cohesive instrument, this type of kinship provided opportunities for a closer interaction between civilians and the military, and reinforced loyalty to and solidarity with the regime.

Members of the officer corps played an important role in expanding kinship through the *compadrazgo* system. Particularly in peasant communities, it was not uncommon for officers to represent Trujillo as godfathers in baptism, confirmation, and matrimony. In addition, soldiers selected officers and comrades to become their child's baptism or confirmation sponsors. This relationship was mutually beneficial to both Trujillo and the soldiers. A soldier might win promotion, land, or a house based on his kinship with Trujillo or an officer. In addition, such kinship develops a strong bond. It is sacred. One does not betray his or her godfather, godmother, or *compadres*. Hence, the *padrino-compadre* relationship generated loyalty toward Trujillo and led to expectations of political protection for the godchild's family.

In addition to the co-parenthood system, Trujillo used other methods to develop a strong sense of loyalty to him. With hard work, control of all communication media, and an effective propaganda machine, Trujillo developed an image of a generous and grandiose father. Dominicans born after 1930 were called "children of the era of Trujillo," and Trujillo often called the soldiers his "children." Trujillo's personality appealed to and captured the imagination of civilians and military personnel alike. For many soldiers Trujillo was like a father who not only gave them a stable job but also solved their problems in a paternalistic way. He "lives in our heart and we adore him as a god," wrote one soldier.[50]

The loyalty of the military to Trujillo was an intricate relationship based on love, fear, and respect. An ex-captain offered the opinion that the discussion of Trujillo's military was too politicized and that it was not sufficiently studied within the then prevailing socioeconomic context. "People who criticize us," he said, "do not understand us." He explained that he was from *monte adentro*, the heart of the countryside, where life was predestined from dawn to night. But when he enlisted, his life changed. Due to his satisfactory performance as a soldier, he was promoted several times. When asked whether he still maintained his admiration for Trujillo, he said in an ironic tone: "You, the 'scientists,' cannot understand why many wanted to be accepted in the army and why only a few wanted to leave the institution. I will tell you why. The army taught us how to be good citizens and gave us a secure job." Then he expressed his admiration for Trujillo. "We were afraid of the Jefe, but we also respected him. He was a man of character."[51]

Others shared his view. They saw Trujillo as a role model. They also believed that under Trujillo the army became "a caste, a factory of personality, which developed the potential of many who otherwise never would have the opportunity to be someone."[52] They expressed a strong identification with the army and recognized that the organization offered them opportunities for advancement not available to other segments of the population. One such opportunity was education. General Clarence Charles Dunlop, a physician who worked in the National Palace during the Trujillo regime and the Balaguer administration, told me that he entered the army with a bachelor's degree but the organization provided the opportunity for him to become a medical doctor. He added, "Gracias a Dios" (Thanks to God). Rapidly and jokingly he reprimanded himself and changed his last remark to "Gracias a Dios y a Trujillo," as it was customary to say during the era of the Generalissimo.[53]

Military Education

Before 1930 the government attempted on several occasions to build a professional army that would be an effective instrument of national power. However, the overwhelmingly rural origins of the enlisted men, political instability, and the prevalence of illiteracy in Dominican society worked against the establishment of systematic procedures for the education of military men. The formal education of most enlisted men was not beyond the sixth grade. For nearly their entire career, these illiterate soldiers, called *los cajotas* by their comrades, spent their time taking orders because the lack of a formal education prevented them from career advancement. On the basis of Linz's theory, the low level of education of so many soldiers may help explain how Trujillo's paternalistic image acquired a new dimension after November 1932 when the regime distributed the *Cartilla cívica*, considered the "most impressive literary production of Trujillo." The dictator proudly acknowledged that he had composed the *cartilla* to elevate the moral character of the citizens, and the content intended to destroy the old man and to mold a new one.[54] A sort of indoctrination manual, the book was officially promoted as a text for the civic education of the Dominican people. Spreading the ideology and philosophy of the regime, the Partido Dominicano distributed the volume to urban and rural schools and barracks alike. It was imperative for all Dominican homes to have one. Among other ideological elements, the text stressed the brotherhood between soldiers and civilians, directing civilians to see *un hermano* (a brother) in each soldier.[55] The *cartilla* did not teach the soldiers how to read and to write but taught them that Trujillo, the Benefactor, favored education and studies. Despite this propaganda, a program to teach basic reading and writing to adult citizens, known as Programa de Alfabetizacion Nacional, did not materialize until the 1950s. The government pushed the program vigorously. Many "volunteered" their time; others received a small salary for their work. The secretary of education appointed public employees, teachers, students, and private individuals to teach and to encourage the people to overcome their educational disabilities.

The military adopted the general literacy program at the end of 1952, but the organization had already embarked on the project. In fortresses and garrisons across the country, illiterate military personnel received instruction in reading, writing, basic mathematics, geography, history, and civics. The government also had established schools for the instruction of officers and enlisted men. To produce efficient company officers and soldiers familiar with common military tactics and procedures, both military instruction and physical training were provided annually. Trujillo himself supervised part of the training program.[56]

Educational Centers and the Curriculum

Soldiers received military instruction at several locations around the country, primarily in the capital. In 1931 the government created a teaching center, bearing the name General Educational Center General Trujillo, to teach officers and recruits how to perform their duties. With its motto, "Todo por la Patria y por Trujillo" (All for the fatherland and for Trujillo), military education also reflected a military celebratory subculture of glory and honor.

Within this context, at the end of 1942 the professional training of officers took place in the cadet school of the National Army, located in the General Educational Center General Trujillo. The cadet school, aimed at developing a cohesive and professionally trained officer corps, which responded to the need for military expansion of the regime, played a significant role in the academic instruction of the military. The curriculum required two years of intensive studies, during which cadets learned about military topography, infantry and cavalry tactics, artillery, and the military code of justice. The program also included general studies and physical education. After completion of their studies, graduates were considered for promotion to second lieutenant.[57]

To enhance military education, at the end of December 1944 Executive Order No. 80 created a bachelor's degree in military science and lengthened the cadet program to four years. The creation of the Military Geographic Institute in October 1949 stressed the importance of geography and cartography, especially as they pertained to the border area between the Dominican Republic and Haiti. Trujillo demanded that junior officers become well acquainted with the topography of the region, its military posts, towns, agricultural production, and any other matter related to the border. Failure to reach proficiency in these areas was grounds for punishment or dismissal. Occasionally, Trujillo himself questioned officers about the frontier area. If an officer failed to respond appropriately, he soon found himself in one of the posts along the 310-kilometer-long border.[58]

The future officers attending cadet school pursued their studies under the strict rules of military education. To facilitate concentration on their studies, the military code required that students remain single until the completion of the program. They had to maintain good academic standing and comply with inspection rules, military exercises, and rigid discipline.

The program integrated standard military disciplines with baccalaureate degree requirements. The first part of the academic program concentrated on military courtesy and discipline, maintenance and use of weapons, military topography, cavalry, physics, chemistry, mathematics, and the English language. The knowledge of basic English enabled the future officers to read tactical manuals and instructions for the use of weapons produced in the United States. The first part of the curriculum also relied heavily on physical education and athletics, leading to health maintenance and fitness. In the second part, cadets continued the study of military and technical subjects of artillery and cavalry but also took classes in liberal arts, communications, law, and military history.[59]

In 1943 the naval school at Las Calderas Naval Base opened its doors, offering training in seamanship, navigation, and command. Some of the first naval officers distinguished themselves with their intellectual production and political engagements. One of them, Ernesto Vega Pagán, became a historian and Trujillo's military biographer. Another, Luis Homero Lajara Burgos, surfaced as a controversial political leader during the 1970s. To better serve the military, some officers combined their military education with other professional studies at the University of Santo Domingo, becoming lawyers, physicians, pharmacists, and engineers. Similarly, army and air force officers also had the opportunity to obtain a university degree.

The air force operated an aviation school as well. In 1928, in honor of Charles Lindbergh's visit to the Dominican Republic that February, the government selected the famous aviator's landing site as the place to build an aviation school.[60] Originally named the Military School of

Aviation, it did not develop any training program and stopped functioning a year later. In 1930 Trujillo sent a group of officers and privates to
learn the art and mechanics of flying at the Columbia Aviation School of
Cuba. Captain Anibal Vallejo and Lieutenants Frank A. Félix Miranda
and Julio E. Tejada were among them. At the end of eighteen months,
they graduated on December 13, 1931. A few days later Trujillo himself welcomed back the first Dominican military aviators. Vallejo and
Felix piloted their own aircraft. Captain Enrique Valverde, who studied
aviation in the United States in 1931, was the pioneer of Dominican
aviation. In 1927 he represented the Dominican Republic at the International Convention of Commercial Aviation held in Washington DC.
Devoted to aviation studies, he learned about commercial aviation and
drafted a blueprint for an airplane.[61]

Although military aviation was beginning to take shape in 1931, there
was not a noticeable improvement in this area until a small group of
cadets began to receive practical and theoretical instruction from foreign
instructors and the first group graduated in 1937. The second group,
whose instructors were mostly Dominicans, graduated in 1939, but the
aviation school did not train students in earnest until 1946. Its main
goal was to develop students' skill at piloting aircraft.[62] Together with
the General Center of Military Training, which was in charge of the
administration of the different military schools and training centers, the
aviation school taught technical proficiency to the cadets.

Since the 1880s, the training staff of the Dominican armed forces had
been a multinational blend of Europeans, Latin Americans, and Americans. But in the early 1930s, fearing a conspiracy, Trujillo barred foreign
officers from military instructor positions. Later, owing to the lack of
qualified Dominicans to teach military science, the government had no
choice but to hire foreign instructors and to send officers abroad to
complete their military education. In 1932 the Dominican government
hired Major D. Glenn Miller, formerly an officer in the USMC, as a military instructor. The same year, a French officer, whose "name is given as
Captain Tomassini," assumed his duty as an instructor of the cavalry.[63]

In 1943 eighty officers sent to the United States began their studies
in artillery, field maneuvers, engineering, and military drawing. In 1947
the Dominican government hired ten young U.S. pilots to teach and
train Dominican pilots. Among the instructors was Lorenzo Berry Jr.,
who later conspired against Trujillo.[64]

In September 1947 retired Brigadier General Victor F. Bleasdale,

USMC, signed an agreement with the Dominican government to serve as a technical advisor to the president of the Dominican Republic on matters pertaining to the training of the Dominican armed forces.[65] In the middle of June 1948, two Brazilian officers, Miguel Assis and Paulo Oliviera Silva, were also under contract to train military personnel in the use of the Brazilian weapons just acquired by the Dominican government.[66]

Military Academy Batalla de las Carreras

The education of the officer corps was crucial to the development of the armed forces. One of the most important steps in the professional formation of officers took place in 1956 when the military academy Batalla de las Carreras opened its doors. (The name Las Carreras, as mentioned, has a nationalist and patriotic connotation with the wars of independence.) The best officers from both the army and the General Educational Center were transferred to serve as instructors at the academy, which quickly became the center of military education. As stated by active and retired officers, the academy was and still is a prestigious center of high military standards. So important was the academy that when I asked General Ramiro Matos González, a former secretary of the armed forces, in an interview in December 1996 what Trujillo's most important contribution to the military organization was, he quickly responded, "the creation of the Academy." He divided the history of the military during Trujillo's era into two periods: before and after the creation of the academy. Matos González explained that before the academy, officers spent most of their time marching, practicing shooting, and controlling subordinates and people in general. Afterward the academy governed almost every aspect of the cadets' lives but also instilled professional standards and discipline in the corps. Eugenio Guerrero Pou, a former air force officer, recalled in vivid detail the dining code of behavior. Every day, under the scrutiny of a superior officer, the cadets entered the dining room in martial order. Then they stood firm behind their assigned chairs.

> Each table had six chairs; heading the table was a senior officer, regularly one who came the year before; the officer of the day had a separate table, with a view that allowed him to see the entire dining room; the order to be seated came from this officer. We sat on the edges of our seats, legs tied with heels together, chests firm, and hands on the edge of the table. Then, the cadet heading the table gave the order to serve our portion of food. To put the food

in our mouths, we had to move the fork or the spoon in a straight line to the mouth, forming a right angle from the plate to the mouth and vice versa; to put the utensils down on the plate, we had to place them at a right angle with the line to the mouth. Not behaving strictly according to good military table manners could constitute a reason for dismissal.[67]

Etiquette was important, but the primary goal of the academy was to create a new military by opening access to leading positions for young, educated, well-trained officers who were more professionally and technically oriented. In the first five years of the academy's existence, 165 officers graduated. Of them, 96 were from the army, 47 from the air force and 22 from the navy.[68]

In his historico-sociological study *The Military and Society in Latin America*, John J. Johnson establishes that professionalization had produced a new officer whose belief in "the need to modernize involves him so deeply with the welfare of the nation that he feels obligated to take a position on all major issues."[69] Corroborating Johnson's notion, in his analysis of the Dominican military profession, Soto Jiménez argues that according to the needs of society and its aspirations, the professional behavior of the officer corps had profound political consequences.[70] Indeed, professionalism gave a different image to the Dominican armed forces with qualified officers, and, against Trujillo's militarism, in the long run it contributed to the development of the need for social reform and justice among junior officers. Several of the leaders of the revolution of April 1965 came from the academy, including many who sought professional improvement abroad.

Although the curriculum of the Batalla de las Carreras academy was originally designed to follow U.S. standards, military principles and doctrines from other countries were soon incorporated into the program. As revealed in the memoir of Guerrero Pou, the international content of the curriculum and the international mix of the faculty were impressive. In sports, for example, the swimming instructor was from the United States; the boxing instructor was from Cuba; a black belt on judo and jiu-jitsu, Mamoro Matsunaga, was from Japan; and a Spanish champion taught fencing.[71]

As Dominican personnel studied with foreign instructors or attended schools abroad, the armed forces became familiar with the Argentinean, Colombian, Cuban, Chilean, Chinese, French, Japanese, Peruvian, Spanish, Venezuelan, and American military systems. Particularly Spain and Venezuela, under the dictatorships of Francisco Franco and Marcos Pérez Jiménez, respectively, cooperated with Trujillo to improve the professional level of the Dominican officer corps. Those who attended classes with Spanish instructors concentrated on learning about disciplinary rules and principles of military operations. Dominican junior officers attended training courses in Venezuelan military doctrine. Under U.S. patronage, officers were sent to Panama to receive special training in jungle combat, anti-guerrilla tactics, and parachuting into combat areas.[72] Study abroad, foreign military missions, and foreign instructors contributed to professional development and allowed officers to keep abreast of new technology, tactics, and professional literature.

Year after year, a group of officers continued their studies abroad after graduating from the Batalla de las Carreras. Some spent one or two years attending advanced military schools in different countries. Others went overseas to study for a short period of time or to observe annual maneuvers. Officers also went abroad to study the use of new weapons, communication systems, and other military disciplines. In 1957 twenty-five officers who had graduated from the academy the previous year were sent abroad to learn methods used by the most advanced armies from around the world.[73] Despite all these advantages, education became a divisive tool, separating the officers into two groups: academic officers and troop officers. Those who went to the academy reached their first promotion, from cadet to second lieutenant, in four years. However, the great majority of the officers spent the bulk of their careers as company officers and had to wait many years before they could get a promotion. They had experience, but not formal education; they resented the fact that younger men with only few years in the service commanded them. Because of their status and low advancement, academic officers also applied the term *cajotas* to troop officers. Throughout the years, the academy also helped change the perception of the military service. Those who applied to the academy sought to obtain a professional career, compared to those who entered the military as a means to survive.[74]

In addition to formal education, officers and selected enlisted men received religious education. In the 1950s the government built two Catholic retreat centers, Manresa Loyola for men and Manresa Altagracia for women. Military personnel and their spouses regularly participated in a short (a week or a weekend) period of meditation, prayer, and spiritual rejuvenation. Why? There is no clear answer, but perhaps it was part of the indoctrination and submission process. It was certainly a means for military men to establish camaraderie with civilians who also participated in these religious activities.

Responding to the development of the military culture, some officers followed in the footsteps of military writers. Holdings at the Dominican public and military archives offer evidence of the literary production of the officer corps. A good illustration is General Matos González, a respected historian and sculptor who authored several books on military history used in the military academies. His publications also include works on Dominican history in general. Similarly, General Renato Hungría, a historian, and his brother José Joaquín Hungría, a geographer, released several publications in their field of expertise. General Manuel Cuervo Gómez, a historian, published works about Dominican militarism and military history in general. And General Marcos Rivera Cuesta published material dealing with military-civil relations as well as issues related to the agrarian reform.

Unfortunately many officers were unable to use their knowledge and expertise to advance in their careers.[75] The system that propelled the betterment of the military personnel did not respect the prerogatives of professionalization. Depending on changing personal and political variables, the Jefe reserved for himself the fate of the officer corps.

As late as the 1990s, former officers and enlisted men who served under Trujillo viewed the dictator with a mixture of admiration and fear. Those who did not know him well admired him and were fascinated by him. Those who knew him well enough to know what he was capable of expressed the terror and frustration they had lived with.[76] In any case, through a web of formal and informal elements, Trujillo methodologically changed the military and altered society as he established new patterns of civilian-military relations.

6. THE NEW FATHERLAND

Functions of the Army and

the Dominicanización Plan

In 1934 a group of intellectuals compiled Trujillo's speeches in a text called *La nueva patria dominicana* (The new Dominican fatherland).[1] The text now customarily referred to as *La nueva patria* established the foundation of Trujillo's authoritarian state, which was analogously called La Patria Nueva. The new arrangement, an extremely centralized government based on the premise that the military could command disciplined support to achieve political goals (much like European fascism), framed Trujillo's vision of the future with eye-catching slogans and statements that assured Dominicans that Trujillo lead the country toward progress and prosperity.

La Patria Nueva

Designed to promote a new order, *La nueva patria* and La Patria Nueva reconceptualized the notion of citizenship; civic duties were defined in terms of allegiance to the dictator. A good citizen was loyal to the regime. Within this context Trujillo emerged as El Padre de la Patria Nueva (Father of the New Fatherland). The image of Trujillo as a new founding father of the nation added another dimension to his persona and to the cult that surrounded his personality.

The content of the book heightened nationalism and called Dominicans to be proud of their glorious past. The text also spelled out organizational and economic changes the government was pursuing to increase agricultural production and to end financial dependence on other countries (a goal achieved in July 1947 when the government paid off all foreign debt). To capture the people's imagination, Trujillo proudly acknowledged that he had composed *La nueva patria dominicana* to elevate the spirit of the Dominican people, and the content intended to destroy the old man and to mold a new one within a military framework.[2]

In forging the military to fit his political design, Trujillo expanded the armed forces by assigning it new tasks, which elevated its status. While reshaping the military, Trujillo proceeded with the creation of new forces to sustain the regime. With the Partido Dominicano on one side and the army on the other side, he turned to the peasantry to establish the social basis of the regime. Not surprisingly, Trujillo tried to establish a bond between the military and the peasants to provide stability for the regime. The new functions the military, the agrarian reform, the development of agricultural colonies, and the Dominicanización plan highlighted the interrelation that Trujillo attempted to establish between the political-military force and the peasantry.

Functions of the Army

During his long tenure Trujillo used the military as an instrument of control, terror, and torture to suppress the opposition and to guarantee stability. In addition to maintaining internal security and protecting the country's borders, the army went "beyond its ordinary limits," and its functions became "more numerous every day."[3] Trujillo viewed the army as a dynamic organization capable of contributing to the economic development of the country and of aiding him in his quest to create a new nation centered around his political goals. Such an attempt was partially grounded in the fact that when Trujillo became president, he took over a weak civil society with a strong army. Indeed, by 1930 "the army [was] the only real institution in the country,"[4] and Trujillo controlled and reshaped the military to his own ends.

Aiming to create strong institutional links between the military and civil society, Trujillo redirected the center of political action by assigning the military civilian duties and by imposing military principles on civil society. The functions assigned to the military, particularly to the army, were clear indicators of the civil-military interrelation pursued by the regime.

In line with his vision of the "new soldier," Trujillo kept military personnel busy with multiple assignments, such as participating in social and cultural functions, developing and administering agricultural colonies, establishing sanitary brigades to combat contagious diseases, checking personal identity documents, and suppressing contraband.[5] Although these duties were in keeping with Trujillo's political goals and projects, some of the tasks assigned to the military did have some social value. Interacting with members of all segments of the population, soldiers

carried out social and civic services sponsored by the Partido Dominicano, such as distributing food, meals, and medicine to the poor. The
diversity of the army's functions, from military to socioeconomic and
rural-civic actions, which was not unusual in Latin America. The Mexican army, for example, in the 1940s was engaged in a variety of social and
civic actions and took over duties from civilian officials. However, the
Dominican army under Trujillo was still significantly different from the
Mexican army under Presidents Lázaro Cárdenas and Manuel Avila Ca-
macho. The Mexican army dealt with student agitation, workers' strikes,
unrest among peasants, and other types of demonstrations inherent in
the democratic system.[6] In the Dominican Republic, the government
suppressed freedom of expression and the army repressed anyone who
attempted to voice an opinion. Under these conditions, military leaders
believed or were conditioned to think that to some extent Trujillo was the
incarnation of *la patria* and the army was the "incarnation of the people."[7]
The army functioned to accomplish the goals of the government.

The army also became an agency to guarantee the collection of taxes
and fees. Government operations largely depended on the collection of
revenue, and it was a soldier's duty to keep an eye on those who attempted to deceive the government by avoiding taxes or by benefiting
from contraband.[8] The government appointed military inspectors to
supervise the collection of taxes in some localities and entrusted them
with a broad range of responsibility in their districts. They had ample
authority, enjoyed considerable prestige, and obtained financial rewards.
The power of this position could be determined by the peculiar political
character of the regime, which stressed the importance of a collaborative
relationship among political agencies, civilian institutions, and military
authorities.[9] Trujillo believed that the army, as a hard-working, disciplined body, could help elevate the spirit and morale of the nation.

Therefore, it is not surprising that on some occasions, even if for a
short period of time, some officers were in charge of the political activities
of a particular province. For example, in 1931 Colonel Manuel Emilio
Castillo organized political meetings and rallies in Santiago; Colonel
Leoncio Blanco and Major Gustavo Bisonó did the same in Barahona and
La Vega, respectively. The senator from the province of Barahona, Jaime
Sánchez, considered such assignments inappropriate because military
men "should be in the barracks" and not walking the streets recruiting
political supporters. Sánchez claimed that government officials harassed
him, prompting him to go into exile.[10] The experiment did not work,

and six months later the provincial governors were again in charge of political activities. But the practice of assigning civilian duties to military men did not end. For Trujillo the army, among all other institutions, was the only one able to successfully carry out its assignments. Therefore, when Trujillo found out that the civilian authorities were negligent in following his orders, he humiliated, fired, and punished the offenders, and he sent a military unit to do what he wanted done. For example, one time Trujillo called an officer to his office and expressed his dissatisfaction with the performance of some civilian authorities while pointing out his confidence in military leadership. "I just came back from Dajabón. Nothing is working there. The town does not have a social life. Go there immediately and do something," said Trujillo. The officer followed Trujillo's instructions. In a few months the corps of engineers built a swimming pool in a private club.[11] Members of the club were primarily from the upper and middle classes, including public employees and the officers of the army, police, and air force. The army's engagement in this type of activity, even if only for the benefit of one segment of the population, served to establish a bond between civilians and the military.

In addition to military and administrative services, the National Army was also charged with staffing the prisons and with other police services. The executive reported to Congress that the army performed an outstanding police job in 1939. Overall, the number of detentions dramatically increased from 13,464 in 1938 to 24,213 in 1939. According to the report, the difference of 10,749 detentions resulted from the army's role as a police force.[12]

By participating in these diverse activities, the army acquired a new dimension: it became an instrument of dissuasion. The army's imposing presence minimized resistance and diminished border crossings to Haiti. With no threats of social disorder, soldiers interacted with citizens of all social levels; the army became the strongest pillar supporting the political framework of the regime. Reaffirming the hegemony of the military, a soldier wrote that the army was a "new social force" with a political mission.[13]

Redefining the relationship between civilians and military authorities, Trujillo drew a line between higher and lower military ranks. At least in the cities, the higher-ranking officers (from major upward) were primarily in charge of social and political activities, while captains and lower-ranking officers attended mainly to military affairs.[14] But such subtleties may not have been as effective in towns located in isolated areas, where all military personnel, regardless of rank, played an active role in political and social affairs. This active role provided an opportunity for the political activism of the military leaders after Trujillo's death.

The Army as Intelligence Agency

The aim of the discussion here is not to explain the modus operandi of the intelligence services because such an explanation would need to be so complex that it would go beyond the scope of this study. I focus instead on another interpretation of civil-military relations that the Trujillo regime worked out to reshape society. In the early 1930s soldiers acted as agents for Trujillo's espionage network. An intelligence unit within the army was not uncommon in Latin America. The Haitian and Mexican armies performed similar functions almost at the same time.[15] In the Dominican Republic, as in Haiti, the army was charged with maintaining internal order, but in Haiti all military intelligence was "sought by and sent to the intelligence unit of the army headquarters."[16] In contrast, in the Dominican Republic, Trujillo distributed these assignments among the police and the three branches of the military. The presidential office had its own specialized intelligence unit. Another specialized intelligence unit operated through the country's only university, the University of Santo Domingo.

Trujillo kept all the intelligence strings under his control, and it was unknown which office supervised all the intelligence operations. Neither "was [it] known who was directing the service abroad; sometimes it [was] an officer of the Army, sometimes a civilian, and usually none of them [was] a professional in the intelligence service."[17] Nonetheless, the army, through the Military Intelligence Service, assumed leadership over military intelligence activities and political-police surveillance.

In controlling the people, the army responded as Trujillo expected: effectively. Soldiers and officers imposed tight surveillance over almost every aspect of Dominican life, instituting a system of domestic terrorism, which also extended to the military. For example, in 1952 Sergeant Cristóbal Cohen, a member of the transportation unit, became the subject of suspicion when he acquired a new car. Cohen could not afford such a luxury based on his salary, his superiors assumed. He maintained that his relatives had helped him purchase the vehicle, but the authorities were not convinced and sent him to military jail.[18] It was not politically correct for a soldier to show financial independence from El Jefe.

Surveillance of union leaders, potential political figures, and university students, as well as censorship, were jobs assigned to the army and shared by the intelligence division of the navy and the air force. Trained civilian spies and a vast network of informers, ranging from public and private employees occupying high positions in society to cab drivers and domestic servants, also worked for the intelligence agency. During World War II, after declaring war against Germany, Italy, and Japan, the regime imposed even more surveillance measures to curb pro-Axis activities and propaganda within the country. To prevent disturbances, the opposition was beaten down by mass arrests and hundreds of assassinations. There were allegations that "the killings were carried out under the auspices of the army" and many prisoners were tortured and killed "near the national lunatic asylum where any screams would not attract attention."[19]

The army directed internal political espionage until 1957, when the Department of Security took over. The new department was in charge of the coordination of all matters related to intelligence, counterintelligence, law enforcement, and immigration. Johnny Abbes García, a civilian who worked undercover as a diplomat for Trujillo's espionage system in Mexico and in Central America, assumed the top position of the agency. Before him, Generals Federico Fiallo, Fausto Caamaño, and Arturo Espaillat took turns directing the military intelligence services. Overnight Abbes received the rank of colonel of the army, a title that indicated how important Trujillo considered this position.

Described as a man who combined "the role of an *eminence grise* with the operational functions of a triggerman," Abbes took control of the repressive apparatus when the regime was facing open resistance from different fronts.[20] Under Abbes's management, the new Department of Security (SIM) created its own unit of terror to do Trujillo's bidding. Many of Trujillo's opponents were the children and relatives of Trujillo's close collaborators. For their *ingratitude*, they suffered physical torture and human degradation beyond description. Abbes's barbaric methods and violence against Trujillo's enemies in general caused some to think that the dictator was mad. In Ramfis's view, Abbes represented the worst of all Trujillo's men.[21] During the last five years of the dictatorship, despite all of the repression they had suffered, the people continued to defy Trujillo and his regime, suffering massive brutality and cruelty as never before.

Revistas Cívicas
In establishing varying degrees of political control, early in the dictatorship, in collaboration with the Partido Dominicano, the army leaders

in rural areas organized gatherings at which peasants met with agricultural experts and discussed issues of concern. At first these meetings, called *revistas agro-políticas*, usually revolved more around politics than agricultural issues. Later the meetings evolved into *revistas cívicas*, which had been around since the nineteenth century. In the past, however, the *revistas cívicas* served to measure the political leverage of the regional or national leaders as they competed for the masses' loyalty and support. But after 1930, the meaning and appearance of these meetings acquired a new tone. Huge and well orchestrated, these gatherings served several purposes. First and foremost, they were an essential part of the regime's ideological offensive to organize the rural masses. As covert actions to disseminate political topics important to the regime, the *revistas cívicas* played an important role during Trujillo's reelection campaigns as they mingled state employees, bureaucrats, and peasants across the country.[22] For example, in 1938 this mixture was spectacular. On horseback, heading the event in ranking order were members of the cabinet followed by senators and congressmen, judges from the Supreme Court, governors, mayors, officers, soldiers, other state employees, peasants, and the public in general. In the capital, members of the diplomatic corps also participated. The show began early in the morning, and very often a heavy breakfast—roasted pigs, plantains, chocolate, coffee, and a wide range of other foods—was served to the participants, many of whom had traveled long distances. Smokers received cigars and cigarettes of their choice.[23] Small and symbolic as these gifts were, they not only demonstrated Trujillo's generosity but they also implied that the recipient incurred an obligation: loyalty. Trujillo expected that the beneficiaries would not bite the hand that fed them.

Trujillo's style of *panem et circenses* (bread and entertainment) also served to indoctrinate the masses, to control them, and to exercise surveillance over them. By telling the peasants what Trujillo wanted them to hear, the *revistas* also served as an "effective means" to deceive them.[24] Seeking to transform the peasants into unpaid soldier-spies (as denunciation became more and more pervasive and institutionalized), during the meetings audiences were encouraged to discuss what was going in their villages. But afraid of speaking "inconvenient" words, the peasants sat and listened but said nothing that could be harmful to anyone in their communities.[25]

Asserting control over the rural communities, highways, and underdeveloped infrastructure helped military intelligence agents, particularly at time of armed uprisings, to gather information and conduct covert activities. Even in the 1950s, the three main highways and the secondary roads covered an area of only about 2,500 square kilometers, so that many rural villages could be reached only with military vehicles.[26] These conditions helped the military hold on to its control over the tightly governed Dominican rural society.

Despite the control it wielded, the army had no political voice of its own and no political decision-making power, as was the case in other Latin American countries. In a society without strong civilian institutions, such as the Dominican Republic, the army had some autonomy to act abusively and capriciously, provided that their actions were in line with what Trujillo wanted. The army became so unpopular that by the end of the dictatorship the military was wholly distrusted by civilians. There were, however, times during the three decades of the dictatorship when the military interacted amicably with civilians, particularly those with an interest in agriculture.

Soldiers as Colonists

In addition to all their other duties, Dominican soldiers also served as a labor force. Aware that a high percentage of soldiers came from rural areas, Trujillo did not disconnect them from their agricultural background. On the contrary, he fostered the bonds between the soldiers and their social backgrounds by assigning them an active role in the implementation of his agrarian policy. Officers and enlisted men became objects and subjects of the colonization program by cultivating and supervising colonies. Furthermore, in view of the fact that most of the soldiers had a rural background and some type of agricultural knowledge, some of them were trained to become agricultural instructors in rural schools.

Having soldiers cultivate the land served political and economic purposes. The regime linked the military to the economic development of the country as soldiers produced goods and services for the state. The government expected the soldiers to pay for at least 50 percent of the cost of maintaining and operating the barracks.[27] In connecting politics with the economy, Trujillo played the double game of giving and receiving. Some soldiers obtained their own piece of land on which to cultivate a variety of vegetables for themselves, their families, or the barracks where they were stationed. Given the country's history of landless peasants, Trujillo gained the support of the soldiers who benefited from his land distribution program. Indeed, the distribution of land greatly benefited military men, particularly the officer corps. Early in 1930s, for example, General Simón Díaz received about 1,000 *tareas* and Carlos R. Fermin, a retired officer, got about 500 *tareas* of confiscated land.[28] (A *tarea* is equal to approximately 629 square meters.) Thus, as Trujillo put it, to encourage agricultural development, the institution used to "destroy the enemy" could also be used to achieve material progress.[29] In effect, agricultural colonies became ladders for social and economic mobility, vehicles for socialization and interaction between civilian society and the military, and a means of promoting military ways and methods in rural areas.

Soldiers and officers not only received land but they also actively participated in the distribution of land and were partially responsible for enforcing the agrarian policy of the state. They also organized and supervised the *juntas protectoras de la agricultura* (associations for the protection of agriculture), the municipal boards in charge of land distribution. The *juntas* to some extent represented a bridge between the peasants and the state and they were meant to "provide free access to idle lands on the basis of contracts whose conditions . . . depended on whether the lands in question were state lands, *terrenos comuneros* or privately owned."[30] The *juntas* were also conceived as a means of active propaganda to promote agricultural development and as a center for the denunciation of those who did not want to work the land.[31] Through the *juntas* officers played an important role in linking soldiers and civilian citizens to accomplish the economic policies of the state. In carrying out Trujillo's agricultural project, some officers embraced the agrarian policy and influenced the government in a reformist direction. As an illustration, Major Rafael Carretero, one of Trujillo's first commissioners for the implementation of the agrarian reform, worked to raise the poor conditions of the landless peasants. Given authority to distribute land, by the middle of 1936 the *juntas* under Carretero's leadership had distributed 107,202 hectares of land. By then there "were already 54,494 recipients, representing an impressive 29 percent of the nation's farms." By 1945 the distribution of land affected 2,842,815 hectares that were given out to 85,554 colonists.[32] Indeed, although Trujillo was never short of words to distort and magnify his ideas and actions, the colonization program promised, and partially delivered, the distribution of free land to those interested in agricultural development, including soldiers, who served as models for other colonists. In addition, the government also provided houses, seeds, tools, machinery, irrigation facilities, and technical assistance to the colonists.

As a result, production for the domestic and external markets increased, and some peasant groups obtained economic benefits.

The Benefactor and the Peasants

To foster support for his regime and *La nueva patria dominicana*, Trujillo drew on popular culture to charm the rural masses. Enchantment of the peasantry began early in 1930. During his first presidential campaign, Trujillo traveled with a musical group that played merengue, the preferred music of the rural population.[33] After he became president, Trujillo continued to use popular culture, emotional speeches, and personal letters to court the peasants. On January 1, 1932, Trujillo addressed a message to the peasants thanking them for their willingness to cooperate with the government's plan for national reconstruction, particularly for their cooperation in augmenting rice production.[34] Rice, an essential element of the Dominican diet, was imported, and during the critical initial years of the regime, reducing the cost of food imports was a priority. For this reason, the government launched a campaign to motivate peasants to produce rice for domestic consumption. In some colonies the state required a portion of the land to be used to cultivate rice. Peasant-soldiers and civilian-peasants worked together in colonies designated for rice production. As a result of productivity, market incentives, and state coercion, rice became a profitable crop, and the country turned from importer to exporter of the product.[35]

Pursuing his objective of establishing a bond or rapport with the peasants, on November 17, 1932, during a public meeting, Trujillo declared that the workingmen were his *mejores amigos* (best friends) and that for the first time in Dominican history a head of state called the workingmen his *amigos.* He also stated that it was a civic duty and moral obligation of his friends to work in agricultural projects.[36] Like other governments before and after him, the topic of development of the agricultural economy became an essential part of Trujillo's political discourse. It was not limited to the speeches in *La nueva patria*. In 1935 during the inauguration of the Industrial and Agricultural Exposition Fair in Santiago, Trujillo declared agricultural development his top economic priority. In conjunction with this policy, he defined his conceptualization of government: to govern was to feed.[37]

Fusing substance with symbols, Trujillo linked his administrative machine to the peasants, offering them land, opportunities to increase production, access to new markets, and profitability.[38] Oriented toward this end, the regime designed programs to integrate the rural areas and the national economy, which aroused enthusiasm and support for the government.

While the implementation of Trujillo's agricultural policy rested on the leadership of capable officers, who enforced the law and authorized and supervised the distribution of land, the articulation of such policy depended on the talents of many of his officials. Rafael Espaillat and César Tolentino, for example, served as secretaries of agriculture and formulated the basis of the agricultural policy of the regime. Both opposed the ownership of large estates and promoted land tenure reform and massive distribution of land to Trujillo's "best friends," the peasants. The distribution of land was so emphatically defended by the promoters of the agrarian policy that government records and newspapers referred to the implementation of their policy in terms of the *socialization* of the land.[39] Officers and officials working together stressed the collaborative relationship that Trujillo sought to establish between the military and civilians.

Promoting Trujillo as Benefactor of the Fatherland, the regime grafted the agricultural policy into an imaginary vision of Trujillo as a populist leader, advocate of the peasants. Peasants received encouragement to write directly to Trujillo in regard to land tenure, legal problems, and personal matters. Did landowners or the authorities abuse the peasants? If so, peasants wrote to Trujillo. Did the community need a new road or a school building? The peasants informed Trujillo. Records of the secretary of agriculture and other secretaries contain hundreds of letters from peasants asking for land, water for irrigation, property titles, and other favors.[40] The language used by the peasants in these letters reflects the effect of the official rhetoric, projected in the political discourse of *La nueva patria* and other texts. Presenting themselves as hard-working parents, loyal to the regime, peasants addressed Trujillo as their sole leader, spiritual father, great Benefactor, and the only government that had showed interest in the less fortunate sector of the population. For example, one letter states that Trujillo taught citizens the proper work ethic, and the peasants, like soldiers, felt that they owed El Jefe and his government their loyalty.[41] Clearly the agrarian policy of the regime had its appeal among landless peasants who received land and assistance from the agricultural secretary and the *juntas*.

The land used for Trujillo's agricultural programs belonged to the state or was given or sold by private owners. Some did so voluntarily;

others were forced to adopt the agrarian policy of the state. Regardless of productivity, large or small estates were subject to different ways of expropriation. A common practice was to offer to buy the land for less than the real value.[42] In some cases, peasants who owned fertile land were forced off their properties, and the state or military men took over.

The Dominicanización Plan and the Haitian Massacre

Trujillo's plan for national rehabilitation was aimed mostly at inhabitants living along the Haitian border. Trujillo's Dominicanización plan, which had the appeal of a crusade, was designed to repopulate the area with Dominican citizens, to foster socioeconomic development, and to minimize Haitian influence. Bolstering nationalism with racial misconceptions, Trujillo's rhetoric encouraged violent actions against the Haitians and reinforced Dominican racial myths.

Traditionally, intellectuals and different social groups strongly honored the Spanish culture and emphasized the Hispanic heritage of the Dominican people to the point of lessening reference to their African heritage. At the end of the nineteenth century, the *indigenista* literary movement sought to celebrate the Indian cultural tradition and focused on the Dominican Indian heritage. Embracing their Indian ancestry, in terms of color, Dominicans began to call themselves *indios*.

This fictitious identification not only distorted history but nourished a chauvinist nationalism. In discussing the indicators of militarism and militarization, Thee classifies chauvinism as an element of ideology.[43] Chauvinism reinforced the Dominican racial attitude against the Haitians, known as *antihaitianismo*. *Antihaitianismo*, considered the racial ideology of Trujillo's regime, has been defined as "a set of socially reproduced anti-Haitian prejudices, myths, and stereotypes prevalent in the cultural makeup of the Dominican Republic."[44] But *antihaitianismo* is so complex that it requires more than one theoretical approach to be explained.[45]

The *antihaitianista* ideology combined with accumulated tensions and animosities, which originated during the period of invasion (1801–5) and the Haitian domination period (1822–44), as well as economic problems and geographic and demographic realities. Occupying one-third of the island, almost four million inhabitants lived in Haiti by 1937 while two million Dominicans occupied two-thirds of the island. The lack of relative space and the need for work resulted in a massive population movement to the east. By 1937 hundreds of Haitians worked as laborers in the sugar fields, as domestic servants, or were itinerant merchants selling goods in the markets and in the streets. Along the border, intermarriage and commercial interchange were customary.[46] Considering the growing Haitian presence along the border as the antithesis of *dominicanidad*, or as Balaguer calls it, "the most powerful instrument of moral disintegration to which Dominican society [had] been exposed,"[47] Trujillo tried to stop Haitian influences by signing two agreements with Haitian President Stenio Vicent (the documents were, in fact, clauses added to a border treaty signed by President Vásquez and President Louis Borno of Haiti in 1929). The Trujillo-Vicent agreement did not stop the crossing of the border, however. Determined to drive the Haitians out and to assert his control over the border, Trujillo ordered a reduction on the percentage of Haitians and other non-Dominican laborers working on the sugar estates. The Congress passed a law to expel Haitians who were working without the appropriate legal documentation. Trujillo's efforts "to clean" his nation of any Haitian presence or influence did not produce the expected results. Perhaps, ahead of Hitler's extensive pogrom of 1938 that allowed Nazi groups to murder Jews, the Dominican dictator envisioned in 1937 a "final solution" for all Haitians living in the Dominican Republic.

Accounts of the massacre report that beginning on October 2, Dominican soldiers and civilians armed with machetes, clubs, knives, and guns slaughtered an estimated twelve thousand to twenty thousand defenseless Haitian citizens living in the Dominican Republic. The killing lasted for about two weeks. It was pure genocide—a holocaust.

What urged Trujillo to order the massacre? How did it start? According to Balaguer's account of the event, early in October 1937 Trujillo was in Dajabón, surrounded by courtiers and beautiful women and drinking a large amount of Carlos I, his favorite cognac. In the midst of the orgy, a high-ranking army officer told him that Haitians trespassing the border were stealing cows and pillaging in Dominican territory. A furious Trujillo ordered the extermination, without exception, of all Haitians established *illegally* in the Dominican Republic.[48]

As expected, the Dominican-controlled press published numerous declarations in which Trujillo minimized the seriousness of the massacre or denied that he had ordered the killing, claiming that frustrated and angry campesinos, using only machetes and knives, were the culprits.[49] These statements implied that a sector of the civilian society had taken over military assignments and that military culture was deeply rooted into the mind and psyche of the citizenry. Civilians did participate in the killing, but according to U.S. sources "bullets from the Krag rifles were found in Haitian bodies," and only Dominican soldiers had access to this type of rifle.[50] Trujillo could not destroy this irrefutable evidence. In the midst of the crisis, Haitian President Stenio Vicent requested international mediation, mainly from Cuba, Mexico, and the United States. In the end, with the participation of Monsignor Maurilio Silvani, the Vatican representative in Haiti, the Dominican Republic agreed to pay Haiti an indemnity of $750,000.[51]

The aggression against Haiti became an albatross around Trujillo's neck. Internationally repudiated and condemned for his ruthlessness against the Haitians, Trujillo stepped aside in the national elections of 1938. However, he retained authority through two of his men, Jacinto Peynado and Manuel Troncoso de la Concha, who were the only candidates and received 100 percent of the votes. (Peynado became president.)

Despite these and other tactics used by the regime to diminish the gravity of the crime, the effect of the massacre did not fade away. Seven years later in November 1945, the Dominican senate renamed the town of Dajabón "President Roosevelt." The U.S. State Department considered the change a political maneuver aimed at enhancing Trujillo's prestige by capitalizing on his relations with the United States. More important, U.S. officials viewed the action as particularly inappropriate; although "the motives may or may not have been relatively innocent, . . . the town is near the scene of the Haitian massacre of 1937."[52] Facing U.S. disapproval, the Dominican senate reluctantly rescinded its action after the town bore the name of President Roosevelt for only eight days.

The massacre's atrocities and the international repercussions that followed have made it the most well-known event in the history of the Haitian-Dominican relations and of Trujillo's regime.[53]

Guardians of the Border

After the Haitian massacre, economic revitalization of the border became a priority. Essential to the politics and policy of the Dominicanización program was the development of agricultural colonies, a process that began during the administration of Ramón Cáceres (1906–11).

In attempting to centralize the military, as explained in chapter 1, Cáceres also sought to expand central control over the peasants by applying drastic measures first and then by establishing agricultural colonies to neutralize their political activities and to develop the agricultural economy. After Cáceres's death the colonization program went into a dormant period, but it was revitalized under President Vásquez. Vásquez based his plan for agricultural development on migration. Vásquez and his secretary of agriculture, Rafael Espaillat, who also served as Trujillo's secretary of agriculture, encouraged Dominicans and foreigners to settle along the border with Haiti in government-sponsored colonies.[54] Their efforts did not pay off and failed to accomplish the government's agricultural goals.

Favoring both agricultural development and Dominicanización of the border, Trujillo gave the army a new role as cultivators and agricultural administrators. They also functioned as vigilantes. Indeed, military men stationed in the frontier territories acted as dissuasive forces, not only preventing Haitian penetration into Dominican territory but also discouraging Dominicans, particularly those attempting to avoid political persecution, from crossing the border.

The colonies, which were established not only along the border but across the country, were organized according to three different models: ones strictly cultivated by the military; ones administered by the military; and ones under civilian administration. Examples of the first model were the colonies of Los Guayos in Sabana de la Mar, and Juan Pablo Duarte and Guayabal in Barahona. The main product of Los Guayos was rice, while Juan Pablo Duarte and Guayabal were destined mainly to produce coffee.[55] The first category also included penal colonies, generally those with inmates serving long sentences who were forced to work the land. In 1932, for example, the government sent more than three hundred prisoners along with about two hundred military men to work at the colony of Sabana de la Mar.[56] Administrated by the military and supervised by the secretary of agriculture and industry were the colonies of Capotillo in Montecristi, Pedernales in Barahona, and Mariano Cestero, Hipólito Billini, and Trinidad on the northern border. Trujillo reported that the productivity of these colonies was so impressive that the staff of the secretary of agriculture believed that all "the colonies should be administered by the military."[57] Most of the colonists were Dominicans but after the Spanish Civil War and World War II, the agricultural development of the regime also included the implementation of a controversial immigration plan that attracted Spaniards, Jews and Hungarian refugees, and Japanese settlers. The Jewish colony of Sosua and the Japanese colonies of Constanza, Jarabacoa, and Dajabón are examples of the third model. Scholars still debate whether Trujillo used some of these immigrants as a barrier to limit migration of Haitians to the Dominican Republic and to "whiten" the Dominican side of the border.[58]

Combining free labor and forced labor, Trujillo's colonization plan forced poor peasants, petty criminals, and others without jobs or property to work on state farms. Prisoners who had earned the trust of the military chiefs, known as *presos de confianza*, were sent to work at the officers' farms. Many ex-prisoners, having completed their prison terms, were "called again" to work in the military colonies or in Trujillo's sugar and sisal hemp plantations where they lived in abominable conditions.[59] The army and the police enforced labor conscription by compelling people to move from city slums to the countryside to cultivate the land. Many of those working at the sisal plantations were "recruited" under such procedures. Once in the plantations they became prisoners and suffered horrendous acts of violence and deprivation. For example, in May 1953 Colonel José María Alcántara, director of operations at the plantation, ordered soldiers to stamp with a hot iron the words "EL SISAL" on the bodies of the prisoners. The workers were basically slaves, working from sunrise to sunset under the tropical sun with limited food and frequent punishments.[60]

Many soldiers who thought they were being recruited to defend the fatherland often ended up as peasant laborers producing goods for Trujillo.[61] (Soldiers also labored on Trujillo's farms and those of his top officers.) The army was also actively engaged in civic action programs including the literacy programs and instruction in agricultural methods in rural schools. Military physicians directed health and sanitary units, offering medical services to peasants, many of whom could not afford to visit a doctor in the city.[62]

By establishing new communities and nearly one hundred military installations, Trujillo offered peasants a chance at economic prosperity, though on his terms. Once-isolated rural areas became connected to cities and towns, and production increased, changing the lifestyle of the peasantry and revitalizing their social and economic life.[63] Before the Dominicanización project and development of the colonies, the peasants on the border were isolated. Without good roads and transportation, except horses, burros, and mules to carry them and their agricultural products to the local market, peasants lived in a closed community. The colonies linked the frontier communities with the administrative and communication system in the capital and other cities and towns. In addition, reflecting the fashion of the time—entertainment to serve a political purpose—local and national artists performed a variety of musical productions, recitals, and other cultural activities in the new colonies.

In ideological and social terms, the variety of political, economic, and social duties assigned to the military produced equally diverse results. On one hand, judging from my interviews with former members of the military, the involvement of the army in so many activities had a negative effect on the organization. Former officers believed that compared with the navy and the air force, the army had too many tasks, were more dispersed, and had less time for intellectual endeavors. On the other hand, by assigning a variety of functions to the military, the execution of these duties contributed to Trujillo's plan to reshape society. Soldiers and peasants, officers and bureaucrats interacted by working together on agricultural projects.

Accordingly, the Dominicanización plan embodied the ideological cohesiveness of La Patria Nueva. By examining the project, one sees how Dominicanización served as a bridge to link civilians and the military as guards of the border, and thereby deepened the military ethos of society even further. In this respect, the permanent establishment of soldier-colonists along the Haitian-Dominican border fulfilled Trujillo's goal of Dominicanización of that border.

Mision Fronteriza

Another important element of Dominicanización was the expansion of church-supported schools. Reinforcing his good relations with the Catholic Church, Trujillo built churches, endowed schools and seminaries, and supported religious teaching in public schools across the country. The border received special attention; numerous schools were built there.

The establishment of some of these educational centers was a result of the efforts of the Jesuits, who promoted the education of the youth in rural areas through the Misión Fronteriza program. Father López de Santa Anna enthusiastically promoted the work of Misión Fronteriza, and proposed that Trujillo build religious schools along the border. The dictator responded positively as he assumed priests and nuns, together with soldiers, would contribute to enhance the educational aspect of the Dominicanización project. The main goal of the educational program was the social, cultural, patriotic, and religious formation of young people living along the border.[64] Trujillo also expressed with satisfaction that the civic-social function of Misión Fronteriza would contribute to form a "new generation of Dominicans" useful to their family and to the fatherland.[65] Consequently, in Dajabón the Colegio Nuestra Señora de la Altagracia, a school for girls, opened its doors in 1943, and Colegio Agrícola San Ignacio de Loyola, a technical school for male students, began to function in 1946.

Independent of Trujillo's political motives, these educational centers contributed in no small way to the intellectual development of the youth and the economic development of agriculture. San Ignacio de Loyola, with its curriculum focused on theoretical and practical agricultural techniques, carpentry, and cabinet-making, became known for its technical education. By the end of 1995, the school had graduated 1,066 agricultural professionals who had worked or were working in both the private and public sector as teachers, experts, and consultants in agronomy.[66]

The female students at La Altagracia, in addition to the standard grade school curriculum, learned about home economics, nursing, and manual arts. Both schools also provided cultural activities and amenities for the enjoyment of the general public. For example, almost every week San Ignacio de Loyola showed movies free of charge or for a very small fee. Watching these movies was one of few diversions for poor people in the community. Since the films were shown at an open-air theater, they also provided a cultural space and social contact for the inhabitants of Dajabón and surrounding areas. In addition, La Altagracia and San Ignacio de Loyola organized *veladas* or presentations of poetry recitals, comedies, and dramas, sometimes in coordination with the public school. Students of both schools performed shows representing a variety of religious, national, and popular themes that appealed to the public. Students from the public school also participated in these activities. Explicit attempts were made to celebrate military victories, such as Restoration Day, in which soldiers and students would parade together to celebrate the military achievements of the heroes of national independence and the Restoration.[67] Obviously, some of these presentations were destined to elevate the nationalistic spirit of the citizens as well as to glorify Trujillo. Participants carried banners that paid tribute to the dead heroes, as well as to Trujillo, the living hero. Nevertheless, the interest of the government in the Dominicanización program prompted the state to deliver resources to isolated areas and fund education, which had produced positive results. On the other hand, responding to Trujillo's contradictory, paradoxical new order, to provide space for the operation of the schools, the government evicted owners and tenants from the land that they had owned or rented for many years.

7 . PARADOXICAL REWARDS

Promotions, Nepotism, and Racialism

In the context of leadership, militarism under Trujillo manifested itself in the ways in which he exercised his authority over his subordinates. Studies of his authoritarian personality have long asserted that Trujillo used insecurity to keep subordinates moving in the direction he wanted. With his power resting on the complicity or identification of the military with his regime, Trujillo developed a system of patronage to enforce allegiance. Those invited to enjoy the splendor of the inner circle and proximity to the dictator received privileges and rewards. But prominence in Trujillo's regime was capricious and temporary.

Although Trujillo derived his base of power from the military, most officers went through periods where Trujillo humiliated or banished them from high positions. Shifting the commanders became a frequent practice. Once in a new post, officers never knew what was next: fortune or misfortune? They might receive a promotion or fall into disgrace. Bureaucrats and other civilian employees were also shifted around. Congressmen had to sign a letter of resignation, with the date left blank, when they took office. They got up every day not knowing if they had a job or not. Favoritism, nepotism, and racialism polluted the organization. Promotions and nepotism became essential elements of Trujillo's management of the military. In the long run, the reinforcement of these elements contributed to the development of a military subculture, signaling the officer corps' relationship with the political system. This military subculture overlapped with the broader civilian culture of political patronage.

The Politics of Rewards

Trujillo extended to the armed forces the patron-client relations that he began to develop with his USMC superiors at the military academy.

But he did so with a noticeable difference; this time, the dictator did not exchange positions with his subalterns. He was always the patron. On August 16, 1934, Trujillo presented the Dominican Congress with an assessment of his first presidential term. His speech emphasized how the past four years, marked by political stability and gradual economic recovery, demonstrated the government's ability to solve the nation's immediate problems. Most noteworthy, thanks to the watchful eyes of the army, was the fact that the nation was at peace, allowing the government to direct its energy toward a constructive future.[1] Trujillo also praised the army for its cooperation with other departments to further the goals of the government. The cooperation of the army with civilian agencies channeled the transmission of the military ethos to society. Civilian employees, working in close association with military men, internalized the principles of discipline, order, and loyalty. Satisfied with the outcome, the government did not hesitate even for a minute to offer *a manos llenas* (in full measure) all the necessary support to maintain the army's efficiency and prestige.[2] Indeed, under Trujillo's leadership, the government devoted money to ensure that the soldiers were not only well equipped but also comfortably installed. Life in the barracks improved significantly from 1930 to 1961. Soldiers lived in clean quarters and received three meals daily, regular monthly salaries, health services, dental care, and entertainment. Understandably, the state had economic and social responsibilities toward the functioning of its armed forces, but Trujillo distorted these duties and presented them as rewards from him to the military. Fringe benefits and manipulation of the patronage system characterized Trujillo's regime. The construction of a military hospital, the establishment of savings funds, and the development of a housing project exemplify Trujillo's calculated actions to attract the backing of the military.

Hospital and Savings Funds

Early in 1938 Chief of Staff of the National Army Héctor Trujillo wrote to the dictator, explaining that the armed forces needed a hospital for the personnel and their families but the Congress would not approve the requested funds. Trujillo responded with a check for $70,000 and a letter in which he stated that the money came from his personal funds.[3] This announcement had melodramatic appeal. No distinction existed between Trujillo's wealth and the wealth of the state. In addition, during his reign, he maintained a democratic façade by using a rubber-stamp

Congress; congressmen did not deny the funding for any of Trujillo's projects.

The hospital became known simply as El Marion. The name honored a French urologist, Dr. George Marion, who performed several surgical operations on Trujillo in 1934 and 1935. In appreciation for his good services, Dr. Marion received "a vote of gratitude in a Joint Resolution of Congress" and many memorials.[4]

The health services provided to the military were not limited to El Marion. Military physicians worked in public hospitals in almost every province. They offered their medical services to both civilians and military patients. Given the preponderance and prestige of the military, the day-to-day contact of the physician-officers with civilian physicians and nurses exerted militaristic influences over the management of the hospitals.

On September 7, 1934, by decree no. 1056, the regime established a savings fund for enlisted men of the Dominican army. Each member of the army contributed 5 percent of his monthly salary, and funds were available in case of personal emergency. Although the funds came from the personnel, Trujillo's military biographer presented it as more proof of Trujillo's dedication to serving "his spiritual sons."[5] The establishment of the funds benefited the personnel but it also protected the government from having to allocate money for the financial needs of the military men. Besides filling the minds of enlisted men and officers with slogans of gratitude such as *todo se lo debemos a Trujillo* (we owe everything to Trujillo), the establishment of the savings funds represented another way to foster loyalty.

Housing

As in other countries, the Dominican government provided housing for the military. But under Trujillo, the housing program magnified Trujillo's paternalistic role and presented him as a providential ruler with the extraordinary ability to solve personal and institutional problems at will.[6]

Like everything else, housing and residence were used as a means of control. Afraid of conspiracy, Trujillo prohibited former military men from establishing residence in foreign countries without his approval and consent. Following the same line of restraint, in 1948 Trujillo ordered the acquisition of an apartment building in Ciudad Trujillo. Married officers could rent the apartments for a period of six months, with the option of renewal, at DR$30 per month.[7] The short lease duration of six months was tactical; it reflected Trujillo's control of the military. The dictator wanted the military to influence society, but he did not want officers to develop deep relationships that might be used against him; consequently, officers generally lasted less than two years at any given post. Nevertheless, Trujillo said his primary goal was to provide housing and financial help to military personnel, since similar apartments rented from a private landlord would have cost twice as much.

In a long-range program developed in early 1950s in almost every city, the state built houses for public employees and several of them were assigned to the military, particularly to officers. Additionally, in some cities the government built residential neighborhoods, called *barrios de los militares*, for the members of the armed forces only. Commanders awarded the houses to enlisted men and officers based on family size, rank, and seniority. Acknowledging the significance of fringe benefits provided by the regime, Salvador Montás Guerrero, an army captain in 1953, stated that military men, resembling an extended family, shared one idea: loyalty toward the Generalissimo, to whom they owed their prosperity, comfort, and prestige.[8]

The Politics of Graft

By converting ordinary functions of the state into acts of magnanimity from the Generalissimo to the military, Trujillo established a special relationship with the armed forces. This relationship may be traced to the triangular connection established between the Partido Dominicano, the military, and the regime, a connection that underlines Trujillo's ability to maintain authority through the patronage system. This alliance not only had political significance, but it resulted in economic profitability for many who were the recipients of graft. The distribution of oil products, one of the most notorious and most visible economic operations of the venal system, became a source of revenue.

A good example of this is the cold and implacable chief of staff of the army (and one of Trujillo's closest partners), General Federico Fiallo, whose loyalty paid off well. The general "was obsessed with duty and devotedly performed whatever was assigned"; he appeared at midday or midnight in the barracks to correct whatever went wrong.[9] Cruel and efficient, he occupied many positions in the government, among them director of SIM. Early in 1945 he headed the Petroleum Transportation and Control Commission. The general informed the oil distribution companies (Pyramid, Shell, Sinclair, Standard, and Texaco) that to ensure impartial distribution of kerosene to the small rural areas, the distribution would be turned over to individuals chosen by the commission.[10] The beneficiaries were local party officials, their relatives, and people from the community considered politically worthy of receiving Fiallo's fuel authorization. The American and British companies in charge of importing and distributing petroleum products acted in complicity with them. As stated by the U.S. embassy in Ciudad Trujillo, with the "acquiescent attitude of the foreign petroleum companies," the distribution of oil became a lucrative source of revenue for the party.[11] The companies were unable or unwilling to stop the scheme.

The distribution of petroleum and its derived products entailed two methods of graft collection: rural and urban. In the rural areas party officials turned over five pesos to the party for every forty-two-gallon drum of kerosene they distributed. In urban areas petroleum company agents continued with the distribution. To receive kerosene from them, consumers had to prove payment of eleven cents per gallon to the party.[12]

The reinforcement of loyalty through the stimulus-response pattern included a wide range of economic benefits varying from customary profitable businesses to illegal transactions. Within the military, Trujillo's brothers were the main beneficiaries of the illegal operations. Captain Romeo Trujillo operated a gambling business, Major Pedro Trujillo received 8 percent of the funds that were to provide food for prisoners, and Major General José Arismendy Trujillo controlled part of the underworld business. In addition, Trujillo's wife, María, exercised a monopoly over the army's supply of medicine, potable water, and other goods and merchandise. She also managed the army laundry, converting it into a profitable enterprise.[13]

Colonel Charles McLaughlin, one of the U.S military instructors and a close friend of Trujillo's, also profited from the venal system. As a "reward for personal faithfulness over a long period of years," he received the administration of Naviera Dominicana, a company that controlled most of the aviation and merchant shipping.[14] Incidentally, McLaughlin's daughter, Alma, was Héctor Trujillo's girlfriend for twenty-two years; eventually they were married on December 12, 1959.

In Ornes's opinion, there "was no business deal too small for the top brass." Rivalry and competition developed among top officials when some of them exceeded what others considered the "legitimate take of graft."[15] For example, Colonel Blanco, the military commander of the southern region with headquarters in Barahona province, had a lucrative business in the early 1930s that generated wealth and political prominence for him that, as previously explained, caused his ruin.

In the end the patronage system became a double-edged sword. A source of wealth and rivalry, it created a vast array of conflicts. Although the rewarding of favored personnel with economic incentives created resentment, few dared to voice concern or opposition. Furthermore, as military men increasingly dominated several sectors of the economy at the expense of civilian entrepreneurs, Trujillo's military design for society gained another foothold.

Promotions

Trujillo used at-large promotions for patronage purposes. As soon as he became president, all officers were either reappointed or their commissions revoked. At the time of his death, the officer corps included men who had obtained their rank by varying means. Some had made their way slowly from the bottom to the top; others had become officers overnight. In any case, promotion implied more prestige than power, as power was not fully exercised based on rank. Trujillo did not delegate; he manipulated. Therefore, the officer corps was deprived of initiative.

Article 58 of the Ley Orgánica de las Fuerzas Armadas details the procedures for promotion in the Dominican armed forces. Education, training, experience, discipline, performance, and seniority were important factors to be considered, but promotions were nevertheless unpredictable—in keeping with other elements of the regime. A former colonel offered perhaps the best explanation of how the system worked: "[For the] same reason that one got fired, someone else might have gotten a promotion."[16] One scholar has noted that the "main pillar of a despot's power is his ability to promote and degrade."[17] In this sense, Trujillo could be considered a master in the art of promotion and degradation.

Although rules were established and opportunities provided, Trujillo played with soldiers' aspirations to acquire a higher rank or to become officers. Very often, more than a sign of merit, promotion was a reward for loyalty.

The handling of promotions, even among similar ranks, separated officers into three different categories. The first category included those who had obtained their promotions due to seniority and merit. They considered themselves the real military men and drew a line between themselves and those in the other categories. Considered merely men in uniform, the second group included officers who, for whatever reason, had been promoted overnight. The third category comprised men whose promotions had been usurped, relegated, or postponed for political intrigue or for no apparent reason.

The irregularities bred resentment in the officer corps, and officers and enlisted men did not always accept the violation of the Ley Orgánica passively. In July 1943 discontent broke out "among the older non-commissioned officers and certain low-ranking commissioned officers of the Army because of an order which disregarded the rights to promotion of many of these men, and promoted a group of youngsters instead."[18] Nevertheless, the favoritism continued. As late as 1961 some of the lower-ranked officers could date their service back to the days of the U.S. occupation. The regime justified the petrifaction by stating that these officers had accomplished little.[19] In other words, their political involvement did not comply with the goals explicitly or implicitly defined by the government.

On the other hand, some officers were appointed for their services to the government in non-military matters. In December 1954, for example, army officers Rafael Espaillat and Virgilio García Trujillo received promotions from the ranks of brigadier general to major general, and Colonel Máximo Bonetti Burgos was promoted to brigadier general. William C. Affeld, the U.S. chargé d'affaires ad interim, offered that promotions rewarded officers for keeping the Jefe fully informed "on the activities of individuals in and out of government as well as for the loyalty of the recipients in performance of duty."[20]

Nepotism and the "Crown Prince" Ramfis

Trujillo established a system by which his relatives and loyal officers held the most important and crucial military posts. Placing his relatives and closest aides in prominent positions was another way for Trujillo to ensure control of the military institution and, indeed, the people. Although Trujillo's ten brothers and sisters feuded bitterly, his brothers (not all loyal) and other family members played prominent roles in the military and in society.

In 1946 Trujillo's grip on the military hierarchy included several of his brothers and other relatives.[21] By 1952, according to one survey, 30 percent of the officers above the rank of lieutenant colonel were related to the Jefe by blood or marriage. The survey concluded that the use and abuse of nepotism and favoritism went past "the point of diminishing returns and now represent[ed] a dangerous threat" to the organization itself.[22]

Nepotism also contributed to division and conflict among officers, especially among junior officers who did not have blood ties to or a long friendship with Trujillo. When some of these junior officers realized that their prospects for promotion were hopeless and that they could not alter the arbitrary system, they became part of a growing group of officers who resented the institution, the regime, and those who received the benefits of instant promotions. According to one U.S. report, the most dangerous aspect of nepotism in the military was stagnation in the upper ranks of the armed forces.[23] Some of the officers had reached an advanced age and were beyond their years of peak efficiency.

In showing favoritism to relatives, Trujillo elevated his loyal younger brother, Héctor, not only to the highest position in the military but also to president of the republic in 1952. Luis José León Estévez, a graduate of the military academy of Venezuela, received several promotions after he married Trujillo's daughter Angelita in January 1958. In a short time he went from captain to major, to lieutenant colonel and to colonel. Trujillo named him director of the military academy Batalla de las Carreras and the first director of the Centro de Enseñanza de las Fuerzas Armadas (Learning Center of the Armed Forces), CEFA, an elite group within the elite air force. However, no one personified the nepotistic character of the regime better than Trujillo's eldest son, Ramfis.

In 1933 at the age of four, Ramfis became an honorary colonel of the National Army. Five years later he was named honorary brigadier general. He resigned his honorary rank in 1943, entered the army as a cadet, and became a captain at the age of twenty in 1949. His ascent up the military ladder reveals both the weakness of the system of promotions and Trujillo's deepest aspiration: to create a dynasty. "Crown Prince Ramfis," as some U.S. embassy personnel called him, was the immediate heir.[24] Also in the line of succession was Trujillo's youngest son, Rhadamés Trujillo Martínez. Another potential heir was Trujillo's half brother Luis Rafael Trujillo.

Believing in the power of military rule, Trujillo invested great effort in training Ramfis for the military and for political life. As early as October 26, 1935, a *Listín Diario* reporter, knowing Trujillo's love for Ramfis, told the dictator, "Ramfis is like a picture of you." Enchanted with the praise, Trujillo responded, "Yes, he is my pride. I want now to prepare him in the hope that he may be useful to the fatherland at the appropriate time." But Trujillo's dream did not materialize. Ramfis went to military school, but he showed no interest in political affairs or public life, preferring instead a bourgeois civilian lifestyle. Although he was married to Octavia Ricart, the mother of four of his children, Ramfis, like his father and many Dominican men, had numerous extramarital affairs. However, unlike many Dominican men, Ramfis spent an enormous amount of money on parties and gifts to seduce and to please women. Ramfis acknowledged that in Los Angeles, with money, name, and a yacht, he lived in opulence and enjoyed the company and fame of many actresses.[25] His list of mistresses included famous Hollywood stars such as Joan Collins, Kim Novak, Debra Paget, and Lita Milan, whom he married in 1960 after he divorced Octavia the same year. He played polo well and against his father's wishes he learned to fly.

Trujillo's desire to ensure Ramfis's succession to the dictatorship prompted his numerous rapid promotions. In 1951 he was promoted from captain to lieutenant colonel and shortly afterward, owing "presumably to the pride he had conferred to his father for his polo activities during a series of matches held in the Dominican Republic," he ascended to colonel.[26]

On June 4, 1952, Ramfis became brigadier general and chief of staff of Dominican military aviation. The promotion was a present from father to son on Ramfis's twenty-third birthday. One year later he advanced to the rank of major general. That same year Ramfis's younger brother, "the brash" Rhadamés, was appointed honorary major of the army at age ten.[27]

Ramfis's last promotion was yet another frustration for those who were pushed aside to open the path for Trujillo's eldest son. For example, the only other major general, Antonio Leyba Pou, was removed from the line of command and became inspector general of the navy.[28] Ramfis knew that the promotion meant more authority for him but not more responsibility.

Ramfis's unearned promotions infuriated members of the military, especially higher-ranked officers for whom he showed no respect. One such officer was General Fausto Caamaño who, as secretary of defense, was Ramfis's superior. It was reported that when the general criticized some administrative aspects of the Dominican air force, Ramfis contemptuously responded, "Yo mando aquí!" (I am the boss here!)[29]

Ramfis's abuse of his privileged position escalated to the point where it undermined the military organization his father had so carefully crafted. His arrogance made him unpopular, especially when he violated military protocol to take the "place of honor" at military functions even when such distinction belonged to a higher officer. Although he is credited with building esprit de corps among the younger officers and engendering strong loyalty, many senior officers disliked him for his brazen acts.

The frustration of senior officers stemmed not only from Ramfis's arrogant attitude but also from their diminishing prospects for the future. If Ramfis became president, they reasoned, he might create an imbalance of power among the army, navy, and air force. Army officers feared Ramfis might dramatically shift the level of power from the army to the air force or even gradually destroy the army. Should that happen, rather than permit a diversion of power, the officers would resort to any means, including the physical elimination of Ramfis, to retain the army's leadership.[30]

These elder officers also resented Ramfis's lack of military discipline. As a student at the Command and General Staff College at Fort Leavenworth, Kansas, in 1957–58, he felt out of place. Bored with soldierly life, he left Kansas and went to California and dedicated more time to his glamorous social life than to his classes. As a consequence, instead of a diploma he received a certificate of attendance. After that he developed anti–United States sentiments to the extent that his sister, Flor de Oro, confessed in a conversation with a U.S. colonel that her brother's anti-American attitude led him to avoid American assistance and to purchase equipment, both for official and personal use, elsewhere. He even carried "the complex to the extent of refusing to eat hamburger sandwiches because he associated them with the United States," she said. Flor de Oro expressed her views on Ramfis to the U.S. officer, and he reported the conversation to the Department of State.[31]

Ramfis's academic failure coincided with a period of international repudiation of Trujillo caused by the assassination of Jesús de Galíndez, a Spanish lecturer at Columbia University in New York City. Galíndez had lived in the Dominican Republic from 1939 to 1946 and had written his dissertation on the Trujillo regime. The study mentioned the regime's achievements but left no doubt of Galíndez's unfavorable opinion of Trujillo's regime. After defending his dissertation in 1956, he was kidnapped in a New York train station and taken to Trujillo City, where he was assassinated. His death caused an international stir. Relations between the Dominican Republic and the other American nations became increasingly tense.

Perceiving Ramfis's academic failure as an extension of the political animosity toward him, Trujillo responded by also adopting an anti–United States posture. He instructed the Dominican Congress to draft a bill to end the Bilateral Mutual Assistance Program of 1953. It proposed to end military cooperation for the operation of U.S. military bases in the northeastern part of the Dominican Republic and to bring home Dominican officers studying in the United States. Some officers returned home, but the Dominican Congress never approved the draft. After a few tension-filled weeks, Trujillo mentioned in a conversation with U.S. Ambassador Joseph Farland that Trujillo would no longer be the commander of the armed forces. Instead, military power would be in the hands of the president, his brother Héctor.[32] The pretension worked well. After Trujillo's "retirement" the two governments continued doing business as usual.

In the meantime Ramfis's promotions continued to generate more bitterness among the officer corps, particularly after September 30, 1958, when Ramfis became chief of the general staff of the combined land, sea, and air force. With this promotion, the military underwent another reorganization aimed, according to Ramfis, at clearly defining the chain of command. The next day he became secretary of state with cabinet rank. Now "all matters affecting the three services would pass through him as Chief of the General Staff for decision by the government."[33] Among the officer corps the appointment raised the question of whether he had the necessary leadership skills to keep the forces together. His father, they said, was authoritarian and cruel, but at least he had personality. Although many crimes were attributed to him, Ramfis was "charming" if he wanted to be, but he had exhibited a lack of vision.[34]

In the opinion of the U.S. chargé d'affaires ad interim Francis L. Spalding, Ramfis's poor judgment became evident in October 1958 in a discussion Spalding had with Ramfis and his friend Arturo Espaillat about the Military Assistance Advisory Group and Naval Mission programs. In that conversation both Ramfis and Espaillat made negative remarks about some of Trujillo's policies, which led Spalding to observe that they "seemed to be unaware that their power and privilege were due solely to the Generalissimo's strength, and they appeared oblivious of the fact that when he [left] the scene things [would] be different."[35]

Ramfis's personality and attitude also led to conflict between father and son. The nature of the tension can be traced to Ramfis's birth. He resented the fact that he was "a natural" son, born out of wedlock. Trujillo's desire to establish a dynasty also became another source of problems. Ramfis expressed that he disapproved of the idea of establishing a dynasty rooted on his father's dictatorship and for this reason did not accept to the vice presidency of the republic when his father offered the position to him.[36]

The tension between father and son intensified at the end of the regime. After a group of Dominican exiles failed to overthrow Trujillo's regime in 1959, for political propaganda and, perhaps, to obtain more information about the plot, Trujillo decided to keep the survivors alive. Defying Trujillo, Ramfis ordered the execution of almost all those who were taken prisoner. After this insubordination and other incidents, realizing that his plan for eventual succession was flawed, Trujillo abandoned his design for making Ramfis his political heir and shifted his attention to Rhadamés.

Ramfis's dependence on his father and his lack of leadership soon became apparent after Trujillo's death in May 1961. Several military rebellions erupted, including one at the San Isidro Air Force Base, the center of Ramfis's operations.[37] By November the Trujillos, including Ramfis, had left the country. Despite his failure as a political leader, Ramfis had played a decisive role in strengthening the air force.

Parameters of Racism in the Armed Forces

Within the complexities of the militarist value system, "there is a link between militarism and racism."[38] To former Dominican president Juan Bosch, Trujillo was a man "of few ideas," but they were deeply ingrained.[39] By analyzing the racial dimension of the Haitian massacre and sociohistorical studies dealing with Trujillo's racial attitude, one may conclude that one of these few ideas was racism.[40]

Although color was not a decisive factor for membership in any branch of the military during the era of Trujillo, the desire for identification with white Spanish heritage and the concealment of black ancestry was extended to the military. Nevertheless, since colonial times, prejudice based on color had been expressed directly or indirectly in society in general as well as in the military culture in particular. During the colonial administration, concern arose about the potential political force of a racially mixed colonial society; therefore, only soldiers who came directly from Spain were part of the colonial militia. After 1738 Creoles were accepted, but only those whose parents had been born in Spain. During the nineteenth century the newly organized voluntary forces tended "to apply the same determinants for social promotion—of which physical appearance was one—as did society as a whole."[41] We may glean another explanation from events during the U.S. occupation. From the Marines' point of view, Santo Domingo was a conquered land populated by racially inferior people, a bias that extended to Dominican enlisted men.[42] The Marines' racial attitude generated enough resentment to bring about the name change of the security forces from the USMC-given Policía Nacional Dominicana (PND) to Policia Nacional in 1927. The nationalists interpreted PND as *pobres negritos dominicanos* (poor little black Dominicans).[43]

Stressing the importance of whiteness, Trujillo himself initiated the practice within the military of disavowing African ancestry. The enlistment record of the Guardia Nacional Dominicana discloses that Trujillo described himself as white when in fact he was mulatto. According to Trujillo, his genealogical profile included a family tree that linked him mostly to his "noble Spanish lineage of his surnames, Trujillo and Molina." The name Trujillo came "from Extremadura, as those of the great *conquistadores*, Cortés y Pizarro . . . and Molina, the name that alongside that of Vizcaya is borne by the Spanish kings."[44] Photos and portraits of Trujillo were retouched to present a whiter Trujillo. Nevertheless, in 1939 during the inauguration of the U.S. Marine Corps Avenue in Ciudad Trujillo, Trujillo admitted that he was mulatto. For the occasion, U.S. General Brigadier William P. Upshur and Colonel Roy S. Geiger visited the Dominican Republic. Trujillo invited them to his office and showed them a sword owned by President Ulises Heureaux. Surprisingly, Trujillo told his guests, "[T]his sword was used when the Republic was governed by a black president, not by a mulatto like me."[45] The interpreter, knowing how Trujillo previously tried to deny his black heritage, did not dare translate the phrase.

As a result of the policy of racial concealment adopted by the regime, it is difficult to determine the racial composition of the armed forces simply by studying available records of enlisted men. The records list only two colors: white and *indio*. To compensate for the lack of written documentation, I conducted interviews with scholars, former military men, writers, and political figures.[46] Reviewing oral history and photographic records, one sees that racial discrimination occurred in the military, particularly in the officer corps. Certainly blacks, mulattoes, and whites moved up within the ranks, but most air force officers were white or light mulattos; mulattos in general seemed to be predominant in the army; and navy personnel tended to be mixed, but apparently more mulatto or dark-skinned men were navy officers. Almost all the former officers I interviewed at first categorically denied the suggestion of racial discrimination within the military. Nevertheless, many disclosed crucial information to fill in the gaps of the documentary evidence.[47] In answering a question about racial discrimination among the armed forces, a former navy officer responded, "En la Marina no era cuestión de color sino de preparación" (in the navy it was not a question of color but preparation). He explained that the navy personnel were the most qualified because navigation demanded technical knowledge. He admitted that once in a while, however, officers of any branch of the military received preferential treatment because of their color.[48] Another officer told me that a group of officers customarily accompanied Trujillo while he was traveling abroad. The group varied for every trip, and it represented the different branches of the armed forces. In 1954 Trujillo traveled to Spain and Italy. Among the officers accompanying him was the aide-de-camp, who happened to be black. With no explanation, a white officer replaced him.[49] This action clearly revealed racial discrimination even if an explicit policy did not exist. The officer who told me the story believed that the substitution of a white officer for the black officer demonstrated Trujillo's vanity and his desire to present "a better" image of the Dominican Republic abroad.

Army officers expressed that from a racial point of view, the army best represented the Dominican people because of its high percentage of mulattos.[50] The officers also indicated that expressions and stories charged with racial connotations abounded within the military. For example, because of his somatic characteristics, a particular captain was known as the "Capitán blanco bembú" (white, thick-lipped, captain). The sarcastic speaker was in fact making reference to a popular notion that all Dominicans, even whites, have some black ancestor, or as the expression goes, "todos los dominicanos tienen el negro detrás de la oreja" (all Dominicans have black color behind their ears). In spite of the charged atmosphere, however, there is little indication that racial discrimination within the military caused much disturbance. The racial composition of the air force generated most of the discontent regarding discrimination. In several interviews former army and navy officers referred to the pilots as the spoiled "blanquitos de [little whites of] Ramfis" who considered themselves a superior caste within the armed forces.

La Guardia Blanca

Racial preference was strongly evident in the composition of the presidential guard, which Juan Bosch called la *guardia blanca*. Its primary mission was to accompany Trujillo during his trips abroad and to honor foreign dignitaries during visits to the National Palace. Trujillo demanded that the members of the guard embody three characteristics: they had to be white, good-looking with elegant manners, and educated. Either of the last two criteria could be ignored, however, if Trujillo or his representatives handpicked someone who was white for duty in this elite group.

The policy of preference for whites grew stronger after the creation of the presidential guard. Some men entered the armed forces or advanced in rank primarily because they were white. For example, former colonel Juan Antonio Delgado Hernández, a regular sergeant in 1947 at the time of the selection of the presidential guards, was at first rejected because other soldiers with similar rank and more qualifications were already chosen. However, because Delgado's physical appearance closely met Trujillo's ideas for the presidential guard, Héctor Trujillo, by then secretary of war and navy, and in charge of selecting future officers, ordered Delgado's promotion to first sergeant on the spot.[51] Delgado's promotion was not an unusual case. The regime used color to recruit, to promote, and especially to impress foreigners who visited the dictator in his office. Trujillo wanted outsiders to believe that whites predominated among Dominicans.

In what would prove to be an ironic twist, to create the presidential guard Trujillo sent his brother Héctor to the Ozama Fortress to select two hundred white men from the five hundred already preselected by the military chiefs from all over the country.[52] Héctor was also known as "Negro," a popular nickname in the Dominican Republic. Although the word means "black," it does not necessarily have a racial connotation, but is often a term of affection among Dominicans, similar to "Sweetheart" or "Buddy" in the United States. But "Negro" is also frequently the appellation of the darkest member of the family, as it was in Hector' case. During the selection process, Héctor referred to the irony of the situation his brother had put him in. He, the Negro, was to select a group of white men to serve his mulatto brother.

How could this incongruence be explained? It implied that in accord with the racial ideology of the regime and Trujillo's vanity, the dictator wanted those close to him to be representative of the phenotypic characteristics that he considered attractive. The best example of an officer preferred by Trujillo was Arturo Espaillat, who was "intelligent, white, of elegant manners, and educated to obey" at West Point.[53] Espaillat was also a strict disciplinarian who commanded respect by inducing fear. Referring clearly to his authority in comparing him with a double-edged razor, Espaillat's associates gave him a nickname: "Navajita" or "La Gillette." Being white was not always a protection against harassment because, as will be shown, the regime in some instances also discredited high-ranking white officers.

Although the practice of filling certain positions in the armed forces exclusively with white men was unfair and controversial, this discrimination did provide opportunities for social mobility for some Dominican officers. Poor, young white men rising rapidly in rank enjoyed the benefits of transferring to one of the most desirable posts in the armed forces.

Color as Janus

There is also evidence that color was used to promote and to denigrate soldiers as well as officers. Rewards and/or reprimands at times were handed out based on color. Discrimination was also used to weaken white, high-ranking officers. The story of General Fausto Caamaño illustrates the problem. A close friend of Trujillo, Caamaño once directed the intelligence services, but he fell from grace in 1953. On September 29 the Foro Público, a section published in *El Caribe* to denounce those who had fallen into abasement, called Caamaño the "blond Secretary" of the armed forces and presented the general as a segregationist who improperly exempted "wealthy persons of light color" from obligatory military service. Tutú Valera, who signed the letter in the Foro, also questioned General Caamaño's military and professional ethics.[54]

Thus, this racial issue goes beyond color to the special mark of being blond. The Foro also accused Captain Cesar Simó Clark, in charge of payroll at the army factory, of being a racist. On September 28, 1953, *El Caribe* published a letter suggesting that the captain believed that because he was blond, he could violate other people's rights. The letter did not describe the charges against the captain but the author demanded such practices to stop immediately.

Why did Trujillo play with color within the military? His racial policy was inconsistent, so it is difficult to discern the answer. One explanation is that Trujillo and those around him tried to build nationalism by selecting some pieces of history and hiding others. History, then, was reconstructed according to Trujillo's ideology. In addition, looking at racism raises the question of whether Trujillo used color to "divide and rule." Militarily, was his theory that as long as officers and enlisted men were fighting with one another they would not join in opposition to his regime? In any case, Trujillo's racial ideas were so ingrained that they even reached his own family, splintering the group into two branches: *Trujillos blancos* (whites) and *Trujillos prietos* (blacks). The *prietos* did not belong to Trujillo's inner circle of relatives and lived confined in a neighborhood "like a ghetto in the Ensanche Ozama" east of Ciudad Trujillo. They had little opportunity for education, though some of the men went into the military.[55] Trujillo forced his family—and by extension society in general—to think of their relation to his person and to the regime in terms of color. However, although Trujillo's racism was clear, his discriminatory practices were unpredictable. He replaced a black officer for a white one while traveling abroad, but one of his personal physicians was a black officer whom I met at the National Palace in 1990. These inconsistencies showed that Trujillo's racist behavior cannot be summarized in two or three paragraphs or shaped into a specific theoretical framework. Each action needs to be studied individually in order to determine the overall racist picture of the regime.

8. A NEW DIMENSION OF
CIVIL-MILITARY RELATIONS
Expansion of the Armed Forces

The creation of a strong military reflects an important dimension of militarization—the socioeconomic impact of the armed forces on civilian institutions. Believing that the preponderance of the military over civilian society was essential to the existence of his regime, Trujillo spent millions of dollars to increase the size and strength of the armed forces with modern equipment, armaments, and sophisticated military technology.

With the assistance of several countries, Trujillo accordingly built the most impressive war apparatus in the Caribbean. He bought weapons in the international market and built his own arms factory, known as La Armería, at great cost.

Military scholars assert that the quality and quantity of the armament is a determining factor on the degree of superiority that armed forces exercise over the unarmed population.[1] Although the population was disarmed, and although the country was at peace with Haiti, as soon as Trujillo took power, he began a military buildup that lasted until the end of the regime. The systematic expansion of the regime's manpower resulted in an army about fifteen times the size it had been in 1924 when the U.S. occupation forces left the country.[2]

The following examination of the reorganization of the armed forces reveals the nature and complexity of Trujillo's military project, as well as the great expenses he incurred in doing so. Compared with other Latin American countries, the Dominican Republic spent a higher than average percent of its budget for military expenditures.[3]

The Army and the Chasing of Weapons
During the process of expansion, of the three branches of the military (army, navy, and air force), the army had priority during the first half of

Table 1. Expansion of the National Army, 1929–1938

Year	1929	1932	1935	1937	1938
Men	2,125	2,179	2,770	3,029	3,212

Source: Memo prepared by Robert Mills McClintock, Third Secretary of the U.S. Legation in the Dominican Republic, December 12, 1938, USNA, RG 59, 839.20/82.

the regime. During the second half, the navy gained importance and the air force tremendously increased its power.

As the mainstay of the Dominican armed forces, from 1929 to 1938 army personnel grew by 33 percent, from 2,125 men to 3,212, as shown in table 1. The data do not include 627 policemen, a semi-military force, and the reserve corps.

Expanding the army included acquiring military equipment. This strengthened the military but also led to a series of tribulations and troubles. These confrontations developed from Trujillo's militarism using weapons as an expression of power but also from Trujillo's passion for arms, an interest he had had since his youth. Once he was the president, the passion became an obsession. For three decades, overtly and covertly, he searched for weapons around the world.

Trujillo's emissaries traveled to Europe, Latin America, and the United States, arranging transactions with a variety of people, ranging from diplomats to "individuals with shady reputations."[4] In the 1930s part of the problem was the scrap warranty arms program, which allowed the sale of surplus military equipment to U.S. citizens, with the specific provision that it be scrapped. Some of the "shady operators," however, managed to "turn around and sell [the weapons] to foreign governments."[5] These actions led to confrontations between the U.S. State Department and foreign governments. In the particular case of the Dominican Republic, U.S. officials tried to prevent this type of transaction by forcing the Dominican government to deal with "reputable firms," for which the Office of Munitions had a list on hand.

Instead of accepting the U.S.–mandated limits, Trujillo acquired arms and ammunitions through other avenues, including his former USMC instructors George Brett, Cutts, MacLaughlin, Watson, as well as other Marines and U.S. citizens worked as Trujillo's arms agents. In the early 1930s Trujillo wanted to replace the old 1898 Krag-Jorgenson rifles, which were reported to be in poor condition, with new weapons. Besides the Krag-Jorgenson rifles, the army also used Lee-Enfield .30 caliber and

Springfield rifles. Acting as a sort of double agent, Watson worked for both Trujillo and the U.S. government. He suggested that the United States sell Springfield rifles to Trujillo because the transaction would allow the U.S. government "to control or limit the ammunition supply to the Dominican Republic."[6] Major Watson's strategy aimed to please both Trujillo and the United States. The United States thwarted Watson's plan, however. Considering that the population was disarmed and the army was moderately equipped with arms and ammunition, the State Department determined that the Dominican Republic did not need more weapons and refused the petition for the sale of Springfield rifles.[7]

The U.S. act of June 5, 1920 also helped block the sale of weapons to the Dominican Republic. This document established that U.S. weapons should be sold to the Dominican Republic at one-third of their list price. For instance, in October 1933 the Dominican government bought arms valued at $5,162.00 for only $1,720.00.[8] Clearly, the regulation offered no incentive to arms dealers, and some of them refused to sell weapons to the Dominican government. The refusal did not discourage Trujillo, however, and the U.S. War Department, the State Department, and other governmental offices received persistent arms purchase and export license requests from Dominican businessmen, diplomats, and officers, as well as Trujillo's former instructors and other agents.

The flood of arms requests generated a debate among U.S. officers working in the Dominican Republic and those in charge of Latin American affairs in Washington. Early in the dictatorship, the State Department argued that it was politically inappropriate for the Trujillo regime to spend money on weapons when the national economy was in shambles, whereas Trujillo's defenders advanced the argument that enemies abroad were ready to invade the country, making an increase in military strength a necessity.[9]

While the debate on the military strength of the Dominican Republic was taking place in the United States, Trujillo's men searched for weapons on the international market. In Spain they bought 2,000 new Mauser rifles for approximately $100,000. These rifles not only offered the advantage of being compatible with the Krag-Jorgensen rifles used by the Dominican army, but "these [new] rifles [were] offered in competition with the same quantity of Second Hand Springfield 1906 rifles from the United States."[10] The Dominican government also bought rifles, carbines, cartridges, aviation weapons, and uniforms from Mexico and other military equipment from France.[11] In acquiring weapons from

France, the Dominican government instituted economic measures that caused serious diplomatic and political friction.

Tobacco for Weapons

In Trujillo's regime, as in other systems, the process of militarization went beyond the military organization. Trujillo's militarism increasingly dominated the economy at the expense of civilian institutions. In 1934, for example, he wanted to acquire two million French francs' worth of artillery. Among the weapons for purchase were 3,500 Lebel rifles (1919 model), 10 fifty-centimeter mortars, and 6 eight-centimeter mortars. The French arms dealer through whom the Dominicans wanted to purchase the weapons refused American paper currency and demanded solid gold or its equivalent. The Dominican government ended up paying the equivalent of 1.3 million in gold francs with tobacco for the French rifles, delivered not directly from the French government stock but from a reserve stock in Poland.[12]

What appeared to be a routine transaction eventually developed into a domestic monopoly and an international imbroglio. Domestically, the Dominican government took control of the tobacco industry, which in 1934 consisted of two companies competing for production and export of cigarettes and cigars: Tabacalera Dominicana owned by Anselmo Copello, and the Dominican Tobacco Company, largely controlled by Amadeo Barletta. Dominicans were involved in the domestic commercialization of tobacco, but foreigners like Copello and Barletta dominated the export market. After the transactions with the French arms dealer, the government imposed control on tobacco production and trade. As interpreted by the French chargé d'affaires, the regulation was established in order "to take control of this commodity for the purpose of meeting the obligation incurred by the Government in the purchase of the French armaments."[13] Table 2 shows that the volume of tobacco exported to France in 1934 vastly exceeded the volume exported to other European countries. Although traditionally Germany was the main importer of Dominican tobacco, to pay for the weapons the government had to channel most of its exports to France.

Applying the principle of economic protectionism, Trujillo explained in a speech to tobacco producers that the government's direct participation in the commercialization of tobacco would benefit the tobacco producers, end speculation, and protect the agricultural working class in general.[14] In the end, however, Trujillo's monopoly worked mainly

Table 2. Tobacco Exportation, 1934

Exporter	Volume (kg)	Value (U.S. $)
France	[5,992,542]	232,385
Germany	449,658	19,012
Spain	275,074	28,900
Holland	1,387,003	.76,239
Belgium	801,460	43,194

Source: República Dominicana, Secretaría de Tesoro y Crédito Público, *Exportation of To-bacco for the Period 1920–1938* 1939.

against the tobacco exporters; it did not benefit producers. On the contrary, the measures caused the strangulation of private enterprise.

The Barletta Incident and the Strengthening of the Army

Trujillo's militarization reoriented the commercialization of tobacco, but it also provoked an international crisis that landed Barletta in jail. In addition to being a businessman, Barletta also served as the honorary consul of Italy in the Dominican Republic and as president of both the Santo Domingo Motors Company and the Dominican Tobacco Company. Since the U.S. General Motors Export Company was the main owner of Santo Domingo Motors, and the Penn Tobacco Company of Wilkes-Barre, Pennsylvania, owned 50 percent of the Dominican Tobacco Company, U.S. investors had a substantial interest in the two companies.

In a position to compete with Compañía Tabacalera, a company in which Trujillo had acquired a large percentage of shares, the Dominican Tobacco Company found itself subject to a government-enforced suspension of its rights to manufacture cigarettes. This resulted in a clash between Barletta and Trujillo. The Dominican government claimed that Barletta organized a conspiracy and soon arrested him, held him incommunicado for a month, and ultimately sentenced him to two years in jail for his involvement in the plot and for an alleged internal revenue violation.[15]

The Italian government held that Barletta's treatment violated international diplomatic agreements and demanded the immediate release of Italy's honorary consul. Mussolini went so far as to threaten to shell Dominican ports, claiming "the Italian Government could not permit such an affront to go unchallenged."[16] The *New York Times* reported the departure of the Italian cruiser *Gaeta* for the Dominican Republic, which intended to stage a naval demonstration.[17] Thus, Barletta's incarceration became a cause célèbre and triggered an international imbroglio involving the administrations of Benito Mussolini, Franklin Roosevelt, and Trujillo.

Siding with Italy, the U.S. government also exerted pressure on Trujillo to release Barletta. According to Secretary of State Cordell Hull, "[T]he Dominican Government could hardly expect any sympathy from the United States or the other American nations" should the Italian government resort to drastic measures.[18] And because Barletta's detainment weakened the interests of the Penn Tobacco Company in the Dominican Republic, the State Department also considered legal action against the Dominican government.[19]

On May 29 a court of appeals reversed the lower-court decision against the tobacco company and its president, and, to free himself from the complicated political problem, Barletta moved to Cuba after he paid a visit to Mussolini in Rome. In an attempt to distance himself from the incident, Trujillo dismissed the secretary of foreign relations, Arturo Logroño. At the same time, the dictator received applause for his hardline position against foreign investors. But by the time the case drew to a close, it had, according to Bernardo Vega, generated one of the worst crises in the Trujillo–U.S. relationship.[20]

The Barletta case clearly shows how determined Trujillo was to expand the military. The regime did not take covert measures in pursuit of its goals, even if dealing with diplomats and foreign civilians. More important, the monopoly of the tobacco industry showed the extension of Trujillo's militarization project. It was beyond the military itself. It altered society by channeling one sector of the economy from private to governmental control.

U.S. Assessment of Trujillo's Weaponry

The United States was one of Trujillo's main suppliers of weapons. However, for legal and political reasons the United States responded negatively to Trujillo's requests for more weapons. But this did not stop Trujillo from acquiring war material; he obtained artillery from other sources.

By the time the Barletta incident drew to a close, Trujillo's military hardware became a major concern of the United States and Latin American countries. What was the real military strength of the Dominican

Republic? Why did it cause political tremors in the region? To begin with, the military strength of the Dominican Republic was a secret "jealously" guarded by the regime. Trujillo did not disclose data about military expenses, personnel, or equipment to the Dominican people or to anyone else. But since 1930s the United States had been accumulating data regarding the military strength of the Dominican forces. The U.S. reports provide a glimpse into Trujillo's well-guarded secret.

U.S. records indicate that by 1938 Trujillo's weaponry was insufficient to effectively meet any outside aggression other than that of Haiti. Robert Mills McClintock, who compiled the data for one report, estimated that in 1938 the Dominican armed forces had between 3,000 and 4,000 shotguns, about 45,000 rounds of rifle and revolver ammunition, about 15 heavy machine guns, 10 light machine guns, and 20 submachine guns. The army also owned one light tank "of erratic performance" and about 50 trucks for the transportation of troops. In addition, the 2,715 enlisted men were armed with Spanish *mosquetón* rifles, also considered unsatisfactory because of their bad firing pin and faulty magazines.[21]

The unsatisfactory performance of the Spanish rifle served as justification for Trujillo's personal request for four thousand Springfield rifles during his first visit to United States in July 1939. On July 11 President and Mrs. Roosevelt held a reception for Trujillo, after which he met with Lawrence Duggan, chief of the Division of the American Republics. The first issue Trujillo brought up was the acquisition of Springfield rifles. The petition, presented when the U.S. Congress was reviewing military materiel that might be supplied to Latin American countries, received a negative response. The legislators excluded the Springfield from the list of weapons for exportation to Latin America.[22]

The events of World War II, however, changed U.S. policy regarding arms provision to Latin America. Arguing hemispheric defense, the United States built military bases in several Latin American countries and obtained raw material for the U.S. arms industry from its southern neighbors. In exchange the Latin Americans received loans to expand defense capacities, equipment, and military training programs. Like other Latin American countries, the Dominican Republic signed bilateral mutual defense agreements with the United States, and granted air and naval base privileges and transit rights to the Allies. For its support, and given U.S. concern with hemispheric security in terms of countering the Communist threat, the Dominican government received bank loans for military purposes and other benefits. In 1940, for example, the Trujillo government received a loan of $5 million for the arms purchases and for the construction of military bases for mutual use. On May 6, 1941, the Dominican Republic became the first Latin American country eligible for Lend-Lease aid. Based on two agreements signed with the Dominican Republic, the United States agreed to transfer $1,600,000 in armaments and munitions to the Dominican military.[23]

U.S. military intelligence released another report on Dominican military strength on March 15, 1942, indicating that the country's military reserves featured meager quantities of all equipment, including eight kinds of rifles and ten kinds of machine guns. Both the 1938 and 1942 reports rated the Dominican officer staff as highly efficient by Latin American standards, but described the equipment as old, in poor condition, unserviceable, and affected by "age and tropical deterioration." The 1942 report indicated that the transportation system for personnel, which was partly dependent on hired buses, was unreliable.[24] The Dominican government challenged the accuracy of the report and argued that the transportation system functioned efficiently.

Amid the disagreements with the United States over arms and equipment, Trujillo continued his policy of strengthening the military by increasing its size. Another U.S. report of 1942 estimated the manpower of the Dominican armed forces at about 4,120 active forces, including 900 policemen. Eight thousand men, many of them former soldiers, and 80,000 "chiefly illiterate peasants" were ready to perform some type of military service if necessary.[25] By 1944 the total figure for the armed forces, including the 900 policemen, reached 6,380. The expansion of the army began to concern U.S. Ambassador Joseph F. McGurk. Believing the army was overstaffed for its defensive mission, he suggested an arbitrary reduction to 1,800 men.[26] Trujillo responded with the announcement that the government had planned to gradually expand the army by 41 percent, from a brigade composed of 7,000 men to a division of 12,000 men. He also stated that the government planned to create two mobile divisions of 12,000 men each.[27] The expansion of manpower and the amount of resources devoted to war-like purposes were in line with Trujillo's use of military power as a political instrument.

In studying the dimensions of militarism, scholars have indicated that an oversized military is a "significant part of militarism."[28] The enlargement of the armed forces also reflected the escalation of militarization in Dominican society.

Table 3. 1944 National Budget

Secretary of war and navy	$ 3,140,856.22
Secretary of commerce (and public debt)	$ 1,872,000.00
Secretary of education	$ 1,844,508.84
Public works	$ 1,435,312.50
Secretary of interior and police	$ 1,249,420.93
Judicial	$ 1,228,200.61
Secretary of commerce and treasure	$ 1,090,844.08
Health and welfare	$ 1,045,609.92
Secretary of agriculture, industry and labor	$ 901,875.22
Secretary of foreign relations	$ 616,979.00
Secretary of the presidency	$ 429,233.84
Special funds	$ 298,000.00
Legislative	$ 282,919.76
Executive	$ 239,360.00
Chamber of accounts	$ 28,526.00
Central electoral office	$ 10,224.96
Total	$15,713,871.88

Source: Gaceta Oficial, December 30, 1943.

Budget and Military Expenditures

The expansion of the armed forces drained a substantial amount of money from the national budget. The military budget surpassed the budgets of the rest of the institutions and represented Trujillo's idea of political power: greatly enlarged armed forces. In 1944 the secretaries of war and navy and of interior and police received almost one third of the national expenditures (see table 3.)

After World War II the United States refused to sell weapons to the dictator. Trujillo then turned to Brazil and negotiated an arms deal 10,000–12,000 rifles, 350 machine guns, and other equipment. Fearing Trujillo's potential use of the weapons for external aggression against neighboring countries, specifically Cuba and Haiti, the governments of Cuba, Costa Rica, and Venezuela objected to the purchase. The Dominicans addressed these concerns by assuring the international community that the weapons had been acquired for defensive purposes only. Afterward the regime managed to get arms from Europe and later from the United States.

When exiled Dominicans tried to overturn the regime in 1947 and

Table 4. Budget of the Central Government, 1958–1960
(DR$ million)

	1958	1959	1960
Estimated revenue	152.3	152.5	138.2
Selected secretaries	68.4	72.5	71.8
Armed forces	30.4	38.7	25.2
Education and fine arts	12.1	12.2	10.4
Public works	12.1	9.4	14.3
Agriculture	5.3	3.9	8.7
Public health and social welfare	8.5	8.3	13.2

Source: *Gaceta Oficial*, Ley de Gastos Públicos, December 1958, 1959, 1960.

1949, in the name of national security Trujillo expanded the armed forces and consequently the military budget to about 25 percent of the national budget by the early 1950s. Unfortunately, the true extent of military expenditures is all but impossible to determine. Although data have been gathered, both in absolute figures and percentages, they may not correspond to reality because Trujillo used so many different mechanisms to distort facts. For example, for the fiscal year 1956–57, military expenses ostensibly were close to $29 million, or almost 25 percent of the entire national budget. But this amount, already considered phenomenally high for a poor country, did not include $1 million in military aid the United States had provided to the republic.[29] Moreover, funds set aside for the purchase of military hardware were not included in the military budget. The government considered the tanks, ships, and airplanes as gifts from Chief Commandant Trujillo to the armed forces.[30]

Even with the less than reliable expenditure estimates, they do help establish some correlation between the defense budget and the strengthening of the forces. These figures also give us some guidance in reconstructing the interrelations of the military budget and the national budget.

Table 4 reflects, in millions of pesos, the proportion of the total Dominican output that was devoted to military spending during the last three years of Trujillo's administration. To better understand the investment in the military, in 1947 the Dominican peso replaced the U.S. dollar, which had been employed since the U.S. occupation in lieu of the national currency, but after the monetary conversion, the peso maintained at par value with the dollar almost until the end of the dictatorship.

In the 1940s the government spent large amounts on weaponry and the construction of military facilities. Training centers, academies, radio stations, naval bases, military aerodromes, and, in the 1950s, the arms factory became part of Trujillo's military complex. The challenge posed by a group of Dominican exiles who invaded the country in June 1959 prompted Trujillo to spend more than 80 million pesos on weapons and military supplies.[31] The amount represented a little more than half the national budget of 1959, estimated at 152.5 million pesos. Thus, claiming national security, the government reinforced militarism and spread militarization, not only spending a substantial amount of money on the military but emphasizing the need for military preparedness and requesting that soldiers and citizens be ready to respond to outside aggression.

This militaristic project of national defense was a source of some controversy. From an economic point of view, the fact that the armed forces had at its disposal the largest percentage of the national budget in some ways separated the military from the rest of the society, adding a new angle to civil-military relations. The members of the military were the "pampered children of the regime," whose lifestyle offered a "glaring contrast between the dire poverty of the masses and the prosperity of the military caste."[32] The economic compensation granted to members of the military helped to ensure loyalty to the government. Of the 3,047,000 million Dominican inhabitants, over 30,000 men were employed in the military, including police and paramilitary forces.[33]

Combining domestic and international factors, during War World II the U.S. military aid program assisted Trujillo in his buildup; the navy and air force, in particular, underwent an imposing modernization process. To better understand the improvement of these two branches of the armed forces, one must keep in mind that there was no air force and only a fledgling navy when Trujillo became president.

The Navy

The Dominican navy was as old as the army. Both were organized in 1844, but the U.S. occupation suppressed the navy. The gradual expansion of the navy began during the 1930s with the acquisition of the modern vessel *Guantánamo* (later renamed *President Trujillo*) from Empress Naviera of Cuba.

At the end of 1934 the government organized the navy command and appointed the first group of officers. The navy had national appeal because of the patriotic role it played during the military campaigns for

independence, and its reestablishment afforded Trujillo political leverage. Both the press and the people applauded his interest in restoring
the navy.[34]

In 1942, according to a U.S. assessment of the Dominican Republic's
national defense system, the navy with its seven coast guard boats and
seventy men could not provide adequate coastal observation and patrol
services.[35] To bolster the expansion of the navy, in 1943 the government
transferred several army officers to the navy and awarded them the rank
of navy cadet. The same year, at Trujillo's request, a naval mission composed of an officer from the USMC and one from the U.S. navy assisted in
training the Dominicans at Las Calderas Naval Base. After World War
II, with the assistance of the Canada, England, Spain, and the United
States, naval training improved even more. These countries offered a
more efficient organization format and more advanced technical methods. To improve the operational efficiency of the navy, enlisted men and
commissioned officers went abroad, mainly to Panama and the United
States, for professional training.

Training improvement was accompanied by a gradual expansion of
the navy's personnel from 180 in 1947 to 3,000 in 1955. The expansion
also included a Marine battalion and a unit of frogmen commandos.[36]
Trained by Europeans instructors, the frogmen, prepared and equipped
to undertake prolonged underwater missions, were valuable to Trujillo's
intelligence services. With their radios and radars, they could carry out
underwater espionage maneuvers and demolish unfriendly ships. In the
late 1950s there were 4,000 men in all ranks of the navy. They commanded and manned 39 combat and auxiliary vessels, including two
former British navy destroyers and several Canadian-built frigates and
corvettes, making the Dominican navy superior to even the Mexican
navy and, in Latin America, second only to that of Venezuela.[37]

The military capability of the Dominican navy caused international
tensions. Neighboring countries became suspicious of the sudden improvements, fearing that Dominican naval strength would be used
against them. In an attempt to assuage their fears, the Dominican government assured them that the mission of destroyers, frigates, and corvettes
was to defend the coast, to preserve order along the coastline, and to
prevent smuggling. The government also argued that Dominican naval
strength could do much for the defense of the country and, indirectly,
for the Caribbean regional defense.[38]

Trujillo's potentially dangerous naval predominance may, in part, have grown out of the Mutual Defense Assistance Agreement of 1953, which allowed the Dominican Republic to receive military assistance from the United States in the form of weapons and military missions. The agreement also provided for the training of Dominican officers at U.S. military schools, where they learned to "handle equipment furnished under the mutual defense agreement."[39] As the navy increased its military strength, it also developed its infantry and other units; as a consequence, in the late 1950s the Dominican navy ranked "fourth among the American Navies."[40]

To increase naval power and independence of action, Trujillo ordered the construction of shipyards named Astilleros Navales de Haina in 1955. Originally built to repair navy vessels, the Astilleros ultimately became another of Trujillo's commercial enterprises. The combination of military strength and control of another sector of the economy, in direct association with the militarization of society, fortified the political-military machinery.

The Air Force

Of the three branches of the armed forces, the air force underwent the most spectacular transformation. The year 1931 marked the beginning of military aviation, when the first three Dominican pilots—Felix, Vallejo, and Valverde—graduated abroad. The government then slowly began to buy airplanes and to train Dominican pilots.

Five years later in 1936, the Destacamento de Aviación, a branch of the army, boasted 8 aircraft and 31 men, and a budget of $2.5 million.[41] Early in 1937 the first group of cadets who received their training in the Dominican Republic graduated as pilots. That same year, to celebrate Columbus Day, three Cuban pilots and the Dominican Frank Féliz Miranda participated in an international flight called Pro Faro a Colón. The Cubans piloted airplanes named *Santa María*, *Niña*, and *Pinta*, and Miranda flew the *Colón*. The group departed from Ciudad Trujillo, but in Cali, Colombia, a storm surprised them. The *Santa María*, *Niña*, and *Pinta* disappeared, but Miranda and his copilot, Ernesto Tejeda, survived the accident. Dominicans lamented the tragedy, but it did not discourage them from forging ahead with military aviation. The government continued to improve both civil and military aviation, acquiring more airplanes, training more pilots, and building more facilities.[42] For example in 1944, to celebrate the one hundredth anniversary of the declaration of national independence, the government organized parades, ceremonies, recitals, civic acts, and other festivities across the country. The celebrations also included the inauguration of several new aviation facilities; among them was the modern General Andrews Airport in Ciudad Trujillo and several others in the interior.

On September 29, 1950, military aviation became independent of the army, changing its name to the Dominican air force. Shortly thereafter, this force became the powerful Dominican Military Aviation, with its own armored units, infantry companies, 240 aircraft, its own hospital, and 3,500 men.[43]

Trujillo's eldest son, Ramfis, was a crucial factor in the improvement of the air force. After Ramfis's appointment as chief commander of the air force in 1952, the San Isidro Area Base became his own military unit— with marked differences from the army and the navy, particularly in its relations with the United States. At first Ramfis accepted U.S. assistance and he developed a good relationship with Sam Hale, the chief of the Military Assistance Advisory Group (MAAG). This relationship ensured that the air force had at its disposal "every kind of technical service needed for its proper functions, and its aircraft ranged from the simple training craft to the latest type of jetfighter."[44] The elite troops of the air force learned how to fly, shoot, drill, and even "think American-style."[45] In addition, through the Mutual Assistance Act of 1953, the United States sold a variety of fighter planes to the Dominicans and sent technicians to help the Dominicans service these aircraft.

By 1956 Ramfis shifted his alignment. He and Espaillat began to voice their opposition to MAAG policy, particularly the Naval Mission agreement. Ramfis did not trust the navy, underestimated its military capacity, and wanted the MAAG program to benefit the air force. Both Ramfis and Espaillat tried to stall the agreement as long as they could, which caused serious problems with Trujillo, who had requested the Naval Mission in 1955, and with U.S. officials in the Dominican Republic.

The agreement was finally signed in December 1956, but Ramfis did not change his view about the U.S. mission. On the contrary, after his academic failure at Fort Leavenworth in 1957, he adopted a more openly anti–U.S. attitude and tried to suspend the U.S. military aid program. Unlike his father, he argued that a "little country" like the Dominican Republic could not "make any substantial contribution to hemispheric defense with the planes and ships" the Dominican Republic had in its possession and that the Dominican armed forces "had sufficient equipment to defend [themselves] from any possible enemies for 30 or 40 years."[46] In Ramfis's view, the presence of the MAAG and the Naval Mission benefited the United States, not the Dominican Republic. U.S. officials stated, in contrast, that Ramfis was trying to institute "a new concept in the Dominican armed forces" whereby the air force would dominate the navy and army.[47] The Dominican air force had its own combat troops, the only tanks in the country, its own secret service, and powerful European machinery that not only separated it from the army and navy, but also rejected the U.S. objective of maintaining uniformity among Latin American weaponry.

Indeed, with its shift in organization and strength, the Dominican air force distinguished itself markedly from both the army and navy by acquiring weapons and equipment primarily from Europe rather than the United States. Furthermore, Dominican pilots, more so than army or navy officers, were exposed to Latin American and European military concepts and to Japanese martial arts. Otto Winterer, a veteran German pilot of Hitler's Luftwaffe, became one of Ramfis's main advisors, which may explain the similarities in organization, clothing, and functions between Trujillo's Dominican air force and Hitler's German air force.[48]

It appears that exposure to European military culture reinforced elitism in the air force. The CEFA (Learning Center of the Armed Forces) had under its control the best equipment and the best and the brightest officers. Created in 1958, the CEFA was originally intended to defend the country from outside military aggression and to train reservists. Soon after, the CEFA became an independent unit used by Trujillo to keep a vigilant eye on the army, the air force, and the navy.[49]

By 1960 the Dominican air force reached its highest level of power, with well-fitted and well-trained pilots in dashing uniforms, more than 200 combat aircraft, including 30 MK-I Vampires, about 50 P-51 Mustangs, and 25 P-47s. Especially noticeable was the increase in the number of military bases. In addition to San Isidro, nine more airfields operated across the country. There was also an aviation school, a body of parachutists, and a well-organized aircraft squadron for transport, rescue, and bombardment.[50]

In conjunction with the expansion of the air force, the increasing militarism and high level of militarization of the Dominican Republic concerned many Latin American nations. The Dominicans could engage in air combat against Haiti or another country. The immediate danger, however, was internal: the use of such a force against the opposition.

The power of the air force was well demonstrated when Air Force

Table 5. Trujillo Regime's Manpower, 1961

Branch	Personnel
Army	12,310
Navy	3,560
Air	3,720
Police	9,170
Total	28,760

Source: Office of Current Intelligence, Report no. 1063/64, LOC 86/217.

General Ramfis temporarily became the commander in chief of the armed forces after Trujillo's assassination. This situation was unique in the military history of the Dominican Republic. Traditionally the army commanded the armed forces.

As he strengthened the military, Trujillo also completed an enormous program of public construction. Although many of these projects were useless, like the hundreds of monuments and statues honoring Trujillo, they symbolized a dimension of militarism—the glorification of power. The building of airports, churches, highways, hospitals, hotels, railroads, ports, schools, sewage lines, telephone lines, and water networks vastly surpassed the accomplishments of previous governments.[51] Material prosperity was evident in many cities and towns. Ciudad Trujillo, for example, was transformed into a modern city with historical colonial buildings, museums and monuments, art centers, ballet schools, and theaters. Orderly and clean, the capital represented "the cosmopolitan heights that the Dominican people could achieve under Trujillo's tutelage."[52] The city also was the center of the regime.

Pageantry and Power
The acquisition of military hardware by the Dominican government relied primarily on its friendly relations with the United States. After War World II, in conjunction with the United Nations, the United States tried to enforce the resolution of February 13, 1947, of the Security Council of the U.N., which placed a ban on supplying weapons to several countries, including the Dominican Republic. In response, lacking of all the weapons that he wanted, Trujillo built La Armería in 1949.

The arms factory provided the regime with a variety of conventional small weapons and munitions, and empowered the government to exercise more control over the population. At a deeper level, La Armería helped to permeate the military ethos in society, as civilians in the work area, like soldiers, performed the different tasks assigned to them unquestioningly. The Armería was an ideal place for the regime to discipline society using the military as a model. In the end, by working side by side, civilians and military were instrumental in accomplishing Trujillo's militaristic goals.

The production of La Armería dramatically improved the military capacity of the Dominican Republic. For example, the factory produced 1,000 units of the .30 caliber Carbine San Cristóbal monthly. The overproduction of light weapons placed the Dominican Republic in the international arms market. Trujillo's agents visited several Latin American nations and the United States to promote Dominican weapons, and foreign arms dealers visited the country to investigate the Dominican arms market.[53]

In an impressive parade held during the presidential inauguration of Héctor B. Trujillo in Ciudad Trujillo on August 16, 1952, the Dominican armed forces provided a full-scale display of its strength to the outside world. The army, navy, and air force exhibited more than twenty thousand men in numerous showy or combat uniforms. Representing the army, ten infantry brigades armed with carbines and bayonets and one motorized brigade displayed an impressive array of artillery. One cavalry squadron, one transportation battalion, and other units turned out for the parade as well. Naval units demonstrated their strength with their naval brigade of five corvettes, two destroyers, two frigates, twelve patrol and coast vessels, and assorted launches. Finally, the air force presented a spectacular demonstration when it "flew in mass formation with a B1-plane trainer squadron, a B-17 flight, and an A-16 squadron."[54]

The Dominican press reported that thousands of citizens from all over the country witnessed the impressive maneuvers and the well-dressed troops in olive combat and military dress uniforms. (There are two different figures for the number of men that participated in the parade. The Dominican press reported 30,000 and the U.S. embassy about 20,000.) To U.S. embassy personnel, however, the parade represented more military pageantry than actual military strength. By U.S. standards, the equipment was old and the transportation battalion was "composed of painted-over trucks owned by the Haina Sugar Central." In comparing the Dominican parade with similar parades in the United States, a diplomat concluded that the Dominicans were more than a century behind. Dominican military capacity and personnel, he suggested, were reminiscent of the late 1830s in the United States. The equipment was old and varied. The troops, although young and physically fit, were inexperienced but well prepared to defend the country against external aggression and to keep internal order.[55]

Within the framework of militarism, the parade showed the profound connection of military culture with civil society as military and civilian authorities marched ahead of soldiers, reservists, and civilians, who, representing different segments of the population, like soldiers were also required to participate in the event. Some civilians, such as teachers and women, wore white suits and white dresses for the occasion. Symbolizing the civil-military milieu, peasants from some rural communities wore khaki pants and white shirts.

Similar displays of military strength took place in 1955, a year of pomp, pageantry, and ceremony in the Dominican Republic. Trujillo's regime celebrated its twenty-fifth anniversary that year. The nation spent millions of dollars building the Feria of la Paz y Confraternidad del Mundo Libre (The Fair of Peace and Confraternity of the Free World) to honor Trujillo, to promote the Dominican Republic as a secure place for investments, and to display agricultural and industrial products, as well as cattle development. Many countries, representing a cultural diversity of art and economic progress, advertised their technological development and the multiple attractions that their nations had to offer. The inaugural ceremonies glorified Trujillo with a display of lavishness. Guests and special delegates enjoyed sumptuous state receptions, luncheons, dinners, balls, and concerts. Foreigners and Dominicans were thrilled by the glamorous, imaginative displays of people, pavilions, and floats. The fair showed Trujillo's increasing "extravagance and love for the grandiose."[56] His daughter Angelita was the queen of the event. For her coronation she wore a white silk satin dress, "sprinkled with rubies, diamonds, and pearls" and "bordered with 150 feet of Russian ermine."[57] Wagons carried goods and merchandise symbolizing the economic achievements of the era. Thousands of men, women, and children participated, waving the Dominican flag, banners, and photos of Trujillo. The showcase of the parade, as expected, was the military. Columns of soldiers and officers in brilliant uniforms moved along George Washington Avenue to salute Trujillo and his guests. Naval vessels maneuvered along the Caribbean shoreline, and military aircraft offered another impressive show.[58] In the exhibition area, the armed forces displayed tanks and other military vehicles, but the artillery produced in the La Armería, particularly the Carbine San Cristóbal, was a great symbol of military pride. These demonstrations were also aimed at demonstrating the regime's capacity for defense and to warn Trujillo's enemies of his power and perhaps, as he thought, his infallibility. Ornes believes that by 1955, "if pressed, Trujillo could make good his boast of putting 100,000 men on a war footing."[59]

How large was the military in 1961? As table 5 indicates, the regime's manpower, including the police, was estimated at over 28,000. By then, according to Crassweller, the Dominican armed forces could be compared with the army of Frederick the Great: "A body that was all muscle and no fat. Its discipline was strict, its morale high. The weaponry and other equipment were excellent."[60]

Although the Dominican military was large, it lacked the autonomy to determine military policy, and it did not have political decision-making power as did the military in other Latin American dictatorial regimes contemporaneous to that of Trujillo. In Argentina, for example, on several occasions the army voiced its political position in favor of or against Perón.[61] Under Trujillo, however, military personnel were expected to support the regime, not criticize it. In Nicaragua, Somoza maintained good balance and control between the ranks, but "the most important issue [was] not Somoza, but the Guardia Nacional."[62] In contrast, Trujillo unquestionably dominated the armed forces. Nevertheless, like Trujillo, Somoza's leadership rested on the internal cohesion of the armed forces, especially loyalty to the dictator. Unlike that of Nicaragua or Argentina, however, the military capability of the Dominican Republic became a threat to the political stability of the region. When Costa Rica, Cuba, Guatemala, Haiti, Venezuela, and other Latin American countries expressed their concern about the increase of Dominican military strength, Trujillo responded by asserting that the military of the Dominican Republic had an international mission: to defend the country and the Caribbean region against the spread of communism. U.S. cold war leaders supported Trujillo's self-proclamation as the first anticommunist of the New World. Militarily, Trujillo's manipulation of the anticommunist ideology was profitable. At first with the assistance of the United States and then against the will of this influential partner, the Dominican Republic became the best-armed nation in the Caribbean.

9. CITIZENS AND SOLDIERS

Militarization, Resistance, and Paramilitarism

With the expansion of the military and the conceptualization of La Patria Nueva Trujillo glorified the military in the eyes of the nation. He envisioned the nation as a military post. Within this framework, his speeches and annual reports to the secretaries of the interior, war and navy stress the importance of the collaboration between the military and the government and offered ways to impose military principles on the citizenry. These documents also mention Trujillo's pride in the fact that the military protected the nation from those who wanted to destroy La Patria Nueva with "anarchist" ideas. Trujillo also encouraged civilian-military interaction; soldiers and civilians had to put their shoulders together to work toward the rebirth of the nation as planned by his government.[1] Despite these attempts and although a military ethos was instilled in a large portion of the population, there was also dissention and opposition to Trujillo's militaristic scheme.

Militarism, Militarization, and Indoctrination

Reconstructing a detailed picture of Trujillo's plan for the militarization of society can help us understand Trujillo's new order as he created mechanisms to impose military discipline on all aspects of public life. For example, with a policy of zero tolerance for tardiness, the government conducted official functions on a precise schedule, and employees went to work on time. Trujillo himself, even if he only slept a few hours the night before, would be in his office at 8:00 a.m. Punctuality is certainly important for the efficient functioning of any business, but in fashioning his authoritarian state, Trujillo used coercion to guarantee punctuality and to compel citizens to behave like soldiers. Applying military principles to the general population, for example, civilians who did not stand up when the national flag was raised or lowered in public risked public humiliation or incarceration. The regime considered resistance both anti-patriotic and anti-Trujillista offenses, and the offenders received punishment "in the same spirit of a commanding officer meting out disciplinary action. And anti-Trujillo activity, to the Old Man, was the same as a soldier committing mutiny." Within this arrangement Trujillo systematically imposed a military discipline "which turned the population into an army" ready to obey orders.[2]

Believing that a widespread military presence was necessary to shape the nation's future, Trujillo ensured that some of the functions assigned to the military coincided with the workings of civil society, allowing the military to be present at different activities sponsored by the regime or by the community. By giving a large space to the military, Trujillo ensured that his officers and enlisted men interacted with people everywhere. Officers and soldiers could be seen in backward villages or in the most enlightened institutions and private clubs alike. They danced, drank, and socialized with peasants and working classes as well as with the upper crust of society. The public appearance of military personnel, imperative in political rallies, in religious activities, and in multiple social events, symbolized Trujillo's dream of La Patria Nueva.

By the end of Trujillo's reign, the military was at the center of social and political life. With their elegant uniforms, martial pace, and flair, at all levels—national, provincial, and local—the officers participated in carefully staged ceremonies or informal parties. They became the objects of attention and distinction; the pilots in particular became la crème de la crème in social circles. Socioeconomic reasons may explain why people admired the officers. In general they represented a broad segment of the population and embodied the promise of advancement. Indeed, the mobility through the officer corps, from the lower class to middle, and even to the upper class changed the traditional social order. Concomitantly, the dictator led the nation on a path toward militarism, using the officers to guide the citizens in the direction that his government wanted, a disciplined society framed in a martial culture.

Perhaps the most visible indicators of the pervasiveness of militarist ideas in society were the marches. Emanating from military culture, under Trujillo's totalitarian grip the Dominican Republic became a marching society. Occasions for marching and displaying political identification with the regime were abundant—on Trujillo's birthday, for example, or during his travel abroad. In fact, the dictator's travels were especially fruitful in that each trip afforded the opportunity for two parades: one to say good-bye, the other to welcome him back. With marching bands and marching multitudes, manifestations of public support succeeded one another, month after month. The month of May is a good example of seemingly endless marches and parades. May 1, Labor Day, was an occasion for workers to march and to show loyalty. May 15, the Day of the Agricultural Workers, was the official day for peasants to do the same. On May 16, to commemorate the election of Trujillo as president in 1930, the entire nation marched. On the last Sunday of May, Mother's Day, again the entire nation paraded to honor Trujillo's mother. On each occasion, soldiers and civilians either marched together or gathered to watch. Not all who participated in the marches did so willingly, but choosing not to participate meant courting imprisonment or becoming subject to political indictments ranging from personal humiliation to economic deprivation, from social ostracism to death.

The state applied no class or gender distinction when selecting marchers. In keeping with Trujillo's militarist ideal of La Patria Nueva, the rituals of the state required active participation of all citizens. Women, men, and children of all ages and social backgrounds rehearsed the steady steps of endless parades and rallies. For adults, especially women, a dress code, as in the military, was unavoidable: most women wore white dresses for rallies and parades. Symbolizing love for Trujillo, some women selected heart patterns or decorated their outfits with red hearts, as shown in the book *Gran desfile nacional de 1958*. The government encouraged citizens to participate in these ceremonies to show not only respect to Trujillo but also love for the fatherland. But the spotlight leaned toward glorification of power and loyalty. The word *loyalty* was frequently included on the banners. For example, during the national celebrations of August 16, 1958, one banner carried by wives of policemen read, "Illuminated by the light of your glory, the wives of the members of the P.N. [National Police] reiterate the commitment of devotion and loyalty of our husbands."[3]

As sociopolitical phenomena, these marches appealed to the masses and added another dimension to the militaristic tone of the Trujillo regime. In addition, using public space as a theater for effusive demonstrations of loyalty, like Hitler, Mussolini, Stalin, and other European fascists, Trujillo tried to unify the nation around his goals with mass meetings and parades. These assemblies also served to show how, little by little, the society assimilated Trujillo's political and military notions of respect and reverence. Dominicans were so conditioned by propaganda and slogans to see the dictator as a superior human being that when he appeared in public, men removed their hats, placed them over their hearts, and bowed their heads in reverence to El Jefe.[4]

Furthermore, through a coded public discourse, every day, in many locations (mainly in the headquarters of the Partido Dominicano) across the country, the regime orchestrated many manifestations of public support. With sophisticated language or popular expressions, eloquent speakers with grandiloquent phrases delivered Trujillo's message to the multitudes. Thus, the people became more and more susceptible to demagoguery.

The manipulation of the Dominican people came in various forms. For example, Trujillo danced well and loved merengue. He used it for multiple purposes. Considered one of the most effective means of propaganda, the verses of the merengue made reference to the achievements of the government, the wealth and beauty of the country, the ideology of the regime, the weakness of Trujillo's enemies, the greatness of the dictator, and the importance of the military. The verse of one merengue, for example, expressed that Trujillo created a new army to protect the nation from its enemies.[5]

Politically, merengue also allowed Trujillo to *congraciarse* or to identify with the masses. Considering that a large portion of the population, both civilian and military, loved merengue, the music embodied interaction between soldiers and citizens. On the other hand, the elite disliked and had proscribed merengue from their clubs and parties. Under Trujillo's auspices, composers transformed the merengue "into a kind of salon music" and Trujillo requested merengue when he attended parties, forcing the elite to dance to its rhythms. Gradually, the vernacular content of merengue became "refined, harmonic, and sophisticated."[6] More important, merengue was transformed from country music (*música de campo*) to the national dance and became a cultural symbol of national identity. Composers gave their musical compositions titles such as "Era Gloriosa" and "Viva el General." Not surprisingly, merengues made reference to Trujillo's many roles and qualities, stressing the figure of the general above all. For example, a fragment of Luis Alberti's composition "Najayo" expressed,

Que viva Trujillo	Long live Trujillo
Hombre sin igual	Man without equal
Que viva Trujillo	Long live Trujillo
Nuestro general	Our General
Trujillo Molina	Trujillo Molina
Dios me lo bendiga	May God bless him for me
Así dice la gente	So say the people
Trujillo que viva	Long live Trujillo
General estrella	Stellar general
Eso digo yo	That's what I say
Trujillo en la tierra	On earth, Trujillo
Y en el cielo Dios.	And in heaven, God.[7]

Rendering tribute to Trujillo reached such incredible degrees of adulation that Balaguer claimed that after 1930 the Dominican people were not only under the divine protection of God but also in the providential hands of Trujillo.[8] These ideas of deification were simplified under the slogan "Dios y Trujillo" that was posted in private houses, public buildings, and displayed during the marches. With control of the media (Trujillo owned the newspapers *La Nación* and *El Caribe* and Trujillo's brother Petán controlled the radio broadcasting system and owned the only television station of the country), Trujillo used propaganda to mold Dominicans into a single-minded society. Propaganda and slogans had a "cumulative soporific effect" on the people as they paid homage to the Benefactor.[9] Under these circumstances, the internalization of concepts and elements of the military culture, such as duty and obedience, contributed to the subordination of civilians, and by extension to the militarization of society.

Militarism, Militarization, and Education

Under Trujillo the educational system underwent significant change. More schools were built, industrial, manual, and technical disciplines were introduced, and a strong emphasis was placed on cultural, intellectual, and literary development. Certainly, education did not direct people toward democracy, but the improvement of facilities was impressive. In 1930 there were only 526 schools with 50,800 students. By 1958, however, 4,419 schools had an enrollment of 423,424 students.[10] There were also vocational schools for those with manual skills, normal schools for teachers, and night schools for workers called Universidades

Libres. College enrollment also increased. Enrollment at the University of Santo Domingo climbed from 379 in 1930 to 1,916 in 1954.[11] At all levels a significant proportion of the population had opportunity for educational improvement during Trujillo's regime. For example in 1936, only 20 percent of the population knew how to read and write; twenty years later, 60 percent of the population had some kind of literacy.[12] The renewal of the National Archives, the creation of the National Symphony Orchestra, the National Conservatory of Music and Public Speaking, the National Arts Theatre-School, the Gallery of Fine Arts, the Primary Music Schools, and other educational centers added quantity and quality to the nation's cultural and intellectual life.[13] In remaking the nation, Trujillo posed as a Maecenas, and foreign and national artists and writers received state support that allowed them to develop their skills and to contribute to a cultural revival of the nation.

Despite these substantial educational and cultural advances, instruction stressed character building over scientific learning and was intended to train civilians to obey. Trujillo's ideologists, eulogists, and intellectual collaborators adapted "totalitarian conceptions of education" from other systems and used these ideas to strengthen the regime.[14] Indeed, the indoctrination of students was integrated with the educational philosophy of the dictatorship. As in Italy with Mussolini or Germany with Hitler, indoctrination began in elementary school and continued through the university, complete with propagandist ideas, myths, hymns, and rituals. Schools became ideal settings for the dissemination of the military goals of the regime. Soldiers went to schools to give military instruction to students; and textbooks depicted Trujillo as the Benefactor, the savior of the nation, the father of the new fatherland who had transformed the country from a backward to modern nation. The *Cartilla cívica*, recommended by the secretary of education as a text for moral and civic instructions in the schools, served as a manual for indoctrination. The text stressed the goodness of Trujillo, who "works unceasingly for the happiness of his people, maintains the peace, supports the schools, builds roads, protects all forms of labor, helps the farmer, . . . encourages learning, and organizes the army for the protection of all law-abiding citizens."[15] Furthermore, the text was designed to inculcate the idea that denunciation of disloyal people was a civic duty and each revolutionary was an enemy.

The ideologists of the *Cartilla cívica* established the base of what Trujillo called *la reconstrucción del pueblo dominicano*, which began in the elementary schools. Based on a brainwashing process, classes began with a ritual. Using highly stylized language, each teacher wrote on the blackboard a phrase exalting Trujillo or praising his achievements. In each principal's office, in the classrooms, and in the halls, photos of Trujillo abounded. An anecdote related to the pictures of Trujillo in the schools circulated in the country. The story goes that one day a teacher sought to discipline one of Trujillo's grandsons. Defiantly, the child looked at the portrait of Trujillo on the wall and told the teacher, "He is my grandfather." And the boy continued doing as he pleased.[16] It appears that the young lad was also "indoctrinated" to use the figure of his grandfather to intimidate.

An important component of the education was rigorous discipline. In the schools, as in the barracks, violations of rules were severely punished. In Trujillo's own words, the army was the institution that together with the school should regulate the will of the people, and therefore both institutions had to show restraint and adherence to discipline to serve as a model for the rest of the citizens.[17] Symbolizing similarity between the army and school, public elementary and high school students wore khaki clothing, which closely resembled soldiers' uniforms. They participated in ceremonial and commemorative events to celebrate military and patriotic victories. To exalt national heroes and military battles, the schools offered prizes to students who wrote selected verses and prose for the occasion. Targets of the propaganda machinery, students praised Trujillo with poems, songs, and martial music played by the bands. Students also participated in marching drills and calisthenics to develop a militaristic attitude. The system compelled teachers to praise the regime, too. In public meetings they recited poems, read speeches, and as models for other citizens, pledged allegiance to Trujillo.

Trujillo's militarism and militarization of society reached the University of Santo Domingo. Founded in 1538, this distinguished institution was the oldest university in the Americas. Although it had long provided a comprehensive range of programs with professors who held different political views, once Trujillo came to power he oversaw the hiring and firing of professors. The university awarded him an honorary doctorate on October 18, 1934. In Trujillo's political thinking, military order was an essential part of the education of the civil society because it could establish "the concept of responsibility and honor" in citizens.[18] Therefore, college students tended to emulate the military: they were obedient and loyal to the government. At the university, as in elementary and high schools, indoctrination was the twin sister of education and students had little opportunity to articulate their own ideas. Instead they had to express admiration for and devotion to the dictator.

In this respect, under Trujillo's rule the educational mission of the university became "handicapped by the political gag that impedes all discussion of topics which could inspire restlessness."[19] To take action against those organizing resistance or criticizing the regime, spies disguised as students enrolled in the university and attended classes. Consequently, controversial subjects were not discussed and, afraid of repression, professors and students "whispered" during lectures instead of talking freely.[20] Some members of the faculty and some students, however, bound together by common intellectual and scientific interests, found ways to get around the state censorship and secretly criticized the regime.

In general, however, teachers and students at all levels participated in myriad militaristic activities. For example, June 30 was the official day to honor teachers. But in fact, June 30 was the day for teachers and students to endorse Trujillo as the First Teacher. Each school organized public meetings, presided over by civilian and military authorities, during which teachers exalted Trujillo with panegyrics, poems, and songs. Together with the students, teachers also participated in well-staged parades. These parades, which resembled those of the military, attracted public attention. Dressed in uniforms that simulated the navy uniform, in some cities and towns the Batón Ballet, or group of female students in miniskirts like cheerleaders, accompanied by a music band, danced and performed acrobatics that delighted the public. People loved to see the children of their communities marching like soldiers with their well-ironed uniforms and clean shoes. Students performed these presentations during other festivities honoring Trujillo. Petán Trujillo organized the first Batón Ballet in Bonao. The carefully choreographed events were compatible with Trujillo's ideas of the political seduction of the masses and the interaction that should exist between the military and civilians. Despite all his efforts, Trujillo did not fully indoctrinate society. Resistance against the regime, outside and inside the military, challenged Trujillo's plan to militarize society.

Resistance, Labor Unions, and Political Organizations

Despite the government's wide-ranging efforts to eliminate criticism of the regime, since the beginning of the dictatorship Dominican exiles denounced Trujillo's ruthless and militaristic state. Many in the international community joined forces with them and offered them moral and financial support, but the exiles faced many obstacles. In regard to labor, the regime fabricated false unions whose leaders received official appointments to represent national labor organizations. In doing so, the regime denied the Dominican workers the right to organize, but genuine worker organizations did not give up. Unions survived by working clandestinely. Showing resistance to indoctrination and militarization, in 1942 workers organized a strike against the Central Romana, a large sugar mill. Trujillo responded ruthlessly to the workers' protest; hundreds of workers were killed or tortured at the hands of the army.[21]

Repression did not stop labor union activities. Amid the terror, Mauricio Báez, Justin José Del Orbe, Fernando Hernández, and other leaders continued the struggle. In the late 1940s a combination of factors helped their cause, as well as the campaign of Trujillo's political enemies. Among these factors, a group of Latin American political leaders envisioned the region free of dictators. Similarly, in the United States after War World II, an energetic campaign against totalitarian regimes became a prominent topic of discussion in Congress and in the United Nations.[22] In regard to Trujillo, a U.S. official in Ciudad Trujillo acknowledged that "a ruthless and efficient dictator" governed the Dominican Republic and the U.S. government should not grant favors to Trujillo and thus strengthen him.[23]

Trujillo realized that his dictatorial regime did not fit the international political trend and that some Dominicans were becoming openly defiant. In order to show some political accommodation and to counteract the growing opposition, the Dominican government promised it would allow political opposition and freedom to join labor unions.[24] Consequently, he invited the opposition to organize political parties and labor unions. Trujillo's "liberalization" policy was threefold. First, by theoretically allowing the workers to exercise the right to strike, the dictator might achieve international recognition. Second, it was a political trap that allowed him to easily identify his enemies. Third, Trujillo could test, one more time, the army's loyalty in a moment of crisis.

Challenging Trujillo's militarist order yet again, labor leaders organized the most important strike of the era in 1946. This time they succeeded in winning wage increases and better working conditions. In 1951 the government articulated the so-called Trujillo labor code, or El Código Trujillo de Trabajo, which made provisions for the collective interest of rural and urban workers and guaranteed equal rights for women in the labor market. Workers' rights, however, were never fully acknowledged. In 1954 when workers tried again to demand a wage increase, the government "threatened to drown the movement in blood."[25] The movement began to languish in the face of these threats.

Suspicious of Trujillo's motives, some political leaders invited to organize the opposition rejected the invitation. They believed that if Trujillo were serious about his offer, he would step down. Others, such as the leaders of the Popular Socialist Party and the Democratic Youth Organization, calculated the risks and decided to organize the opposition.

Trujillo did not fulfill his promises. Many of these leaders paid dearly for their actions. Trujillo's press, *La Nación*, attacked their ideas, the army repressed them, and the judges sent them to jail. Trujillo was just testing the strength of the opposition.

Two other parties, the National Labor Party and the National Democratic Party, emerged as Trujillo's idea of political opposition. When elections came in 1947, these two parties and the Dominican Party participated in the election. Of course Trujillo won. In fact there was no opposition, but this type of masquerade gave the regime the appearance of legitimate power. By then the development of the cold war favored Trujillo. To counteract communism and Soviet influence, the United States began to favor rightist dictatorships, pouring money and military supplies into the hands of rulers like Trujillo. Thus the cold war helped Trujillo stay in power, although it did not destroy the anti-Trujillista resistance. On the contrary, Trujillo's abuses generated animosities and temporarily broke the unity of the military.

Military Conspiracy in the 1940s

The members of the Dominican armed forces blindly followed Trujillo for a decade after the conspiracy of the early 1930s. However, signs of unrest reappeared in 1946. In early January an uprising in the army, quickly detected and suppressed, created some commotion even beyond the barracks. The regime accused Captain Marion Dalby of the U.S. Naval Mission of being involved in the conspiracy, but he denied the charge. Because the incident took place during one of the periods of tension between the United States and Trujillo, the U.S. embassy considered the accusation as another attempt to discredit U.S. officials.[26]

Later that same year, First Lieutenant Eugenio de Marchena coordinated a network of military conspirators. Some civilians also participated. Marchena modeled his plan of action on that used by the Trinitaria, the secret organization created by Juan Pablo Duarte in 1844, to bring independence to the Dominican people. As in the Trinitaria, only a few of Marchena's group knew one another. The group selected June 22, the army holiday, to begin the uprising. Knowing Trujillo would be attending a parade, they planned to kill the dictator by blasting away the presidential stand and then taking control of General Andrews Airport and the arsenal at the Ozama Fortress. Word of the conspiracy reached Trujillo well in advance, allowing him to stop the plot in May. Those caught were sent to prison, where most of them eventually perished.[27] To show other officers what would happen to them if they also decided to conspire, the army exhibited Marchena, tortured and disfigured, from military post to military post. He was the last to be killed. No one knows for sure how many enlisted men participated in the plot, or how many were executed. A jailed civilian heard Trujillo ordering subordinates to burn alive all officers implicated in the scheme.[28] Among the participating officers, two were the nephews of one of Trujillo's closest friends, Ricardo Paíno Pichardo. Paíno, whom Crassweller describes as a man born a courtier, had shown "genuine and deep" loyalty to Trujillo and served the regime in many high positions. Despite Paino's status, a firing squad executed his nephews with Paino himself as a witness.[29] Trujillo's regime permitted no opposition and no mercy for military conspiracy. Even so, soldiers and officers took chances to act politically. Sporadic military discontent, whether open or subtle, was met with swift repression. Trujillo managed to stay in power and to control the military, but not without resistance.

Armed Resistance

On May 16, 1947, Trujillo was "elected" president for the fourth time. In the meantime Dominicans in exile, in conjunction with the Caribbean Legion, organized an armed invasion known as the Cayo Confites expedition. As the CIA concluded, the legion, integrated by men from a variety of ideological positions, enjoyed support from Central American and Caribbean leaders.[30] Presidents Juan José Arévalo of Guatemala, Rómulo Betancourt of Venezuela, and José Figueres of Costa Rica emerged as leaders of the Caribbean Legion. Juan Bosch, Juan Isidro Jimenes Grullón, Ángel Miolán, Miguel Ángel Ramírez, Juan Rodríguez, and other Dominican exiles strongly supported the plan.

In preparation for the invasion of the Dominican Republic, an estimated 1,200 men, supplied with adequate small arms, rifles, grenades, machine guns, and aerial bombs, gathered and trained on Cuban territory. However, in the middle of September the expedition failed in Cuban waters before the invaders had the opportunity to land in the Dominican Republic. The CIA offers this explanation for the thwarted invasion: "Immediately prior to the expedition's projected departure for the Dominican Republic, . . . the Cuban Government—prominent members of which had been openly aiding and abetting the Legion's activities—suppressed it, their reasons being internal political maneuvers and United States pressure."[31] Nonetheless the organization gathered strength and reorganized its resistance.

In June 1949 Dominican exiles again coordinated with the legion, this time for an aerial invasion against Trujillo. This attempt to eliminate Trujillo also failed for various reasons, among them bad weather, which forced four of the invading airplanes to land on Cozumel, where the Mexican authorities interned the legionnaires. Of the six airplanes that departed from Guatemala, only one, commanded by Horacio Ornes, reached its target and landed in the town of Luperón on the northern shore of the island. Ornes deployed his group in two directions, but in the darkness, they shot at each other.[32] Worse yet, Trujillo knew of the plan in advance and had mobilized his army. Almost all rebels were killed; the few who survived were taken to prison.

The media portrayed the dissenters as communists, enemies of the fatherland. And the only television station in the country, La Voz Dominicana, owned by Petán Trujillo, broadcasted an extended anticommunist campaign discrediting the rebels and praising Trujillo and the military.

After the invasion of Luperón, the regime imposed severe restrictions on society. Tighter internal security measures, including control of the movement of foreigners, continuous waves of arrests, and incarcerations transformed the republic from a nation into a prison.[33] During the decade of 1950–60, the security forces became an even more brutal force of repression than they had been before.

Arguing that the country was "a victim of communist aggression" and had faced "the most dangerous military attack . . . recorded in Dominican history," the government sent a long list of the arms and munitions captured in Luperón to the OAS.[34] The regime also claimed that in order to respond adequately to internal and external threats, the government had no choice but to strengthen the military capability of the republic. To strengthen the air force, for example, by Law No. 1990 of May 2, 1949, the name of the secretary of defense changed from secretary of war and marine to secretary of war, marine, and aviation.

Paramilitarism

Paramilitary organizations were developed to respond to the increased "threats" to Dominican society. There were two types: those with specific assignments, and those with pageantry-inspired roles. Those with specific duties included the National Police, the reserve forces, and the *alcaldes pedáneos*, or rural police. These organizations shared some military responsibilities with the regular forces. In addition, domestic militias and mercenaries performed military duties along with the regular forces. La Guardia Universitaria was the best representative of the pageantry category.

The National Police

Created in 1936, the National Police was the first paramilitary organization in Trujillo's Dominican Republic. Considered an auxiliary agency, this force employed a significant number of ex-soldiers. Its organizational structure and territorial distribution paralleled that of the army.

The central command, housed in the National Police Palace, a modern building with updated means of communication and transportation, directed the modus operandi of the institution. Primarily in charge of enforcing domestic law, the National Police also had roles in espionage, intelligence services, and other tasks normally assigned to the army. The unclear division between the army and the police generated rivalry and animosity. Adding to the confusion, Trujillo transferred control of the police from the secretary of the interior and police to his most trusted army officers.[35]

In addition, the Police Law of October 19, 1936, allowed Trujillo not only to appoint the police chief but also to award him a higher army rank.[36] For example, a lieutenant colonel could receive a temporary rank of colonel as well as that of chief of the police. The appointment was usually a short-term one; few commanders of the police lasted more than one year in office. Trujillo systematically rotated the most reliable chiefs of the army into and out of the position of chief of the police. Almost everyone had a turn at least once in his military career. In contrast, no police officer was ever given a higher rank in the army.[37]

In spite of or because of the rotation scheme, the police became a well-organized paramilitary force and witnessed steady growth from 578 men in 1936 to 9,170 in 1961. Although the police force was quite large, in the rural areas the *alcaldes pedáneos* (rural mayors) functioned as vigilant policemen.

Alcaldes Pedáneos

In fostering collaborative relationships between civilians and military authorities, the *alcaldes* played an important role in executing the orders of the central government. In the rural communities they were the epicenter of Trujillo's bureaucratic establishment. Representing the state's idea of good citizens, these government employees also functioned as mayors in rural communities, but in a peculiar way. In the new order created by Trujillo, the *alcaldes* performed a wide range of functions over a large territory. They enforced the law, maintained order, took and escorted prisoners, and assisted soldiers patrolling the border to prevent the penetration of Haitians or the escape of suspicious Dominicans. They were also very active in the distribution of land and water for irrigation, as well as in assisting and supervising peasants in the colonies. In addition to these functions, often they acted as witnesses for the prosecution or the defense and their words had a lot of weight in the courts. In other instances, however, the *alcalde* became a protector of members of his community and defended them even if he had to confront military authorities.[38] Certainly, the figure of the *alcalde* was a powerful one. Because of the authority given to the *alcaldes*, their jobs had prominence among the members of the community.

Many *alcaldes* were former soldiers who had returned home after serving in the army. They were often the only ones in their communities with a regular salary—albeit a small one. The *alcaldes* also usually were the only villagers to have a gun, which, along with their military training, strengthened their authority and allowed them to exercise not only police and army duties but to assume political and social power. Because of their authority and relatively high standing in the community, parents looked at them as ideal *padrinos* (godfathers) for their children. By establishing this connection, considered to be sacred and as close as a genealogical one, parents expected protection and, as was customary in rural areas and poor communities, some financial assistance along the way. On the other hand, the bond established with many families helped these agents accomplish their mission more effectively. Through these relationships, directly or indirectly, *alcaldes* exerted their authority over a large number of citizens.[39]

The lack of infrastructure was also on their side. Stationed in communities with limited communication systems, poor roads, and almost no social services, their periodic visits to the city added to their civil and political importance. They became the mailmen and newspaper carriers for the community, as well as the intelligence agents for the state. They kept records of the "agricultural production of each individual peasant in their locality," which could be used to determine the level of cooperation with the regime.[40]

Familiar with everyone in their communities, the *alcaldes* helped enforce conscription and played a paternalistic role, acting as counselors in domestic conflicts and as arbiters in disputes concerning trade and financial matters. Respected and feared by the peasants, the regime relied on the *alcaldes* to exercise control over citizens residing in remote and isolated communities.

Reserve Forces

Under Trujillo's theory that "no enemy is small,"[41] after the Cayo Confites invasion the dictator decided to give military training to civilians. The expansion of manpower included massive conscription, but the idea of using conscription to militarize the population had first been spelled out in 1928. On March 10 of that year, the newspaper *Patria* published an editorial in support of intensive militarization of the working class and obligatory military instruction in schools for all students, male and female. Trujillo made obligatory military service a reality on September 11, 1947. His nation-in-arms plan, aimed at enhancing the military strength of the republic, was enforced vigorously on the male population. Contrary to the Patria proposal, however, conscription did not include women, but as a symbolic gesture women could register their names in the recruitment office. The recruitment of men, who had to register as "volunteers," was intensive all across the country. Each province had had its own reserve unit since the early 1930s.[42] Men between seventeen and thirty-five years of age classified for regular service, and men between thirty-five and fifty-five were part of the special services. Local authority had the power to call on every man who qualified. Thirty thousand participated annually in the training program, which prepared them to be "useful to the fatherland, the government and to defend themselves." In case of war, they had to be in active duty for a year and a lottery system selected those who had to serve. All conscripts, regardless of age, received a seventeen-week course in basic military training. Those who classified for active duty but were not selected by the lottery system received ninety days of training so that they would be ready if their service was necessary.[43]

The main goal was to develop a body of 10,000 civilian reserves.

To this end, the government created a reserve training school in San Cristóbal, and by 1954 more than 500,000 Dominican men had received basic military training.[44] That meant that almost half of the Dominican male population had undergone some sort of military training—according to the 1950 census, the Dominican population totaled 2,135,-872.[45] In 1960 the total population was 3,047,070; 50.4 percent were male and 49.6 percent were female.

The people in general did not welcome the obligatory service and many men reluctantly joined the reserve. It meant two hours of extra work a day, from 6:00 a.m. to 8:00 a.m., for three to four months. Not only did they not receive payment for their trouble, but they incurred expenses. They were responsible for their own clothing, shoes, and transportation. Reservists also had to pay for health certificates.

When the training center at San Cristóbal could no longer accommodate the reservists, Trujillo ordered each province to establish its own regional and local recruitment and training centers. In this way, Trujillo explained, the whole country could share the civic satisfaction of watching the conscripts participating in parades as proud soldiers.[46] Local centers also eliminated the costs of transporting and housing the recruits, and the recruits spent less of their own money.

In reading Trujillo's conscription project, one is struck by his notion of the obligatory military service as a mix of politics, militarism, and pageantry. The training consisted mainly of physical exercises and repetitive explanations of civic duties and the need for loyalty to the Generalissimo. Only occasionally during the training did the reservists handle real weapons; most of the time they practiced with wooden replicas of a carbine. Thus the appearance of the trainees was impressive, but their military readiness was questionable.

One of the main goals of the obligatory service, it seems, was to recruit young men for regular service. According to Major Agustín R. Plúyer Trujillo, chief of the Central Office of Registration of the Military Obligatory Service, his office selected enlisted men in the armed forces from the best of the reserve forces.[47]

When the military training of the reserve moved under the supervision of the CEFA in 1960, reservists began to receive more practical training. Soon the government considered the reserve as an additional force, which, together with the regular army, could defend the fatherland on the battlefield.[48] Paramilitarism, so well suited to the nature and practice of the Trujillo regime, became institutionalized.

Mercenaries and Militias

During the final two years of Trujillo's dictatorship, other paramilitary groups emerged—mercenary organizations and native militias.

Mercenaries

Trujillo militarism had no borders. La Legión Extranjera Anticomunista (Foreign Anticommunist Legion), created in 1959, was made up of men from all social and military backgrounds representing twenty-two nations, primarily Spain but also Austria, France, Germany, Greece, Italy, Yugoslavia, and other European countries. Dominicans also joined the Foreign Legion. The year 1959 was a difficult one for Trujillo. A combination of domestic resistance, economic decline, international pressure, hostility from the United States, and an armed confrontation organized by Dominican exiles set into motion forces that ultimately led to the downfall of the regime. Facing challenges from different directions, the dictator appeared to have lost confidence in his own military organization when he decided to hire soldiers of fortune to defend himself and to invade Cuba and Venezuela, countries from which anti-Trujillo groups were receiving support. The regime also attacked foreign political leaders who provided refuge for the exiles. But Fidel Castro became Trujillo's main target. In his futile effort to eliminate Castro, Trujillo entered into an alliance with supporters of Fulgencio Batista and spent several million dollars establishing connections with all types of agents and paying for expensive weapons, cover operations, and other costly activities, such as hiring soldiers of fortune.[49]

To disguise what they were really doing, the regime placed the hiring of mercenaries within a broad ideological and social context. Early in March 1959, a group of retired army officers (including former top officers such as Federico Fiallo, Fausto Caamaño, Antonio Leyba Pou, Félix Hermida and Arturo Espaillat) informed Secretary of the Armed Forces General José García Trujillo that because of the "subversive climate" created by Communists in the Caribbean area, they had formed the Foreign Legion to respond promptly to any attempt to invade the Dominican Republic or Haiti. The secretary thanked the officers and supported their project because of its importance in the "preservation of continental peace and the preservation of norms which, like that of nonintervention and reciprocal respect in the relations of states, constitute the essence of international order in America."[50] Consequently, General García ordered "without delay and without omissions of any sacrifice" the transfer of funds to support the organization. And García gave orders to the Department of Technological Services of the armed forces to have at the disposal of the Legión Extranjera 25,000 machine guns, 3,000,000 cartridges, and 25,000 machetes.[51] Soon the mercenary enterprise began to function.

Former army general Fausto Caamaño, assisted by Vladimir Cecén, a former colonel from Yugoslavia, directed the organization and operations of the Foreign Legion. Navy Colonel Ernesto Vega Pagán was in charge of recruiting and training the mercenaries. In building the force, Trujillo received support from Spain's Generalissimo Franco, and Spanish personnel, mostly former officers from the Blue Division that had fought during World War II with the German army, helped with hiring and training the mercenaries.

Although Trujillo's goal was to hire three thousand men, only twelve hundred applied, according to the Spanish navy special envoy.[52] And many of those who did enlist complained that their recruiters had deceived them, including a group of Greeks who claimed that a "sharp Greek citizen who told them a lot of lies about the Dominican Republic" had misled them, including the possibility to move to the United States after two years of living and working in the Dominican Republic. Others signed up for farm or factory work and expected a salary of at least $300.00 pesos at month. Instead, they received $165.00 upon signing the contract, and $60.00 per month of service. Some officers, however, received salaries of up to $1,500 pesos, a sum that surpassed the salary of many Dominican employees in high positions.[53]

Harry M. Lofton, second secretary of the U.S. embassy in Ciudad Trujillo, who visited these soldiers of fortune in their compound, offered vivid details of the mercenaries' experiences in the Dominican Republic. According to one of his reports, to discipline the mercenaries, the commanders sent them to the Dominican naval base at Las Calderas for two days, then "to La Victoria prison for fifteen days, then to the training camp of Constanza."[54] In Constanza the mercenaries were organized into a battalion, and four companies of about eighty men each composed the battalion. They appeared to be in good health and were well dressed in clean khaki uniforms, but dissatisfaction with the food, what was "good only for the black people who live in this country," the lack of freedom, and other grievances about the living conditions gradually transmuted the discontent into animosity and disaffection. Disturbed by the regime's policy of killing civilians and consistent with their own un-restricted lifestyle, some mercenaries disobeyed orders. Disgruntled and mutinous, others attempted to organize protests. Consequently, many of them ended their lives in Dominican prisons.[55] Few managed to leave the country; others tried and failed or were killed when they attempted to flee the country. Thus, the presence of mercenaries in the Dominican Republic added another dimension to Trujillo's militarism and added to the already tense political situation.

In the end, however, the hiring of mercenaries paid off for the dictator. In June 1959, when Dominican exiles launched an invasion to overthrow Trujillo, the event served to test the soldiers' ability and readiness in the battlefield. When it appeared that the soldiers were not perform-ing adequately, the authorities called the mercenaries into action.[56] The combination of mercenaries and the army forces led to the defeat of the invaders in areas of the provinces of La Vega and Puerto Plata known as Constanza, Maimon, and Estero Hondo.

The Militias
To counterbalance the presence of the mercenaries and to extend mili-tarization to all segments of the adult population, the regime organized native militias, including a female branch called Feminine Anticommu-nist Foreign Legion. This group appeared to have a symbolic role of moral support; the real militia was made up of six battalions and about 2,000 Dominican men.[57] It included the 50 navy frogmen dressed in black uniforms who had received special training to combat insurgency. Similar to the mercenaries, the militias responded in moments of crisis.

To supplement the paramilitary front, Trujillo's brother Petán orga-nized Los Cocuyos de la Cordillera (Lightning Bugs of the Mountain Range) and presented them as a symbol of loyalty to his brother. This group included peasants and urban workers, and claimed to represent the citizen-soldiers ready to defend the fatherland.

Los Jinetes del Este (Riders of the East) sprang from the association of veterans led by one of Trujillo's henchmen, Felix Bernardino, and retired officers loyal to the dictator. Some landowners and ranchers also joined the Jinetes, whose self-defined mission was to patrol the countryside on horses to detect and prevent infiltration by anti-Trujillistas from out-side the country. The militias, although essentially civilian, were closely connected to the army. The close contact between ordinary citizens and

the officer corps through the rituals of drill and military training provided opportunities to impart the military ethos of discipline and blind
obedience to another segment of the population.

Altogether the paramilitary groups, which also included Los Mili-
cianos and Los Macheteros de la Frontera (Machete Men of the Border),
added approximately 5,000 troops to the republic's military strength.

Combining militarization and repression, Trujillo was able to paralyze
every form of resistance. A U.S. government report at the time noted that
the Dominican armed forces were capable of protecting the government
against any "conceivable combination of enemies in the Caribbean" and
maintaining order against internal opposition.[58]

The Pageantry Force

Trujillo's plan for the militarization of society stretched to the University
of Santo Domingo. At the suggestion of Dr. Enrique Aybar, the dean of
the dental school, La Guardia Universitaria President Trujillo was organized early in 1937. Ideal for extending military culture to society, the
organization from its inception had clear paramilitary mandates to fulfill.
On May 2, 1937, Trujillo presented the flag of the army to soldiers during
a public meeting at the general headquarters of the army in which university students were well represented. Delivering an ideological speech,
the dictator highlighted the political action and common purpose that
existed between the military and university students: "An exceptional
circumstance has given this act an extraordinary significance. Together
with you, soldiers, to receive the flag that will serve as their insignia, are
the students that compose La Guardia Universitaria, organized under
the inspiration of my government, and recognized for its semi-military
character, in the interest of binding the highest academic center of the
country to the institution which more effectively is serving the nation to
readjust the integral functioning of the government."[59] As the banner of
the organization, the flag of La Guardia Universitaria reflected the ideological meaning of its existence and the political interrelation between
the dictatorship and the students: the flag showed Trujillo's insignia and
the University emblem in the middle of four stars.[60]

In supporting the organization, Trujillo sought to bridge the "conservative force represented by the army and the intellectual (the liberal)
force represented by the students" in order to develop a mutual understanding "between the barracks and the university, centers that shared
the mission of training the Dominican youth to defend the fatherland."[61]

This was a way to offer the students a sense of belonging by participating in a great cause: the defense of the country. Since university student organizations in Latin America had been regarded as a breeding ground for revolutionary activities, by offering personal satisfaction and a feeling of camaraderie between soldiers and students, Trujillo prevented student revolts and neutralized their revolutionary impulse. In addition, La Guardia Universitaria served as a vehicle of political control within the academic community and a channel to guarantee loyalty to the regime.

Directed to emulate the army's managerial methods within a fascist framework, the organization, which was led by a board of directors, consisted of professors and students. The president of the board had a military title: commandant. His immediate subalterns were called auxiliary officers. The members of the board were elected by the general assembly of the Guardia Universitaria, but the chief of the army had to approve their appointments and some of the organization's activities.[62]

The first president was Homero Henríquez and the vice president was Adolfo Bonetti Burgos, the first Dominican and highest ranked diplomat to the Third Reich. La Guardia Universitaria was not only a fascist organization but an elite group who dressed in elegant uniforms and participated in important military parades. As described by one of the first members of the organization, the uniforms were of an "aristocratic cut," with a design drawn from an Italian model. These uniforms attracted the attention of the public. The students were very proud when they wore the "dark navy blue jacket; wool blend ivory color pants with blue braids on the sides; golden bottoms on the chest and the sleeves with the national emblem; patent leather shoes; blue caps with golden ornamentation and the national emblem on the front; white shirts and black ties."[63] Although in theory there were no restrictions on enrollment, to some extent the participation was limited to young men and women who could afford the expensive dress of the organization and who had a clear record of no anti-Trujillista involvement.

To incorporate military attitudes and values into La Guardia Universitaria, leaders stressed the importance of discipline in the organization, and all members received military instruction. The training included calisthenics, marches, military formation, and the obligatory military salute, which consisted of the raising of the right hand to the forehead. The students had to behave according to the army's code of courteous behavior and protocol. When participating in parades, rallies, and other public activities, an active military officer commanded the group.[64]

Although militaristic and political goals were at the center of the organization, during the first meeting with the students Aybar noted that the organization had been created to accompany President Trujillo during his journeys of "observation and studies across the country." Trujillo wanted to put the students in direct contact with the geography, the beauty, and problems of each region.[65] Trujillo, who considered the knowledge of national geography as an essential part of the Dominican-ización project, invited a group of university students to go along with him and 100 soldiers and 50 officers to visit the area along the border with Haiti on August 3, 1937.[66] The trip offered an ideal setting for establishing close contact between soldiers and students, joining arms and academics in symbolic expression of congeniality and loyalty toward Trujillo.

Considering that part of the mission of the Guardia Universitaria was "to bring to the university the meaning of the political moment and to contribute to the splendor of the university,"[67] the leaders used the students for the propagation of the Trujillista ideology framed in an academic fashion.

In 1940 the Guardia Universitaria showed its complete ideological identification with the regime when it became a political party: the Trujillista Party. Membership was beyond the university campus; it had reached a national level. Under the leadership of Isabel Mayer and Milady Felix de L'Official, women were very active in the party. But those who wanted to be members of the organization had to go through a process of "purification" to determine their political honesty and their loyalty to El Jefe.[68] The organization, embodying the combination of the academic with the military to perfect society, also had a civic mission: to serve as a model.

Although in some instances university students took a firm position against the dictator, particularly after 1959 when underground cells co-ordinated massive resistance, in general during the era of Trujillo Dominican students did not denounce the dictatorship, which often happens in Latin America where students frequently are at the forefront of opposition to oppressive regimes. On the contrary, with the salute, flag, marches, parades, uniforms, and other military symbols, the government linked the university students with the dictatorship, promoting the regime's ideology by selecting a group of young people to savor honor, glory, and the mystique of pageantry. But all the paramilitary forces represented the most concrete evidence and visible symbols of the insertion of the martial spirit and military culture in society during the Trujillo regime.

EPILOGUE

The End of Trujillo's Dictatorship and the

Transcendence of Military Culture in Society

Trujillo's militaristic policy had a tremendous impact in the Dominican Republic. The resources invested to strengthen the armed forces resulted in the Dominican Republic's becoming a powerful military force in the Caribbean. Even though Trujillo's weapons, with the exception of those used during the Haitian massacre, were not used against any other country, his military establishment drew international attention and aroused fear and speculation that the dictator could organize sufficient military might to attack Caribbean and Central American countries. Internally, Trujillo's military establishment served to control and militarize society, to satisfy Trujillo's whims, and to convert the Dominican Republic into the most repressive state in the region at the end of 1950s.

The violent nature of his rule aroused anxiety, fear, and suspicion among Dominicans to the extent that the Dominican psychiatrist Antonio Zaglul diagnosed that by the middle of the 1970s, many Dominicans were suffering from some form of paranoia. Zaglul traced Dominicans' sense of systematic persecution and their insecurity back to the colonial period, as well as to the precarious political life from independence to the U.S. occupation, but he concluded that the psychological traumas the Dominican people suffered under Trujillo's militaristic state were the real cause of Dominicans' mental anguish.[1]

Elsewhere in Latin America in the late 1950s, internal resistance toppled several authoritarian rulers: Perón of Argentina was forced out of power in 1955; Gustavo Rojas Pinilla of Colombia in 1957; and Marcos Pérez Jiménez of Venezuela in 1958. These and other dramatic events encouraged Dominicans to challenge Trujillo's regime. Crucial to these developments was the triumph of Fidel Castro in Cuba. While visiting Venezuela in early 1959, Castro said that the liberation movement would not stop in Cuba. He told cheering crowds in Caracas, "Everywhere I hear the chant, 'Trujillo next!' "[2]

Another important factor was the election in 1959 of Rómulo Betancourt as president of Venezuela. Personally and ideologically, Betancourt detested the Dominican dictator, and like Castro he wanted to bring Trujillo down. Thus, Venezuela and Cuba, as well as Costa Rica, Guatemala, and Puerto Rico, welcomed Dominican exiles and supported the Dominican struggle against the dictator.

The Latin American anti-Trujillista campaign coincided with a period during which the United States turned a cold shoulder toward dictators. For many policymakers in Washington, it seemed time for the remaining antidemocratic rulers to go as well. Ironically, Castro was first on the U.S. list of dictators marked for removal. To accomplish their goal, U.S. officials realized that they could not strike effectively at Castro while Trujillo was still in power. In addition, afraid that the brutalities of Trujillo would lead to a communist takeover like the one in Cuba, the Eisenhower and Kennedy administrations sought to ease Trujillo out of power. Initially they attempted to convince him to step down, but eventually they resorted to ordering the CIA to supply weapons and other means to those who conspired against the dictator.[3]

Meanwhile, despite widespread militarization, tighter internal security measures—including continuous waves of arrests and incarcerations—repression and weapons could not impede the political awakening of the people. The continued tortures and murders of hundreds of people, including military men, led to several military conspiracies. These conspiracies show that the political and military sectors were not always working together toward the common goal of keeping Trujillo in power. Certainly most of the time the armed forces obeyed Trujillo's orders, but there were many instances, as demonstrated in the conspiracies in 1930s and 1940s, when enlisted men and officers refused to abide by Trujillo's rule and consequently paid with their lives. Embodying the military discontent of the 1950s, in April 1959 Air Force Captain Juan de Dios Ventura Simó flew his Vampire jet to Puerto Rico and requested political asylum, leaving his wife and children in the Dominican Republic. From Puerto Rico, he went to Venezuela and joined other exiles.

By the time of Ventura Simó's defection, Latin American support and the U.S. position on dictators encouraged exiled Dominicans to organize their forces against Trujillo's government. In June 1959 a group of Dominican exiles, assisted by Cuban military commanders who had fought with Castro in Sierra Maestra and revolutionaries from other Latin American countries, landed in the northern part of the country. Permeated by military culture, out of fear, loyalty toward Trujillo, or ignorance, the local population did not support the rebels. Surrounded by overwhelming air and ground forces, the insurgents suffered a devastating defeat. Almost all perished in the areas of Maimón, Constanza, and Estero Hondo. One of the survivors was Ventura Simó, who had come with the rebels to fight against Trujillo.

Upon landing at Constanza, he was immediately taken prisoner and used as a tool by the regime. Trujillo, who had carefully nurtured the officer corps, could not stand the idea that they could turn against him. Claiming that Ventura Simó was not a defector but a double agent, the dictator mounted a charade, decorating and promoting Ventura Simó to lieutenant colonel. At a cleverly conceived meeting, Ventura Simó was introduced to members of the diplomatic corps, including the U.S. ambassador, Joseph Farland. Photographers were on hand to capture the ambassador shaking hands with Ventura Simó. Farland, realizing that Trujillo had used him, sent a protest to the Dominican secretary of state and to the head of foreign delegations established in the Dominican Republic. The photo, distributed broadly, insinuated that in fact Ventura was a double agent. Once Trujillo had achieved his propaganda goals, Ventura Simó was tortured and killed in one of the prisons and then put a plane, which crashed at sea.[4] Trujillo used Ventura Simó's death and the failure of the rebels to send a message: after twenty-nine years, no one could displace him from power.

Although the insurgents suffered defeat, their actions were different from earlier attempts to overthrow the dictatorship. The invasion caused substantial damage to the regime and served as a political catalyst among professionals, college students, and young people in general, motivating them to adopt a militant attitude against the dictatorship. Soon after, several political groups joined forces against Trujillo, provoking a chain reaction of events that weakened the regime and ultimately caused its disintegration.

Two months after the failure of the invasion, repulsed by the barbaric tortures inflicted upon Ventura Simó and other combatants, a military plot unfolded at San Isidro Air Base. Captain Miguel Cabrejas and Sergeant Delmonte y Consuegra, the leaders of the conspiracy, attempted to dismantle the air force by incapacitating the airplanes. As in the past, Trujillo knew about the plot well in advance and about fifty participants were severely tortured and then killed.[5]

Although this conspiracy failed, tensions continued to mount. In January 1960 the chain reaction reached the Catholic Church. Its hierarchy, which had been blessing and praising the dictator for thirty years, issued a pastoral letter, read in churches throughout the country, condemning the excesses of oppression and requesting respect for human rights. (Trujillo thus found himself in the situation of other Latin American dictators. Pastoral letters had preceded the downfall of Pérez Jiménez, Perón, and Rojas Pinilla.) Trujillo responded by launching a campaign to discredit clergymen and nuns and issuing an order for the arrest of all bishops. Two bishops, Tomas Reilly of San Juan of la Maguana and Francisco Panal of La Vega, were harassed and accused of being terrorists. As the dictatorship became increasingly harsh and the pressure against the church escalated, the people gradually turned against the dictator.[6]

A clandestine political organization, the 14th of June Movement, emerged gradually from the underground as a nuclear organization aimed at putting an end to the dictatorship. Strongly supported by the upper and middle classes, the faction included members such as Patria, Minerva, and María Teresa Mirabal, the convent-educated sisters who perished in their struggle against Trujillo. Known by their code name Las Mariposas (the butterflies), they played a key role in organizing the 14th of June Movement and energized the resistance against the regime. For their political activism, along with Rufino de la Cruz, who was driving their car, they were murdered on November 25, 1960. The killing took place on a mountain road while they were returning home from visiting Minerva's husband, Manuel Tavárez Justo, and María Teresa's husband, Leandro Guzmán, who were jailed in Puerto Plata. Like the Mirabals, many other men and women risked their lives to liberate the country from the oppressive regime.

As the resistance increased, the dictatorship vigorously attacked not only those who conspired against the system but ordinary people likewise were jailed or killed. Consequently, the reprisals strengthened the opposition and diminished the level of support that the regime had been receiving from people and institutions for three decades.

At this critical moment, in the middle of the crisis, Trujillo made a dramatic mistake by engineering an assassination attempt against Betancourt, the newly elected president of Venezuela. On June 17, 1960, Betancourt's car blew up in Caracas. The president suffered severe burns on his body, particularly on his hands. As a result, the Inter-American Peace Commission indicted the Dominican regime for several violations of human rights, and the OAS imposed economic sanctions and an arms embargo.[7]

Now the political battle turned into an economic crisis. In addition to the embargo, three years of drought, large expenditures in European arms markets, and the low world price of sugar and other main export commodities began to affect the Dominican economy. After enjoying a strong balance of payments for more than twenty years, the government almost ran out of cash, and the country's international reserve drained quickly. To protect their assets, Trujillo's relatives and friends transferred their savings to foreign banks.[8] To intensify the crisis and increase the pressure, the Kennedy administration deprived the country of $22 million, which the United States had retained from sugar transactions.

Under national and international pressure, Trujillo made some gestures toward liberalizing his policies. President Héctor Trujillo resigned and Joaquín Balaguer succeeded him. Ramfis Trujillo stepped down as chief of staff and left for Europe. However, as tension with the United States mounted, Trujillo initiated a campaign attacking "Yankee Imperialism" over Radio Caribe, a government-owned radio station. Soon after, he decided to ally the Dominican Republic with the Soviet Union and even tried to gain Cuba's support by adopting a conciliatory attitude toward Castro. Considering Trujillo's move as dubious, the Soviet Union rejected the offer to sign a non-aggression pact with the Dominican Republic. Trujillo's political decline was well underway.

As the dictator approached the end of his regime, the government's political difficulties reached the hierarchy of the military. In 1961 several high-ranking officers conspired with civilians to end the oppression. The time of change and struggle had begun.

The symbiosis between the military and the regime and between civilians and the military that Trujillo had tried so hard to establish began to unravel. The leaders of the final conspiracy included three army officers with close connections to the dictator: General Román Fernandez, secretary of state of the armed forces and husband of Trujillo's niece, Mirella García; Lieutenant Amado García Guerrero of the military corps, who worked for Trujillo in the National Palace; and former army general Juan Tomás Díaz, a friend of Trujillo's since childhood. Each of them, as well as their civilian co-conspirators, had benefited from the regime but also had suffered under Trujillo. For example, Román Fernandez had been publicly humiliated by Trujillo on several occasions. García was forced to break an engagement because his girlfriend's brother was in the opposition. It is said that as proof of his loyalty, García's superiors ordered him to fire a shot at someone. He did not know, but that person was his former girlfriend's brother. Since that night he had a mission: to kill Trujillo. Díaz's bitterness stemmed from degradation. He had lost his rank because some of his relatives had joined the opposition. One of the civilian conspirators, Antonio de la Maza, acted in retaliation for the death of his brother Octavio de la Maza, who lost his life during the Galíndez incident.[9]

Against great odds, and together with Luis Amiama, Modesto Díaz, Antonio Imbert Barreras, Manuel Tunti Cáceres, Pedro Livio Cedeño, Salvador Estrella Sadhalá, Huáscar Tejada, Roberto Pastoriza, and others who had also been victimized by Trujillo, they conceived a plan to end the dictatorship. At the end, the U.S. also played a role in coordinating a liaison between military and civilian plotters who directly participated in the killing of Trujillo.

On May 30 they ambushed Trujillo, who was traveling in a car driven by his chauffeur, Zacarías de la Cruz. As reported by de la Cruz from his hospital bed, when he realized that Trujillo was injured he wanted to turn back, but the dictator refused and gave his last order: "Stop. I am wounded. We have to fight."[10] Revolver in hand, Trujillo left the car and was killed during an intense firefight. (This version of Trujillo's last moment is a controversial subject. Many believe that Trujillo did not have time to fight back. Others perceive the story as part of the myth surrounding Trujillo.)[11]

In the aftermath of Trujillo's death, Ramfis Trujillo returned home from Paris, took control of the armed forces, and led the investigation into his father's assassination. Within days all the conspirators, except Amiama and Imbert, who found refuge in a friend's house, suffered horrendous torture or were killed.

Meanwhile, Balaguer, allowing the exiles to return, political parties to organize, and the press to have free expressions, began to lead the country gradually toward democracy. However, dismantling the dictatorship was a difficult and painful process. Amid unrest, chaos, and repression, thousands of lives were lost and many properties were destroyed. In November two of Trujillo's brothers, Hector and Petán, together with diehard Trujillista officers, attempted a swift coup against Balaguer. In response, another group of officers, supported by the political parties, rebelled against the Trujillos. Pressure against the Trujillos escalated. With 1,800 Marines aboard eight vessels three miles off the Dominican coast, the U.S. navy threatened to intervene if the Trujillos managed to take over. Consequently, by the end of the month, Héctor, Petán, Ramfis, and most of the Trujillo family had gone into exile.

After the Trujillos left the old network collapsed, shaking the sociopolitical fabric of the nation. The military, like society in general, went through an agonizing period of definition and redefinition. Officers and enlisted men found themselves in an untenable position. Formed, trained, and educated to maintain the dictatorship, they were not prepared for drastic political change.

Responding to intense political pressure during the crisis that tore the Dominican Republic in two over a period of four years (1961–65), reform-minded officers known as the Constitutionalists clashed with far-right conservative comrades known as the Loyalists. In the midst of the ensuing chaos, civilian authorities had a difficult task in managing the transition from dictatorship to democracy. After thirty-one years of subjugation, it was particularly complicated to democratize the armed forces. Trujillo, the only leader many soldiers had ever known, had offered them a cushion of security that many wished to maintain. They continued to function within the Trujillista scheme, maintaining many of the values, methods, and procedures of the dictatorship.

In the meantime, the country slowly continued its move toward democracy. Trying to stay in power, Balaguer compromised with the opposition and created and headed a new government composed of seven members. But because of his identification with Trujillo's regime, he was forced to resign and went into exile. Amiama and Imbert became members of the council that governed the country until the democratic election of Juan Bosch in December 1962.

Elections alone did not deliver democracy. Struggling to establish a democratic system, the nation lived in chaos for the next four years. Massive rioting, constitutional changes, civil-military confrontations, and the U.S. intervention of April 1965 left the Dominican people in despair. However, since 1966, Dominicans have exercised the right to vote freely every four years. Democratic laws have been restored and many reforms have been incorporated into the political system. Although the Dominican Republic has seen significant changes since Trujillo's assassination, even by the end of 2002 the military culture in society had endured.

Under Trujillo's regime a whole generation came of age lacking a clear understanding of freedom and democracy. These Dominicans were conditioned to think and act in accordance with Trujillo's militaristic rhetoric. Consequently the military became, perhaps, the most solidly entrenched institution forged by Trujillo. Four decades after Trujillo's death the organization basically still functioned according to the dictator's plan. Specifically, nepotism and favoritism continued to shadow recruitment and promotion, albeit less frequently; soldiers and policemen continued abusing civilians.

The durability of this dictatorial influence can be partly explained by Trujillo's method of using the military institution as a tool for rewarding and providing military men with upward social mobility, prestige, and authority in state and society. Within this framework, Trujillo expanded the size of the armed forces and created paramilitary units, which absorbed a significant portion of the male population.

Naturally, the more numerous they were, the more they influenced and altered society. People from all social levels were affected in one way or another by Trujillo's military policy. For many Dominican men, the military was an occupation, a way to make an often very good living. Thus, many families depended on the Jefe's military establishment, and the bigger it got, more Dominicans were prompted to cooperate with the regime.

In this way, the dictator framed the political participation of the military into a system of unconditional loyalty toward his regime. Trujillo neutralized the military's potential for political action against him. This arrangement was crucial to Trujillo's political survival and a fundamental departure from previous administrations. In the past, military men deposed presidents. Trujillo's military never deposed him, at least not until the very end.

The military became a pivotal force in the development and consolidation of the middle class, a process that began during the U.S. occupation. In addition, many members of the elite, who at first refused to work for Trujillo, became his prominent advisors and servants. Some of them became members of Trujillo's officer corps. Thus, the elite eventually returned to occupy leading positions in the military corps, but no longer as a dominant or separated class. Poor young men were also eligible for promotion to the officer corps. In general, under Trujillo military personnel became part of the elite group possessing economic power and social prestige, although the dictator controlled that power.

One of the most intriguing aspects of Trujillo's regime was the existence of a powerless military institution within an overly militarized state. Even in connection with military administration, including deployment of forces and promotion of personnel, Trujillo retained full control. For thirty-one Trujillo dictated the terms of his relationship with the forces.

By introducing sweeping changes in the allocation of decision-making authority, Trujillo modeled the functioning of civil society on the military principles of obedience and discipline, while simultaneously commissioning soldiers as his agents in almost all matters concerning the political system.

Concomitantly, he used the army's manpower to fight in the political arena as if it were a battleground. For good reason, the people feared the military. And fear mixed with pageantry and ideology acted as a catalyst to promote the martial spirit of the military to citizens.

The military culture in society endured beyond Trujillo's death. In the late 1970s a Dominican social worker who lived in the United States returned to her country and worked for the government from 1978 to 1982. One day she asked a low-ranking officer to run a bureaucratic errand for her. Another employee who overheard what she told the officer advised her: "Next time when you need the service of the military personnel, you do not say *por favor* [please]; you just give them an order." Then, as an indication of the influence of the military culture, he added, "In this society, we are accustomed to obey orders."[12]

The incident clearly manifested the influence of military culture in society that began to evolve from colonial times and was strongly developed throughout the national period, particularly during the era of Trujillo. Only gradually after Trujillo's death did the military begin to join the people in chanting, "Democracia y libertad!"

APPENDIX

Trujillo's letter of application to the Dominican
Constabulary Guard organized by the U.S. Marines

Santo Domingo Diciembre 9 de 1918.

Señor

C. F. Williams
Coronel Comandante, G. N. D.,
Ciudad.

Señor:

El que suscribe, por su digno órgano, solicita un puesto de Oficial en la honrosa institución de la Guardia Nacional Dominicana.

Con perdón de la molestia, debo significarle, que no poseo vicios de tomar bebidas alcohólicas ni de fumar y que no he sido sometido a Tribunales ni siguiera para asuntos de simple Policía.

En mi pueblo natal, San Cristóbal, a 30 kilómetros de esta Ciudad, he pertenecido y pertenezco a la primera Sociedad y mi edad es de 27 años de estado casado.

En San Cristóbal pueden dar testimonio de mis costumbres y maneras de conducirme, personas honorables y de esta Capital, los Señores Rafael A. Perdomo, Juez de Instrucción de la 1ª. Circunscripción, Eugenio A. Alvárez, Secretario del Juzgado de la. Instancia y Licenciado Armando Rodríguez, Consultor Jurídico de la Secretaría de Estado de Justicia é Instrucción Pública.

Le saluda atentamente.
(Fdo) RAFAEL L. TRUJILLO

Santo Domingo, December 9, 1918

Colonel C. F. Williams
Commanding Officer, D.C.G.
Ciudad

Colonel Williams:

I respectfully request a commission in the Dominican Constabulary Guard, worthy institution you command.

I would like to state that I do not drink or smoke and have never been arrested even for minor infractons of the law.

I am married, 27 years old, and belong to one of the best families of my home town, San Cristobal, which is 30 kilometers from the city.

Honorable persons from my home town can vouch for my character. Here you may contact Judge Rafael A. Perdoma, Mr. Eugenio A. Alvarez, Secretary of the Lower Court and Lic. Armando Rodriguez, Legal Adviser to the Department of Justice and Education.

Sincerely yours,
Rafael L. Trujillo

As reproduced in Ernesto Vega Pagan, *Military Biography of Generalissimo Rafael L. Trujillo Molina, Commander in Chief of the Armed Forces*, translated by Ida Espaillat. (Ciudad: Editorial Atenas, 1956), p. 23. Courtesy Archivo General de la Nación.

Medical Examination report of Trujillo

Medical examination report of Trujillo when he applied to La Guardia on December 18, 1918. Courtesy Archivo General de la Nación.

A CHRONOLOGY

1492 Christopher Columbus lands on the island he called La Española on December 5.

1492 Establishment of the Fuerte de la Navidad, first European settlement in the Americas, on December 25.

1496 Foundation of the city of Santo Domingo. It became the capital and the center for the Spanish conquest of the American continent.

1516 African slaves begin to arrive in large numbers in the island.

1538 Santo Tomás de Aquino, the first university in the western hemisphere, is established in Santo Domingo.

1697 Spain cedes the western third of Hispaniola to France in the Treaty of Ryswick.

1795 France gains control over the entire island in the Treaty of Basel.

1801 Toussaint Louverture takes command of the island.

1802 France gains control of the eastern part of Hispaniola.

1804 Haiti declares its independence from France. Jean Jacques Dessalines becomes the first president.

1805 Dessalines enters the former Spanish colony with his troops.

1809 Spain regains control of the eastern part of Hispaniola.

1821 Núñez de Cáceres pronounces independence from Spain.

1822 Haiti begins its twenty-two-year occupation of the eastern part of Hispaniola.

1838 Juan Pablo Duarte organizes La Trinitaria.

1844 The Dominican Republic gains independence from Haiti.

1861 The republic again becomes a Spanish colony.

1863 War of Restoration against Spain begins.

1865 End of the Spanish annexation.

1879 The Blue Party supports Gregorio Luperón for president.

1880 Fernando Meriño wins the presidential election.

1882 Ulises Heureaux is elected president.

1891 Rafael Leonidas Trujillo Molina is born in San Cristóbal on October 24.

1899 Heureaux is killed.

1905 Modus Vivendi is signed between the Dominican Republic and United States.

1906 Ramón Cáceres becomes president.

1907 Cáceres signs the second Modus Vivendi with the United States. Trujillo becomes a telegraph operator.

1911 Cáceres is assassinated.

1913 Aminta Ledesma becomes Trujillo's first wife.

1915 Flor de Oro, Trujillo's first child, is born in San Cristóbal.

1916 Trujillo becomes a security guard at the Boca Chica sugar mill.

1916 The U.S. Marine Corps occupies the Dominican Republic on November 29.

1917 U.S. forces create the Dominican constabulary guard known as La Guardia on April 7.

1918 Trujillo applies for a commission in the constabulary guard on December 9.

1919 Trujillo receives his appointment as second lieutenant of the Dominican constabulary guard on December 18.

1920 Lieutenant Trujillo is sent to the east region, the focus of resistance to the U.S. occupation.

1921 Trujillo confronts the armed guerrillas in La Noria in January. He enters the military academy of Haina in August.

1922 The Hughes-Peynado plan of evacuation of the U.S. troops includes the formation of a provisional government headed by Juan Bautista Vicini Burgos.

1924 The Marines depart. Horacio Vásquez is elected president.

1925 Trujillo replaces Colonel Buenaventura Cabral as commander of the Dominican National Police. He divorces Aminta Ledesma.

1926 Creation of *La revista militar*.

1927 Trujillo is promoted to brigadier general. He marries Bienvenida Ricart.

1928 Club Unión rejects Trujillo's membership application. Creation of the military aviation.

1929 Mission Dawes visits the country from April 2 to April 23. Rafael L. Trujillo Martínez (Ramfis) is born on June 5.

1930 Beginning of the era of Trujillo.
February 23. Trujillo joins forces with the movement against President Horacio Vásquez.
February 28. President Vásquez submits his resignation.
May 16. Trujillo becomes president and Rafael Estrella Ureña becomes vice president.
June 14. Military actions against General Cipriano Bencosme. He dies five months later.
June 1. Assassination of Virgilio Martínez Reyna and his wife Altagracia Almánzar.
August 16. Inaugural ceremonies of Trujillo's administration.
September 3. Hurricane San Zenón devastates Santo Domingo, the capital.
September 5. Martial law is imposed over the country.

1931 April 4. The government is transferred to Santiago.
June 20. Government troops kill Desiderio Arias.
August 16. Party of General Trujillo is formed.
August 25. Estrella Ureña leaves the country.
October 23. Declaration of the Emergency Law.
December 8. Beginning of military deployment across the country.
December 13. Three Dominican military pilots, Félix Miranda, Julio E. Tejada, and Aníbal Vallejo, graduate in Cuba. Earlier the same year Enrique Valverde obtains his diploma in the United States as a military aviator.

1932 January 12. Opening of the first military colony in El Valle, Azua.
March 11. Party General Trujillo changes its name to Partido Dominicano.
November 8. Trujillo is elected president of the Club Unión.
November 11. The Dominican Congress declares Trujillo Benefactor of the Fatherland.
November 17. First distribution of *La cartilla cívica*.
December 18. First *revista cívica* in Rio Verde, La Vega.

1933 May 8. Soldiers arrest General Leoncio Blanco and his group of conspirators.
May 26. The Congress honors Trujillo with the title of Generalissimo of the armed forces.

October 2. Congress passes a law declaring a group of exiles traitors to the nation and their properties are confiscated.
October 18. Trujillo meets Haitian President Stenio Vicent in the northern Dominican-Haitian border.

1934   May. Leoncio Blanco is killed in prison.
June 4. Beginning of land distribution to peasants.
June 10. Trujillo father dies.
July 10. Trujillo announces the enactment of the Tobacco Law.
October 18. The University of Santo Domingo grants Trujillo an honorary doctorate.
December 4. Military and civic reserves pay homage to Trujillo in the Airport Miraflores in Santo Domingo.

1935   February 19. Congress passes a new divorce law, which grants divorce to childless couples after five years of marriage.
April 4. Amadeo Barletta is arrested. A month later he is sentenced to two years in prison.
May 29. Barletta is released from prison.
September 30. Trujillo marries María Martínez, his third wife.

1936   January 8. Santo Domingo is renamed Ciudad Trujillo.
February 22. Inauguration of George Washington Avenue in Ciudad Trujillo.
March 8. Trujillo begins a three-day visit to Haiti.
April 13. President Stenio Vicent of Haiti arrives in Ciudad Trujillo.
April 14. Ratification of new boundary treaty signed with Haiti.
September 21. The highest mountain of the island is named Pico Trujillo.
October 22. Congress declares October 24 a national holiday to celebrate Trujillo's birthday.

1937   March 4. Organization of the Guardia Universitaria.
May 13. Active and former military men pay their respect to Trujillo at the National Palace.
October 2. The Haitian massacre begins.
November 11. To participate in the Pan-American flight Pro-Faro a Colón, three Cuban airplanes land in Ciudad Trujillo.
December 29. The Cuban pilots and mechanics of the Pan-American flight die in Cali, Colombia.

1938 January 31. Dominican—Haitian Agreement signed in
Washington. The Dominican Republic will pay $750.000 to
compensate victims of the Haitian massacre.
July 9. At the Evian Conference, France, the Dominican
republic offers to accept European refugees.
August 16. Jacinto Peynado and Manuel de Jesús Troncoso de
la Concha take the oath as president and vice president of the
republic, respectively.
August 26. Nine-year-old Ramfis Trujillo receives the rank of
brigadier general.
October 14. Inauguration of El Marion.
December 22. Congress approves the construction of the naval
base Las Calderas.
December 28. Taxes of $500.00 imposed on non-Caucasian
immigrants.

1939 February 10. Inauguration of U.S. Marine Corps Avenue.
April 4. Dominican Republic recognizes the government of
Francisco Franco.
March 14. Trujillo and President Vicent travel along the
International Highway.
June 6. Congress declares June 30 Teacher Day.
June 10. Trujillo's daughter Angelita is born in Paris.
June 30. Trujillo departs for his first trip abroad. He visits the
United States and Europe.
July 9. Trujillo is a guest at the U.S. Naval Academy.
July 10. Trujillo visits the naval base at Quantico.
July 11. President Roosevelt receives Trujillo at the White
House. Army Brigadier General George C. Marshall offers a
reception in honor of Trujillo.
August 2. Trujillo leaves the United States for Europe.
October 21. The Dominican Republic declares its neutrality in
World War II.
October 28. Trujillo returns from abroad. Days later a
multitude of 35,000 persons parades to welcome him back.
November 7. Two hundred eighty eight Spanish refugees
arrive in Ciudad Trujillo.

1940 January 30. Agreement to establish Jewish refugees at the
agricultural colony of Sosúa.
February 19. First publication of *La Nación*.

February 23. Beginning of celebration to commemorate the tenth anniversary of the era of Trujillo.

February 26. Invited by the Marines, Trujillo goes to the Culebra Island to see military maneuvers.

March 7. President Peynado dies of complications from diabetes.

March 8. Troncoso de la Concha becomes president.

September 2. Trujillo departs for the United States.

September 24. Trujillo signs the Trujillo-Hull Treaty, which returns control of customs to the Dominican government.

October 14. Creation of the Trujillista Party organized by the Guardia Universitaria.

November 2. Trujillo receives the title of "Restorer of Financial Independence."

1941   April 1. The United States officially transfers customs to the Dominican government.

June 19. About seven thousand women gather in Ciudad Trujillo to pay tribute to Trujillo.

April 29. Trujillo's fifth trip to the United States.

August 4. Creation of the National Symphony Orchestra.

September 4. Trujillo meets President Lescot of Haiti in Elías Piña.

October 1. The first five hundred literacy schools for adults begin to function.

October 26. Opening of the Reserve Bank.

November 16. General José Estrella and former vice president Estrella Ureña are accused of participating in the murder of Virgilio Martínez Reyna and his wife.

November 21. Trujillo departs for the United States.

December 12. Trujillo declares Dominican Republic support for United States in World War II.

1942   January 20. Workers strike at the sugar fields in La Romana and San Pedro de Macorís.

May 3. German submarines sink the ship *San Rafael*.

May 16. Trujillo is elected for the third time. Dominican women exercise the right to vote for the first time.

May 19. Isabel Mayer, first woman to serve in Congress, is elected as representative of the Montecristi province.

May 21. The ship *Presidente Trujillo* is sank by German submarines.

June 16. The schooner *Nueva Altagracia* is sunk by German submarines.

June 23. Congress declares a state of emergency.

June 25. The first Sunday of June is declared Father's Day.

August 16. Trujillo takes the oath of president for the third time.

August 17. Trujillo receives an honorary doctorate from the University of Pittsburgh.

December 1. Rhadamés, Trujillo second son with María Martínez, is born.

1943   January 25. Agreement with the United States for the installation of Naval Mission.

February 27. Naval school opens at Las Calderas Naval Base.

April 4. Dominican legation in Washington is elevated to an embassy.

November 15. Trujillo requests a half million pesos from the senate to build the Ciudad Universitaria.

December 11. Accompanied by diplomats, Trujillo visits the northern border and the Mision Fronteriza.

1944   January 31. Construction of Ciudad Universitaria begins.

January 24. Miraflores airport is renamed General Andrews in honor of General Frank Maxwell Andrews.

February 27. Centenary celebrations to commemorate one hundred years of national independence.

March 4. Creation of the feminine branch of Partido Dominicano.

June 3. Ellis Briggs presents his credentials as U.S. ambassador to the Dominican Republic.

November 1. Nelson Rockefeller arrives in Ciudad Trujillo.

December 23. Creation of the bachelor degree in military sciences.

1945   March 8. Dominican Republic establishes diplomatic relations with the USSR.

June 6. Creation of the Banco Agrícola e Hipotecario.

September 24. Trujillo is proclaimed Liberator of the Workers.

October 18. Venezuela breaks its diplomatic relations with the Dominican Republic.

November 16. The Dominican government proposes to rename Dajabón as Roosevelt Province.

November 17. The government requests that U.S. sugar mills denounce the communists.

December 28. The United States refuses to provide more weapons to Trujillo.

1946   January 7. Labor unions organize a strike in the sugar mills of San Pedro de Macorís and La Romana.

January 29. Creation of social security.

April 20. Inauguration of the Hospital Dr. William A. Morgan for workers.

June 6. The San Ignacio de Loyola agriculture school opens its doors in Dajabón.

June 14. Military uprising led by First Lieutenant Eugenio de Marchena fails.

June 15. Trujillo talks about political aperture and allows Dominicans and Cuban communists to have a meeting in Ciudad Trujillo. The Socialist Popular Party (PSP) is allowed to organize.

August 4. An earthquake causes severe damage across the country.

September 14. First public meeting of the PSP.

September 24. First National Congress of the Workers.

October 26. National persecution against labor unions and political leaders of the opposition.

November 29. Trujillo announces that exiles were organizing an invasion of the Dominican Republic.

1947   February 10. Beginning of the arms factory as the Hispaniola Corporation.

March 6. The Spanish Naval School ship *Juan Sebastián Elcano* begins a twelve-day visit to the Dominican Republic.

May 16. Trujillo becomes president for the fourth time.

July 21. The government pays off foreign debt.

July 23. Guatemala breaks diplomatic relations with the Dominican Republic.

August 17. Inauguration of the Ciudad Universitaria.

September 11. Congress approves obligatory military service.

September 30. Cayo Confites invasion.

October 2. Creation of the Marina de Guerra.

October 10. The Central Bank and the Dominican peso are created.

December 12. Congress denounces Presidents Arévalo, Betancourt, and Grau San Martin as enemies.

1948   April 14. First publication of the newspaper *El Caribe*.

May 8. Costa Rica breaks diplomatic relations with the Dominican Republic.

August 13. The Dominican government accuses Cuba of harboring the Cayo Confites expedition.

1949   June 19. Exiles attack by air the north coast of the Dominican Republic. The event known as the Luperón invasion is another failure similar to the Cayo Confites.

December 12. Trujillo requests power to declare war.

December 26. Congress authorizes Trujillo to declare war.

1950   February 2. Trujillo asks for the revocation of his power to declare war.

February 25. Five survivors of the Luperón invasion are pardoned and freed from prison.

August 6. Third census.

August 11. Aviation, Flights of Military Aircraft Agreement with the United States.

September 29. Separation of the air force from the army.

December 10. Assassination of Mauricio Báez in Cuba.

1951   February 20. Technical Cooperation Agreement with the United States.

June 11. Trujillo Code of Labor is promulgated.

December 12. Cuba and the Dominican Republic reestablish friendly relations.

1952   January 21. Beginning of construction of Basilica of Higuey to honor La Virgen de la Altagracia.

May 12. Fourteen members of the Cayo Confites are freed.

May 16. Héctor Trujillo is elected president of the republic.

August 10. Anastasio Somoza and his wife arrive in Ciudad Trujillo for the inauguration of Héctor Trujillo.

August 16. Héctor Trujillo takes the oath of president of the republic.

October 18. Obligatory Literacy Program for Adults begins to function.

December 3. Trujillo departs for the United States.

1953   January 5. Trujillo visits President Truman in the White
       House.
       March 6. Trujillo signs the Mutual Defense Agreement with
       the United States in Washington.
       March 6- President Eisenhower receives Trujillo in the White
       House.
       March 15. Trujillo returns to Ciudad Trujillo.
       March 16. Festivities across the country celebrate his return to
       the country.
       March 22. Inauguration of San Isidro Air Force Base.
       September 28. Ramfis receives the rank of major general.
       November 16. General Valin of France departs after visiting
       the Armería.

1954   March 31. Inauguration of the Agricultural and Industrial Fair
       La Paz de Trujillo in Santiago.
       May 14. The Congress declares 1955 as the "Year of the
       Benefactor."
       June 3. Trujillo arrives in Spain. Later he signs an agreement
       with Franco.
       June 16. Trujillo signs the Concordat agreement between the
       Holy See and the Dominican government in Rome.

1955   January 1. Beginning of celebrations of the Year of the
       Benefactor.
       January 7. Over seven hundred Spanish immigrants arrive.
       January 16. Trujillo announces a vast plan to bring Italians,
       Japanese, and Spanish immigrants to the Dominican Republic.
       March 1. U.S. Vice President Nixon and his wife Patricia visit
       the Dominican Republic.
       April 6. The army begins an active role in teaching and
       enforcing the literacy campaign.
       May 14. Beginning of celebrations of the twenty-fifth
       anniversary of the era of Trujillo.
       May 14. Trujillo is declared Father of the New Fatherland.
       September 16. Domingo Perón goes to exile in the Dominican
       Republic.
       December 20. Opening ceremony of the Fair of Peace and
       Confraternity of the Free World.

1956   February 28. International Congress of the Catholic Culture
       in Ciudad Trujillo.

March 12. Jesús Galíndez is kidnapped in New York City and flown in a plane piloted by Gerald Murphy to the Dominican Republic, where he is murdered.

July 25. First group of 185 Japanese immigrants arrives in Ciudad Trujillo.

October 7. Military Academy Batalla de las Carreras begins to function.

December 3. Gerald Murphy is murdered in the Dominican Republic. Fellow pilot Octavio de la Maza is arrested for the murder.

1957   January 7. Octavio de la Maza is murdered in prison. His brother, Antonio, promises to retaliate.

May. Hungarian refugees arrived.

May 5. Héctor Trujillo is elected president and Joaquín Balaguer as vice president.

1958   January 23. President Marcos Pérez Jiménez of Venezuela flees to Ciudad Trujillo.

March. The United States suspends the sale of arms to the Dominican Republic.

November 7. The Dominican Congress demands the cancellation of military agreements with the United States.

December 3. Trujillo proposes to reestablish military agreements with the United States.

1959   January 1. President Fulgencio Batista, the dictator of Cuba, flees to Ciudad Trujillo before Fidel Castro's forces seize power in Havana.

March. Formation of the Foreign Legion.

April 21. Trujillo asks the Congress to declare a state of emergency.

June 6. The OAS accuses the Dominican Republic of human rights violation.

June 14. Dominican exiles land in Constanza and launch an armed offensive against Trujillo.

June 19. Another group of exiles lands in Maimón and Estero Hondo.

July 17. Ramón Marrero Aristy is assassinated.

August. Batista departs for Portugal.

September. Accusation of subvention against members of the U.S. naval diplomatic mission.

September. A complot within the air force is disclosed.

September. Trujillo's agents enter the Santo Tomás de Aquino Seminar and conduct arrests.

November 19. The Dominican government initiates a campaign against Betancourt.

December 12. Héctor Trujillo marries Alma McLaughlin.

1960 January 1. Creation of the 14 of June (1J4) movement.

January 4. Hundreds of 1J4 members are rounded up and tortured by the SIM. International repudiation of Trujillo follows the event.

January 12. TV and radio propaganda campaign against the United States.

January 26. Perón leaves the Dominican Republic and goes to Madrid.

January 31. Priests throughout the country read the famous pastoral letter to their congregations.

March 3. Trujillo replies to the pastoral letter.

March 6. Second pastoral letter. Harassment of bishops, nuns, and priests.

May 4. Trujillo expels U.S. Embassy Press Officer Carl Davis. President Eisenhower approves a contingency plan to aid a domestic coup against Trujillo. Dominican dissidents request that the Unites States provide arms to eliminate Trujillo.

June. Trujillo directs an assassination attempt against President Betancourt of Venezuela, which fails.

August 3. Héctor Trujillo renounces the presidency. Balaguer becomes the interim president.

August 6. OAS member states vote to sever diplomatic relations with the Dominican Republic and to impose economic sanctions. The United States downgrades its embassy to a consulate general.

August 26. The United States breaks relations with the Dominican Republic.

September 4. Petán organizes the Cocuyos de la Cordillera.

September 9. Haiti suspends relations with the Dominican Republic.

November 1. Suspension of financial support to Colegio San Ignacio de Loyola de Dajabón.

November 25. Trujillo's agents murder Patria Mercedes, Minerva, and María Teresa Mirabal.

1961 January 12. U.S. "Special Group" approves arms delivery to Dominican dissidents.

January 18. The government requests for Trujillo the title of Benefactor of the Church.

January 4. OAS imposes economic sanctions against the Dominican Republic.

February 2. U.S. Consul McNamara is declared persona non grata.

March 4. Monsignors Panal and Reilly become the main targets of the anticlerical campaign.

May 30. Trujillo is assassinated.

May 31. Trujillo's son Ramfis assumes control of the military. The conspirators in the assassination begin to be captured. Huáscar Tejeda is the first to be arrested by SIM agents.

June 1. Fifi Pastoriza is captured. Many friends and relatives of the implicated in Trujillo's death are arrested.

June 2. Amado García Guerrero is shot by SIM agents.

June 4. Tunti Cáceres surrenders. Salvador Estrella is captured. Agents of the SIM shoot Juan Tomás Diaz and Antonio de la Maza.

July 5. Ramón Castillo, Angel Miolán, and Nicolas Silfa, leaders of the Partido Revoluccioanrio Dominicano, PRD, arrive from exile.

July 9. University students have their first political meeting. The 1J4 becomes a political party.

July 11. Viriato Fiallo leads the organization of Unión Cívica Nacional, UCN.

October 20. Juan Bosch, president of the PRD, returns to the country after more than twenty years in exile. Street riots and strikes supported by the UCN begin.

November 18. The remaining Trujillo assassins are massacred at the Hacienda María. Amiama Tio and Imbert Barrera survive. Ramfis Trujillo flees the country.

November 19. The U.S. Atlantic fleet arrives.

November 19. Most of the Trujillo family leaves the Dominican Republic for exile under a U.S. military guard to the United States, Puerto Rico, Spain, and Portugal.

November 27. The capital is renamed Santo Domingo again.

December 17. Ramfis Trujillo, seriously injured in a car crash outside of Madrid, dies of pneumonia.

1962   January 1. A council of state takes over the government and begins the preparation for elections.

January 4. The OAS removes the sanctions against the Dominican Republic.

January 17. General Rafael Rodríguez Echaverría establish a military junta. The people repudiate the act.

March 8. Balaguer goes into exile.

December 13. Impasse between Bosch and Father Láutico García.

December 20. Juan Bosch is elected president.

December 28. In Palma Sola, a religious group accused of disrupting public order, is killed.

1963   February 27. Inauguration of Juan Bosch government.

June 11. Pablo Casals and his orchestra visit the Dominican Republic.

May 21. Beginning of public meetings called Christian Reaffirmation.

September 25. A military coup deposes Bosch. He goes into exile in Puerto Rico.

September 26. A civilian triumvirate, presided over by Emilio de los Santos, replaces Bosch.

October 23. Manolo Tavárez leads an uprising in the Manaclas.

December 22. Tavárez dies during a confrontation with the army.

December 23. Donald Reid Cabral replaces de los Santos at the council of state.

1965   April 24. Violent manifestations against Reid Cabral rock the country.

April 25. Civil war begins. Constitutionalists, who favor the return of Bosch, fight against the Loyalists, those who oppose Bosch.

April 28. Second U.S. intervention. President Lyndon Johnson orders Marines to land in Santo Domingo.

May 4. Francisco Caamaño Deñó takes the oath as the Constitutionalist president. Elías Wessin y Wessin presides over the military junta government.

May 6. The OAS creates the Inter-American Peace Force.
May 7. Creation of National Reconstruction government, which replaces the military junta.
June 28. Balaguer returns to the Dominican Republic.
August 31. Both sides in the conflict sign the Act of National Reconciliation. Ten months later Balaguer is elected president.

NOTES

Introduction

1. For quotation and definitions of militarism, see Skjelsbaek, "Militarisms, Its Dimensions and Corollaries," 81–86.
2. Stepan, *Military in Politics*, 6–20; Loveman and Davies, *Politics and Anti Politics*, 61–128; Lieuwen, "The Problem of Military Government," 7. A classic work is Vagts, *A History of Militarism*. For military officers as politicians, see pp. 293–323.
3. Regehr, "What Is Militarism?" 129.
4. Huntington, *The Soldier and the State*, 177.
5. Nunn, "On the Role of the Military," 44–45.
6. Otley, "Militarism and Militarization in the Public Schools," 220.
7. Thee, "Militarism and Militarisation," 20–21.
8. Atkins, *Arms and Politics in the Dominican Republic*; H. Klein, "David del Toro," 25; Rouquie, *The Military and the State in Latin America*. These sources and others present the military as part of society, not isolated from politics.
9. Lieuwen, "The Problem of Military Government," 7.
10. Crassweller, preface to *Trujillo*, ix.
11. Statement from U.S. Legation in Ciudad Trujillo to Secretary of State, September 9, 1939, United States National Archives, Record Group 59, 711.39/79 (hereafter USNA, RG, and file number).
12. Three other novels—Danticat, *The Farming of Bones*, Álvarez, *In the Time of the Butterflies*, and Prestol Castillo, *El masacre se pasa a pie*—also stimulated interest in Trujillo's dictatorship. In fact, Álvarez's novel was turned into a TV movie starring Selma Hayek, Marc Anthony, and Edward James Olmos.
13. For example, Franco, *La era de Trujillo*; Roorda, *The Dictator Next Door*; Inoa, *Estado y campesinos*.
14. Linz, "Totalitarian and Authoritarian Regimes," 3:259–62.
15. Rossi and Plano, *The Latin American Political Dictionary*, 127–28.
16. Rossi and Plano, *The Latin American Political Dictionary*, 127–28.
17. This is what Trujillo told the Dominican Congress on December 9, 1930.

See his publication, *El pensamiento político de un estadista*, 2:50–52.

1. Origins and Development of the Dominican Military

1. García, *Compendio de la historia de Santo Domingo*, 1:42–43.
2. For more about this period, see Moya Pons, *La dominación haitiana*.
3. Duarte's political ideas are clarified in Peña, *Así era Duarte*, 64–69.
4. García, *Compendio de la historia de Santo Domingo*, 3:484–85.
5. Campillo Pérez, *El grillo*, 58–59.
6. For more on social class distinction, see Moscoso Puello, *Cartas a Evelina*.
7. Martínez, *Diccionario biográfico*, 456–57.
8. Vega Pagán, *Historia de las fuerzas armadas*, 1:26.
9. Hoetink, *El pueblo dominicano*, 162.
10. *Colección de leyes y decretos*, 1:303.
11. Vega Pagán, *Historia de las fuerzas armadas*, 1:134.
12. Weil et al., *Dominican Republic*, 247. *Compadrazgo* is a Catholic ritual of kinship that requires sponsors for a child's baptism, confirmation, and communion. The ritual implies spiritual and material obligations to the godchild and loyalty to the *compadres* (godparents).
13. Vega Pagán, *Historia de las fuerzas armadas*, 1:140–41.
14. Hoetink, *El pueblo dominicano*, 91–94.
15. Soto Jiménez, *Las fuerzas militares*, 23–37, 47–48. See also Betances, *State and Society in the Dominican Republic*, 20–22.
16. Rodríguez Demorizi, *Hostos en Santo Domingo*, 1:285–88.
17. Cited in Hoetink, *El pueblo dominicano*, 164; Vega Pagán, *Historia de las fuerzas armadas*, 1:218–19.
18. Luperón, *Notas autobiográficas*, 3:404.
19. Malek, "Rafael Leonidas Trujillo Molina," 27.
20. El-Himani, *Santo Domingo*, 169; Frómeta Nina, "El ejército nacional."
21. Vega Pagán, *Historia de las fuerzas armadas*, 1:244.
22. Hoetink, *El pueblo dominicano*, 166.
23. Duff, *Leader and Party*, 51.
24. The government changed hands rapidly between 1899 and 1903: Vice President General Wescenlao Figuereo, who became president, lasted from July 26 to August 30, 1899; a Council of Secretaries, which lasted for one day, August 31, 1899, was presided over by Tomas Morales (the other members were Enrique Henríquez, Jaime R. Vidal, Arístides Patiño, and Braulio Alvarez); Junta Popular (Mariano Cestero, Alvaro Logroño, Arístides Patiño, and Pedro María Mejía) governed from August 31 to September 4, 1899; Horacio Vásquez governed from August 18 to November 15, 1899; Juan Isidro Jimenes governed from November 15 to May 2, 1902; and Horacio Vásquez governed from April 26, 1902, to April 23, 1903.
25. Vega Pagán, *Historia de las fuerzas armadas*, 1:264–65.

26. C. Walcott, Jr., to the Department of State, September 21, 1915, USNA, RG 59, 839.51/806; A. de la Rosa, *Las finanzas de Santo Domingo*, 183–84.

27. See Acevedo, "Lo que vi."

28. Troncoso Sánchez, *Ramón Cáceres*, 309.

29. Memo from C. Walcott, Jr., to Mr. Harrison, September 21, 1915, USNA, RG 79, 839.51/806.

30. Monclús, *El caudillismo en la República Dominicana*, 159; Campillo Pérez, *El grillo*, 128–34.

31. Frederick Douglass to James G. Blaine, February 26, 1890, cited in Malek, "Rafael Leonidas Trujillo Molina," 32.

32. Luperón, *Notas autobiográficas*, 1:202–4.

33. Juan Luis Abascal used these terms while discussing the role of the military during the first republican period with me in July 2001.

2. U.S. Occupation of the Dominican Republic

1. President Theodore Roosevelt's speech to the U.S. Senate, February 15, 1905, in Gantenbein, *The Evolution of Our Latin American Policy*, 667–78.

2. Agreement in House Document of February 15, 1905, United States Foreign Relations (hereafter USFR), 1905, 342–43.

3. Russell letter to the Dominican Minister of Foreign Affairs, November 19, 1915, USFR, 1915, 336–37; Knight, *Los americanos*, 73; Henríquez Ureña, *Los yanquis*, 80–89.

4. See Booth and Walker, *Understanding Central America*, 29.

5. Admiral W. B. Carpeton to Josephus Daniels, Secretary of the Navy, May 13, 1916, USFR, 1916, 226–27.

6. See Jimenes's manifest to the nation in Henríquez Ureña, *Los yanquis*, 97–99.

7. Welles, *Naboth's Vineyard*, 2:779–81.

8. Vega Pagán, *Historia de las fuerzas armadas*, 1:277.

9. Fuller and Cosmas, *Marines*, 28.

10. Calder, *The Impact of Intervention*, xiii.

11. Metcalf, *History of the United States Marines Corps*, 355–56.

12. Calder, *The Impact of Intervention*, 9.

13. Gilbert, *Mi lucha contra el invasor yanqui de 1916*, 41.

14. Military Governor to the U.S. Chief of Naval Operations, July 2, 1920, USNA, RG 59, 839.00/2214–2300.

15. "The Annual Report of the Military Government of Santo Domingo," USFR, 1917, 710.

16. Brigadier General Logan Feland, U.S. Marines, to the Military Governor in Santo Domingo, July 1, 1920, USNA, RG 59, 839.00/2214–2300.

17. Fuller and Cosmas, *Marines*, 28.

18. Ducoudray, *Los "gavilleros" del este*, 102–3; Calder, *The Impact of Intervention*, 181.

19. Peguero, "Participación de la mujer en la historia dominicana," 36.

20. Pepín, *Feminismo*, 47.

21. Military Governor of Santo Domingo to the U.S. Chief of Naval Operations, July 2, 1920, USNA, RG 59, 839.00/2214–2300.

22. Fiallo, *La comisión nacionalista in Washington*, 41–66.

23. "Annual Report," USFR, 1917, 712. Hereafter "La Guardia" will be used when referring to the new force.

24. Vega Pagán, *Historia de las fuerzas armadas*, 2:13–18; L. Mejía, *De Lilís a Trujillo*, 146.

25. Calder, *The Impact of Intervention*, 54.

26. "Annual Report," USFR, 1917, 716.

27. Crassweller, *Trujillo*, 41; Goldwert, *The Constabulary in the Dominican Republic and Nicaragua*, v.

28. Kelsey, "The American Intervention," 178.

29. Rufus Lane, "Civil Government in Santo Domingo," 136.

30. Knapp's position in USFR, 1917, 717.

31. Kelsey, "The American Intervention," 177–78.

32. Quarterly report of the Military Government of Santo Domingo, July 17, 1918, USFR, 1918, 368.

33. Skelton, *An American Profession of Arms*, 44.

34. Vega Pagán, *Historia de las fuerzas armadas*, 2:15.

35. A. Klein, *Sugarball*, 19–20.

36. Medina Benet, *Los responsables*, 9; Vega Pagán, *Historia de las fuerzas armadas*, 2:9–20, 44–45.

37. Report, Logan Feland, July 2, 1920, USNA, RG 59, 839.00/2214–2300.

38. Fuller and Cosmas, *Marines*, 28.

39. Gordon, *Pendleton Papers*, 73.

40. Vega Pagán, *Historia de las fuerzas armadas*, 2:17–18. See also Arvelo González, "Las fuerzas armadas dominicanas."

41. *Listín diario*, October 8, 1921; Knight, *Los americanos*, 98.

42. Renda, *Taking Haiti*, 131–33.

43. Metcalf, *History of the United States Marines Corps*, 355–56.

44. L. Mejía, *De Lilís a Trujillo*, 144–45.

45. Pichardo, *Gallos y galleros*, 34.

46. "Ejército Dominicano."

47. Calder, *The Impact of Intervention*, 58–59.

48. Calder, *The Impact of Intervention*, 124.

49. *Listín diario*, September 23, 1922.

50. Roosevelt's letter dated June 2, 1919, in Vega Pagán, *Historia de las fuerzas armadas*, 2:41.

51. Wiarda, "Aftermath of the Trujillo Dictatorship," 36.

52. Harries-Jekins, "Armed Forces and Society," 86.

53. Zakrzewski Brown, *Culture and Customs of the Dominican Republic*, 143–46; Austerlitz, "Dominican Merengue."

54. Peguero and Santos, *Visión general de la historia dominicana*, 336–37.

55. A. Klein, *Sugarball*, 16.

56. Cited in Vega, *Trujillo y Haiti*, 200.

57. Laguerre, *Military and Society in Haiti*, 75.

3. From Soldier to Commander in Chief

1. Morrison, *Latin American Mission*, 58.

2. Sinks, "Trujillo," 165–68.

3. Padilla D'Onís, *Anecdotario de Trujillo*, 20.

4. Rouquie, *The Military and the State in Latin America*, 4.

5. Wiarda, *Dictatorship and Development*, 42. See also Galíndez, *Era of Trujillo*, 9.

6. Vega Pagán, *Military Biography*, 64.

7. F. Trujillo, "My Tormented Life," 50.

8. Ornes, *Little Caesar*, 72.

9. J. de la Rosa, "El estado." Numerous photos of Trujillo wearing his military uniform at different events are in *Álbum de oro de la Feria de la Paz y Confraternidad del Mundo Libre*, 1956.

10. Espaillat, appendix to *Trujillo: The Last Caesar*, iv. Partial lists of medals awarded to Trujillo are mentioned in Vega Pagán, *Military Biography*.

11. General Order No. 37, November 17, 1922, and Trujillo's promotion in Vega Pagán, *Historia de las fuerzas armadas*, 2:70–72; *Gaceta Oficial*, October 3, 1922, contains the decree regarding promotions.

12. Trujillo's efficiency reports appear in Vega Pagán, *Military Biography*, 49–51, 57–60, 177–91. See also Nanita, *Trujillo*, 30.

13. Millett and Soloman, "The Court Martial."

14. Excerpts from the trial are reproduced in Millett and Soloman, "The Court Martial," 398.

15. Millett and Soloman, "The Court Martial," 400–403.

16. Crassweller, *Trujillo*, 48.

17. *Listín diario*, February 24 and 25, 1924; Hicks, *Blood in the Streets*, 31.

18. Medina Benet, *Los responsables*, 52–53; Vega Pagán, *Military Biography*, 96.

19. Former army colonel Luis Montes de Oca, interview by the author, February 4, 1990, National Archives, Santo Domingo. For Trujillo's political intrigues, see García, *Mis 20 años junto a Trujillo*.

20. *Censo de la República*, 38.

21. Schoenrich, *Santo Domingo*, 177.

22. Crassweller, *Trujillo*, 57.

23. Bosch, *Composición social dominicana*, 301.

24. Logan, *Haiti and the Dominican Republic*, 69–70.

25. Crassweller, *Trujillo*, 129.
26. Nanita, *Trujillo*, 92.
27. Balaguer, *Memorias*, 100–102.
28. Derby, "The Magic of Modernity," 386.
29. Balaguer, *Memorias*, 102.
30. Crassweller, *Trujillo*, 133–35. Julia Álvarez, *In the Time of the Butterflies*, 20–24, offers a fictionalized version of Trujillo's seduction of Lina.
31. In *The Feast of the Goat*, Vargas Llosa fictionalizes the lives of some of Trujillo's functionaries whose wives and daughters were victims of El Jefe's sexual desires. For example, see pp. 398–401.
32. Vega, *La vida cotidiana dominicana*, 157. There are suggestions that despite of his macho image, Trujillo had some bisexual tendencies. See Hernández Flores, *Lecciones de trujillismo*, 151–57.
33. Cutts to the U.S. Legation in Santo Domingo, April 3, 1930, USNA, RG 59, 839.00/3371.
34. U.S. Legation in the Dominican Republic to the State Department, October 1935, USNA, RG 59, 839.20/213.
35. Vega, *Trujillo y las fuerzas armadas norteamericanas*, 276–77.
36. Letter, Colonel Trujillo to Colonel Cutts, in Vega Pagán, *Military Biography*, 126–27.
37. Hillman and D'Agostino, *Distant Neighbors in the Caribbean*, 69.
38. Vega, *Trujillo y las fuerzas armadas norteamericanas*, 49–67; Roorda, *The Dictator Next Door*, 149–91.
39. Commissioner Welles to the Acting Secretary of State, August 29, 1922, USNA, RG 59, 839.00/2591.
40. Medina Benet, *Los responsables*, 53–54. See also Memorandum, J. Dunn, Latin American Division, State Department, to Secretary of State, June 30, 1925, USNA, RG 59, 839.00/4–819.
41. "The Trujillo Regime in the Dominican Republic: An Analysis of Trujillo's Rule in the Dominican Republic during the Past Sixteen Years," *Intelligence Report, No. 4190.*
42. Russell to Secretary of State, 1925, USNA, RG 59, 839.00/2893/6–3025.
43. Rossi and Plano, *The Latin American Dictionary*, 137.
44. Kantor, *Patterns of Politics*, 317. See also Dyer, "Dominican Republic," 179.
45. Vega Pagán, *Military Biography*, 109–12.
46. Trujillo's project of military reform in Vega Pagán, *Military Biography*, 109–12.
47. "La brigada y el brigadier."
48. Vidal, "La República Dominicana."
49. Vidal, "La República Dominicana," 68.
50. Several debates published in *Boletín de la Cámara de Diputados, 1924–1938* 3, no. 48 (October 1927).

51. "El ejército dominicano." Vidal was the editor who wrote the article. Some of his statements during my interviews with him reveal that he did not change the point of view that expressed in 1927. See Vidal, "La República Dominicana," 70.

52. "Diez años de servicio," 1–2.

53. Dato Pagán Perdomo, interview by the author, February 2, 1990, Santo Domingo.

54. *Revista Carnaval* 2, no. 1 (1926).

55. Frómeta Nina, "El ejército nacional."

56. *Memoria del Secretario de Interior, Policía, Guerra y Marina*, 1928, in Vega Pagán, *Historia de las fuerzas armadas*, 2:144.

57. L. Mejía, *De Lilís a Trujillo*, 218; Medina Benet, *Los responsables*, 256.

58. Medina Benet, *Los responsables*, 256.

59. Malek, "Rafael Leonidas Trujillo Molina," 131.

60. Gobierno Dominicano, *Actas del congreso*, October 15, 1924.

61. Several active and retired officers described to the author many aspects of Trujillo's persona and personality. See also Bosch, *La fortuna de Trujillo*, 25; Crassweller, *Trujillo*, 3–51.

4. Road to the Presidency for the Army's Commander

1. Letter from Américo Lugo to Horacio Vásquez cited by Franklin Franco in Pierre-Charles, *Problemas domínico-haitianos y del Caribe*, 86–87.

2. *Población de la República Dominicana*, 17.

3. Linz, "Totalitarian and Authoritarian Regimes," 3:261.

4. *Listín Diario*, May 4, 1927.

5. Cassá, *Capitalismo y dictadura*, 699–700; S. Medina, Méndez, and Paulino, "Análisis socio-histórico," 301.

6. Véliz, *The Centralist Tradition of Latin America*, 280.

7. Medina Benet, *Los responsables*, 144–56; L. Mejía, *De Lilís a Trujillo*, 287.

8. Boin and Ramia, *El proceso de desarrollo del capitalismo en la República Dominicana*, 1:185–93.

9. F. Álvarez, *Ideología política del pueblo dominicano*, 32–33.

10. Dawes et al., *Economic Commission Report*, 4–30; Jimenes Grullón, *La República Dominicana*, 147–50.

11. L. Mejía, *De Lilís a Trujillo*, 218; Crassweller, *Trujillo*, 125; Medina Benet, *Los responsables*, 290.

12. Reported in Jimenes Grullón, *Sociología política*, 3:82.

13. As referred to Jimenes by Vilomar. See Jimenes Grullón, *Sociología política*, 3:82.

14. Rossi and Plano, *The Latin American Political Dictionary*, 135.

15. Crassweller, *Trujillo*, 68; Cutts to Secretary of State, USNA, RG 59, 839.00/3340.

16. See Crassweller, *Trujillo*, 61, 101–2; Galíndez, *Era of Trujillo*, 138–41.

17. *Memorias de la Secretaría de Interior, Policía, Guerra y Marina,* 1928, in Vega Pagán, *Historia de las fuerzas armadas,* 2:143–44.

18. "The Trujillo Regime," *Intelligence Report, No. 4190.*

19. Medina Benet, *Los responsables,* 325.

20. Minister in the Dominican Republic to Secretary of State, December 25, 1929, USNA, RG 59, 839/3340.

21. Acting Secretary of State to Minister Curtis, March 18 and 19, 1930, USFR, 1930, 2:718–19.

22. Medina Benet, *Los responsables,* 330–35.

23. Curtis to Secretary of State, March 18, 1930, USNA, RG 59, 839.00/3335.

24. Acting Secretary of State to Curtis, March 19, 1930, USNA, RG 59, 839.00/3355.

25. Moya Pons, "The Dominican Republic since 1930," 510.

26. Acting Secretary of State to Curtis, March 19, 1930, USNA, RG 59, 839.00/3355.

27. Acting Secretary of State to Curtis, March 19, 1930, USFR 1930, 2:719.

28. Cutts to U.S. Legation in Santo Domingo, April 3, 1930, USNA, RG 59, 839.00/3371.

29. Aybar, "La revolución de febrero"; Tomas Erickson, "El idealismo de la revolución," *La opinión,* February 25, 1936; Hernández Franco, *La más bella revolución de América;* Mejía Ricart, "El significado histórico del 23 de Febrero del 1930," *Boletín del Archivo de la Nación* 10 (1940).

30. Curtis to Acting Secretary of State, USFR, 1930, 2:711.

31. Mateo, *Mito y cultura en la era de Trujillo,* 46.

32. Jimenes Grullón, *Sociología política,* 3:114–15.

33. Minister Curtis to Secretary of State, March 27, 1930, USNA, RG 59, 839.00/3338.

34. Trujillo Molina, "Manifiesto al pueblo dominicano el 24 de abril, 1930," in *Discursos, mensajes y proclamas,* 1:3–5.

35. Balaguer, *Memorias,* 219–261; Mateo, *Mito y cultura en la era de Trujillo,* 67–89.

36. Trujillo's inauguration in *Listín diario,* August 17, 1930; Crassweller, *Trujillo,* 87–88; Roorda, *The Dictator Next Door,* 54–55.

37. Ornes, *Little Caesar,* 61–63.

38. Malek, "Rafael Leonidas Trujillo Molina," 194.

39. Jimenes Grullón, *La República Dominicana,* 201.

40. Vega, *Trujillo y el control financiero norteamericano,* 86–90.

41. Trujillo Molina, "Projecto de ley de gastos públicos," in *Discursos, mensajes y proclamas,* 1:45–56.

42. Eugene M. Hinckle to the Department of State as reported by Robert Mills McClintock, December 9, 1938, USNA, RG 59, 839.20/82.

43. L. Mejía, *De Lilís a Trujillo,* 275; *Baltimore Sun,* February 15–20, 1930.

44. Trujillo Molina, *Discursos, mensajes y proclamas*, 1:15.

45. Trujillo Molina, *Discursos, mensajes y proclamas*, 1:52.

5. Changing the Military, Altering Society

1. Ayuso, *Todo por Trujillo*, 46.

2. Espaillat, *Trujillo: The Last Caesar*, 24.

3. As cited in Nunn, *The Time of the Generals*, 121.

4. Trujillo Molina, *Discursos, mensajes y proclamas*, 1:166; Balaguer, *El pensamiento vivo de Trujillo*, 77–83.

5. Bons, "An Organizational Approach to the Study of Leadership."

6. *Listín diario*, November 20, 1931; Medina Benet, *Los responsables*, 449–55.

7. Osorio Lizarazo, *Portrait of Trujillo*, 122.

8. Trujillo's tactics of destruction are described in Jimenes Grullón, *Sociología política*, 3:146–47; Campillo Pérez, *El grillo*, 169–71; Crassweller, *Trujillo*, 96.

9. Ornes, *Little Caesar*, 147.

10. See, for example, *Listín Diario*, April 17 and 27, 1931.

11. Trujillo Molina, *Discursos, mensajes y proclamas*, 1:142.

12. Inoa, *Estado y campesinos*, 78–79; Rodríguez Demorizi, *Cronología*, 1:77–83.

13. De Besault, *Presidente Trujillo*, 63.

14. Trujillo Molina, *Discursos, mensajes y proclamas*, 3:113–14.

15. Dunlop, "El enganche"; Ramiro Matos González, interview by the author, February 12, 1990, Santo Domingo.

16. Ignacio Gómez Núñez, interview by the author, January 4, 5, and 7, 1990, Santiago.

17. Barnes, *Pawns*, vi–xvii.

18. Soto Jiménez, *Las fuerzas militares*, 172–73.

19. Cuevas Sena, "Gesta contra la tiranía," 4.

20. *Memoria de la Secretaría de Estado, Guerra y Marina*, 1948, in Vega Pagán, *Historia de las fuerzas armadas*, 2:359.

21. Nanita, *Trujillo*, 186.

22. Nunn, *The Time of the Generals*, 47.

23. Eugene M. Hinckle to the Department of State as reported by Robert Mills McClintock, December 9, 1938, USNA, RG 59, 839.20/82.

24. Antonio (Tony) Santos, former sergeant of the National Army, interview by the author, February 9, 1990, Santo Domingo. Other former members of the armed forces confirmed this exaplanation.

25. Order General No. 11, February 20, 1931, printed in *Gaceta Oficial*. For more about the military territorial division, see *La República Dominicana*, 64–68.

26. See "Se reestablece la antigua división de departamentos militares," *Listín Diario*, January 30, 1933.

27. Vega Pagán, *Historia de las fuerzas armadas*, 2:256–70. See also Fontana, *Tru-*

jillo y su obra, 111–15. Incidentally the name of two of these provinces, San Rafael and Benefactor, honored Trujillo and revealed his megalomania.

28. Vega Pagán, *Historia de las fuerzas armadas*, 2:311–31; *U.S. Military Intelligence Reports: Combat Estimates*, "The Dominican Republic," March 15, 1942, Report G-2, W.D., M.I.S.

29. "El Generalísimo Trujillo," 50–51.

30. Alexander, "Primary Groups."

31. Alfaro Reyes, *Álbum comemorativo*. In addition, *La Revista*, *Revista Militar*, and *Revista de las fuerzas armadas* show photographic evidence of political meetings taking place in different fortresses or members of the military attending political meetings in different locations.

32. Trujillo's statement to the Mexican magazine *Continente* on April 21, 1945, cited in Vega Pagán, *Historia de las fuerzas armadas*, 2:334.

33. Penson, *El Partido Dominicano*, 67–75.

34. James Gantenbein, chargé d'affaires ad interin, to the Secretary of State, June 25, 1934, USNA, RG 59, 839.20/57; Labourt, *Trujillo: Seguiré a caballo*, 31. This brutal method was often applied to political prisoners.

35. L. Mejía, *De Lilís a Trujillo*, 315.

36. Arthur Schoenfeld to Secretary of State, June 7, 1934, USNA, RG 59, 839.20/28; Ornes, *Little Caesar*, 146; "La conspiración del Coronel Leoncio Blanco," in Labourt, *Trujillo: Seguiré a caballo*, 31.

37. Vega, *Trujillo y Haití*, 1:186; Hicks, *Blood in the Streets*, 55.

38. Arthur Schoenfeld to Secretary of State, January 31, 1933, USNA, RG 59, 839.20/27; "Se restablece."

39. L. Mejía, *De Lilís a Trujillo*, 315.

40. Crassweller, *Trujillo*, 114. More about Tancredo Saviñón may be found in Hicks, *Blood in the Streets*, 153–54.

41. *Listín Diario*, October 28, 1935; James Gantenbein to Secretary of State, October 28, 1935, USNA, RG 59, 839.001; James Gantenbein to Secretary of State, October 1, 1935, USNA, RG 59, 839.001/232; Crassweller, *Trujillo*, 152; Hicks, *Blood in the Streets*, 150–51.

42. See "Trujillo Was Suspicious of His Brother Virgilio's Ambitions," in García, *Mis 20 años junto a Trujillo*, 2:25–28.

43. Wendell W. Woodbury to Department of State, September 7, 1954, USNA, RG 59, 739.521; Crassweller, *Trujillo*, 284.

44. Crassweller, *Trujillo*, 444.

45. Crassweller, *Trujillo*, 141.

46. Hicks, *Blood in the Streets*, 179.

47. *U.S. Military Intelligence Reports: Combat Estimates.*

48. Nanita, *Trujillo*, 191.

49. Espaillat, *Trujillo: The Last Caesar*, 25–26.

50. Huertas, "Trujillo es el ejército."

51. Anonymous interview by the author, February 19, 1990.

52. Febles, *El primero de abril y el ejército*, 36.

53. Former general Clarence E. Charles Dunlop, interview by the author, February 15, 1990, Santo Domingo.

54. Trujillo Molina, *La nueva patria dominicana*, 273.

55. Excerpts from *Cartilla cívica* in Balaguer, *El pensamiento vivo de Trujillo*, 273–81.

56. Office of Naval Intelligence report titled "The Dominican National Army," June 8, 1931, USNA, RG 59, 839.20/9.

57. Soto Jiménez, *Las fuerzas militares*, 167–71; Vega Pagán, *Historia de las fuerzas armadas*, 2:329–30, 340–41.

58. Former officers Renato Hungría and José Joaquín Hungría, interviews by the author, February 1990, Santo Domingo.

59. Marina Méndez and Elida Jimenes, "Antecedentes: Instrucción, educación, y evolución de la enseñanza de las instituciones castrense dominicanas" (1988), 21; García, *Mis 20 años junto a Trujillo*, 1:105–7; Vega Pagán, *Historia de las fuerzas armadas*, 2:307–8.

60. Secretaría de lo Interior Policía, Guerra, y Marina, *La República Dominicana* (Santo Domingo: La Milagrosa, 1932), 70–71; El-Himani, *Santo Domingo*, 175; Bonetti, "La aviación y el ejército dominicano."

61. El-Himani, *Santo Domingo*, 175.

62. Jorge, "Trujillo creador de la aviación militar."

63. Arthur Schoenfeld to Secretary of State, April 29, 1932, USNA, RG 59, 839.20/22.

64. Jack D. Neal, Chief Division of Foreign Activity Correlation, to E. J. Shamhart, Deputy Commissioner, Investigations and Patrol Bureau of Customs, November 26, 1947, USNA, RG 59, 839.248. The instructors were Hal Muny, Ted Satterfield, D. M. Ray, Hamilton Wilson, Louis Ramey, K. W. Everson, Ellwood Mundy, W. B. Stone, and F. A. Graber.

65. B. L. Austin to Kenneth Anderson, "Agreement between the Dominican Republic and Brigadier General Victor Bleasdale," September 24, 1947, USNA, RG 59, 839.20.

66. Ciudad Trujillo (Burrows) to Secretary of State, June 2, 1948, USNA, RG 59, 839.20.

67. Guerrero Pou, *Yo maté a su hijo*, 31.

68. Alfredo Balcácer Vega, unpublished work related to the Dominican armed forces, 9.

69. Johnson, *The Military and Society in Latin America*, 115.

70. Soto Jiménez, *Temas*, 27.

71. Guerrero Pou, *Yo maté a su hijo*, 33–34.

72. Soto Jiménez, *Temas*, 134–35; Méndez and Jimenes, *Antecedentes*, 51.

73. Méndez and Jimenes, *Antecedentes*, 51.

74. Interviews by the author with several former officers, among them Navy Colonel Alfredo Balcácer Vega (February 8–9, 1990, Santo Domingo), Matos González (February 12, 1990 and December 12, 1996, Santo Domingo), and Montes de Oca (February 4, 1990, Santo Domingo).

75. For an illustration, see Cuevas Sena, "Gesta contra la tiranía."

76. Julio Fortuna Polanco, interview by the author, December 30, 1989, Santiago; Miguel Holguín, interview by the author, February 2, 1990, Santo Domingo; and Ramón Mejía Guerrero, interview by the author, February 20, 1990, Santo Domingo.

6. The New Fatherland

1. Among the intellectuals who worked for Trujillo were Virgilio Alvarez Pina, Joaquín Balaguer, Julio Ortega Frier, Victor Garrido, Porfirio Herrera, Arturo Longroño, Abelardo Nanita, Manuel Arturo Peña Battle, Jacinto Peynado, Roberto Despradel, Manuel de Jesús Troncoso de la Concha, and Rafael Vidal. All of these men had high positions in Trujillo's administration.

2. Trujillo Molina, *La nueva patria dominicana*, 273.

3. Trujillo Molina, *Discursos, mensajes y proclamas*, 1:52–53.

4. Duff, *Leader and Party*, 35.

5. An editorial in *Revista Militar*, April 1935, lists several functions assigned to the army. See also Quezada, "El ejército nacional y Trujillo," 106–7.

6. Ronfeldt, "The Mexican Army and the Political Order since 1940," 65–66.

7. Nunn, *The Time of the Generals*, 120.

8. Order General de Brigada No. 21, August 20, 1930. Cronológico de las Fuerzas Armadas no. 000067, Biblioteca de la Secretaría de las Fuerzas Armadas, hereafter BSFA.

9. Memorandum, Robert Mills McClintock to the Department of State, December 12, 1938, USNA, RG 59, 839.20/82.

10. García, *Mis 20 años junto a Trujillo*, 2:206–12.

11. Montes de Oca, interview.

12. Memorias del Ejército, 1939, Cronológico de las Fuerzas Armadas No. 000064, BSFA.

13. Medina Peña Ramos, "El ejército nacional en la era de Trujillo." See also Álvarez Mainardi, "El ejército nacional."

14. Former officers in the veterans club Hermandad de Pensionados de las Fuerzas Armadas y la Policía Nacional of Santo Domingo, interviews by the author, February 7, 1990. Although these statements, in my opinion, do not reveal any information that may be used against the officers, I have honored their request to remain anonymous.

15. See Laguerre, *The Military and Society in Haiti*, 125–47; Lozoya, *El ejército mexicano*, 81–82.

16. Laguerre, *The Military and Society in Haiti*, 127.

17. Galíndez, *Era of Trujillo*, 166.

18. Memorias del Ejército, 1939, Cronológico de las Fuerzas Armadas No. 000065, BSFA.

19. "The Trujillo Regime," *Intelligence Report, No. 4190.*

20. Crassweller, *Trujillo*, 329.

21. Balaguer, *Memorias*, 254; León Estévez, *Yo, Ramfis Trujillo*, 51.

22. Inoa, *Estado y campesinos*, 82–83.

23. An interesting description of one of these events is in F. Mejía, *Vía crucis de un pueblo*, 164–66.

24. Cassá, *Historia social y económica*, 2:259–60.

25. Former officers, interview, February 7, 1990.

26. Pagán Perdomo, *Por qué lucha el pueblo dominicano*, 181.

27. Trujillo Molina, *Discursos, mensajes y proclamas*, 1:265.

28. San Miguel, "The Dominican Peasantry and the Market Economy," 295–96.

29. Trujillo Molina, *Discursos, mensajes y proclamas*, 1:265–66.

30. Turits, "The Foundations of Despotism," 273. See also his explanation of *terrenos comuneros* (idle land) on pp. 163–68.

31. Inoa, *Estado y campesinos*, 84–85.

32. Turits, "The Foundations of Despotism," 273, 283–84.

33. Pacini Hernández, *Bachata*, 39.

34. Trujillo Molina, "Proclama del jefe del estado a los agricultores de la república," in *La nueva patria dominicana*, 97.

35. Inoa, *Estado y campesinos*, 65–66; Turits, "The Foundations of Despotism," 474.

36. Trujillo Molina, "Proclama del jefe del estado a los agricultores de la república," 165.

37. Trujillo Molina, *Mensajes, discursos y proclamas*, 2:151.

38. San Miguel, "La paradoja de la democracia dominicana," 84–85.

39. For example, see *Listín Diario*, January 9, 1935.

40. Espaillat, *Trujillo: The Last Caesar*, 25. Some of these letters are cited in Turits, "The Foundations of Despotism," 462–67.

41. Cited in Turits, "The Foundations of Despotism," 464.

42. In 1954, to expand the properties of the Colegio San Ignacio de Loyola in Dajabón, my father received an offer to sell his land for about one half of its real value. When he refused we were evicted, and the land, as well as the land of five of his neighbors, was declared property of the state. See also Turits, "The Foundations of Despotism," 315–16.

43. Thee, "Militarism and Militarisation," 20.

44. Sagás, *Race and Politics in the Dominican Republic*, 4.

45. Among the scholars who produced these and other interesting ideas about *an-*

tihaitianismo are Cassá, "El racismo"; Despradel, "Las etapas del antihaitian-ismo en la Republica Dominicana," 83–96; and Vega, *Trujillo y Haiti*, 23–39.

46. J. Cuello, *Documentos del conflicto dominico-haitiano*, 8–10.

47. Balaguer, *Dominican Reality*, 120.

48. Balaguer, *Memorias*, 71–72.

49. In October, November, and December 1937 *Listín Diario* and *La Opinión* published several of these declarations. For example, see *Listín Diario*, November 5, 1937, and *La opinión*, November 29, 1937.

50. *U.S. Military Intelligence Reports: Combat Estimates*, 5. See also letter from Balaguer, Subsecretary of the Dominican Foreign Relations Office, to Evre-mont Carrie, Plenipotentiary Minister of Haiti, October 10, 1937. Letter in J. Cuello, *Documentos del Conflicto, dominico-haitiano*, 51–52.

51. For a well-documented history of the events, see J. Cuello, *Documentos del Conflicto dominico-haitiano*. For U.S. press coverage of the conflict, see Swilley, "The Haitian-Dominican Republic Incident of 1937."

52. See *Intelligence Report, No. 4190*.

53. In addition to J. Cuello, *Documentos del conflicto dominico-haitiano de 1937*, see Inoa, *Bibliografía*; Capdevila, *La dictadure de Trujillo*; Maríñez, "Relaciones dominico-haitianas y raíces histórico culturales africanas en la República Dominicana"; Swilley, "The Haitian-Dominican Republic Incident of 1937."

54. See Vásquez's policy on colonization in *Gaceta Oficial* no. 3872, July 2, 1927.

55. Trujillo Molina, *Discursos, mensajes y proclamas*, 1:265–66.

56. Rodríguez Demorizi, *Cronología*, 1:84.

57. Trujillo Molina, *Discursos, mensajes y proclamas*, 1:265–66.

58. Gardiner, *La política de inmigración del dictador Trujillo*, 15–32.

59. Julio (Julito) Reyes, interview by the author, January 1990, Dajabón.

60. R. Cuello, *El Sisal*, 82. For some of the actrocities committed by General Alcántara, see pp. 130–36.

61. Interviews with former enlisted men in Santiago, Dajabón, Santo Domingo, and New York City in 1989 and 1990.

62. Balaguer, *Dominican Reality*, 68.

63. For an explanation of theories linking economic development to democ-racy, see Espinal, "Classes, Power, and Political Changes in the Dominican Republic," 11–16; Cambeira, *Quisqueya la bella*, 185.

64. Sáez, *Loyola*, 27.

65. López de Santa Anna, *Misión Fronteriza*; Trujillo Molina, *Discursos, mensajes y proclamas*, 3:31–32.

66. In 1996 former students from all over the country returned to Dajabón to celebrate the Colegio San Ignacio de Loyola's fiftieth anniversary. See Sáez, *Loyola*, 16.

67. From my recollections growing up in Dajabón and participating in many of these activities.

7. Paradoxical Rewards

1. Balaguer, *El pensamiento vivo de Trujillo*, 57–58.
2. Trujillo Molina, *Discursos, mensajes y proclamas*, 7:25.
3. Vega Pagán, *Historia de las fuerzas armadas*, 2:276–78.
4. Crassweller, *Trujillo*, 115. See also "Las fuerzas armadas," in *Álbum del centenario de la República*, 62–69.
5. Vega Pagán, *Historia de las fuerzas armadas*, 2:237.
6. Joaquín Balaguer presents Trujillo as providential in Nanita, *La era de Trujillo*, 61.
7. Gobierno Dominicano, *Memorias de la Secretaría de Estado Guerra y Marina*, 1948, 28, See also "Sortean 50 casas entre alistados de fuerzas armadas."
8. Montás Guerrero, "El desenvolvimiento militar de la frontera."
9. Crassweller, *Trujillo*, 264.
10. U.S. Embassy in Ciudad Trujillo to Secretary of State, September 13, 1945, USNA, RG 59, 839.633.
11. Ambassador Joseph McGurk to the Secretary of State, "Partido Dominicano Graft from the Petroleum Distribution," September 13, 1945, USNA, RG 59, 839.633.
12. See Vega, *Trujillo y Los Estados Unidos*, 127–29; see also McGurk to the Secretary of State.
13. Bosch, *La fortuna de Trujillo*, 77–116. See also Ornes, *Little Caesar*, 141.
14. McGurk to the Secretary of State, September 13, 1945, USNA, RG 59, 839.633.
15. Ornes, *Little Caesar*, 141–45.
16. Montes de Oca, interview.
17. Andreski, *Military Organization and Society*, 137.
18. Caribbean Defense Command, Army Intelligence Project, October 2, 1943, USNA, RG 319, 1941–1945, box 51, entry 47.
19. *U.S. Military Intelligence Reports: Combat Estimates.*
20. William C. Affeld, Jr., to the Department of State, December 10, 1954, USNA, RG 59, 739.551.
21. "The Trujillo Regime," *Intelligence Report, No. 4190*. These included brothers Héctor B. Trujillo, chief of staff of the National Army; José Arismendi (Petán) Trujillo, major in the National Army; Pedro V. Trujillo, captain in the National Army; and Aníbal Julio Trujillo, former general in the National Army. Among other well-known relatives were José García, a brother-in-law (married to Marina Trujillo), major general in the National Army and at one time secretary of state of the interior and police; García's sons, José and Virgilio, respectively a major and a lieutenant in the army; and Fernando Manuel Castillo, a brother-in-law (married to Nieves Luisa Trujillo), a captain in the Aviation Corps.
22. Richard Johnson to Department of State, August 28, 1952, USNA, RG 59, 739.11/8–852, box 3387.

23. U.S. Embassy Dispatch No. 571, January 22, 1953, USNA, RG 59, 739.551, box 3387.
24. Johnson to Department of State, August 28, 1952.
25. León Estévez, *Yo, Ramfis Trujillo*, 44–45.
26. William Belton to Department of State, Bureau of Inter-American Affairs, June 5, 1952, USNA, RG 59, 739.551; Crassweller, *Trujillo*, 303–5.
27. Belton to Department of State, June 5, 1952.
28. Belton to Department of State, June 5, 1952.
29. Richard A. Johnson to the Department of State, September 29, 1953, USNA, RG 59, 739.551.
30. U.S. Embassy to Department of State, September 29, 1953, USNA, RG 59, 739.551.
31. Francis Spalding to the Department of State, February 14, 1959, USNA, RG 59, 739.551.
32. U.S. Embassy to Department of State, September 29, 1953.
33. U.S. Embassy to Department of State, September 29, 1953.
34. Reconstruction of officers' views of Ramfis from interviews with Balcácer Vega, Montes de Oca, and Matos González in February 1990. Historian Bernardo Vega expressed similar ideas during an interview in February 1990.
35. Spalding to Department of State, February 14, 1959.
36. León Estévez, *Yo, Ramfis Trujillo*, 21–36.
37. *Hispanic American Report* 14 (July 1961): 609.
38. Skjelsbaek, "Militarisms, Its Dimensions and Corollaries," 91.
39. Juan Bosch, interview by the author, February 27, 1990, Santo Domingo.
40. For sociohistorical studies dealing with Dominican racism, see Sagás, *Race and Politics in the Dominican Republic*; Tolentino Dipp, "El prejuicio racial en Haití y en la República Dominicana"; and Torres-Saillant, "The Tribulations of Blackness."
41. Hoetink, "The Dominican Republic," 120.
42. Calder, *The Impact of Intervention*, 124–25.
43. Ibid.
44. Nanita, *Trujillo*, 77.
45. Vega, *Trujillo y las fuerzas armadas norteamericanas*, 228.
46. The group of scholars included Roberto Cassá, Danilo de los Santos, Abraham Lowenthal, Pedro Mir, Dato Pagán Perdomo, and Carmen Durán, among others. Bosch, Matos González, Joaquín Hungría, Renato Hungría, and Ramón Font Bernard all generously shared with me their ideas during interviews and conversations in 1990.
47. Racial "subdivision" of the armed forces based on interviews with Bosch, Bernardo Vega, Balcácer Vega, Matos González, Pagán Perdomo, and several other members of the armed forces who spoke under condition of anonymity.
48. Balcácer Vega, interview by the author, February 8, 1990.

49. Information provided under anonymity by a former army officer.
50. Matos González, interview, February 12, 1996.
51. García, *Mis 20 años junto a Trujillo*, 1:375.
52. García, *Mis 20 años junto a Trujillo*, 1:371–72.
53. Ayuso, *Todo por Trujillo*, 42.
54. The Foro was the most well-known instrument of denunciation, but Trujillo's machinations and taste for intrigue included a variety of mechanisms. For more details, see Derby, "The Magic of Modernity," 302–33.
55. Ayuso, *Todo por Trujillo*, 43.

8. New Dimension of Civil-Military Relations

1. Andreski, *Military Organization and Society*, 35; Thee, "Militarism and Militarisation," 23–24.
2. Dyer, "Dominican Republic," 185; Latorre, *Política dominicana contemporánea*, 65–66.
3. Weil et al., *Dominican Republic*, 207.
4. John C. Dreier to Charles C. Hauch, February 20, 1948, USNA, RG 59, 839.24.
5. Jack D. Neal, Chief Division of Foreign Activities, to Edson J. Shambart, October 24, 1947, USNA, RG 59, 839/248.
6. Thomas Watson to Minister Charles Curtis, March 20, 1931, USNA, RG 59, 839.24.
7. Walter Thurston to Francis White, March 30, 1931, USNA, RG 59, 839.24/63.
8. War Department to the Secretary of State, October 20, 1933, USNA, RG 59, 839.24/95.
9. Vega, *Trujillo y las fuerzas armadas norteamericanas*, 253–74.
10. Thurston to White, March 30, 1931.
11. Memorandum, Luis E. Nicolás to the Remington Arms Company, New York City, June 1, 1931, USNA, RG 59, 839.24/93.
12. Arthur Schoenfeld to Secretary of State, August 1, 1934, USNA, RG 59, 839.24/03; *Revista de Agricultura y Comercio*, 57 and 58 (June–July 1934).
13. Cited in Schoenfeld letter to Secretary of State, August 1, 1934.
14. Trujillo Molina, "A los agricultores en interés de evitar la ruina de las zonas tabacaleras," in *Discursos, mensajes y proclamas*, 2:64–65. See also Rodríguez Demorizi, *Cronología*, 1:129.
15. Galíndez, *Era of Trujillo*, 30; Crassweller, *Trujillo*, 109–10.
16. Memorandum, Chief of the Division of Latin American Affairs, May 5, 1935, USNA, RG 59, 839.115.
17. *New York Times*, May 21 and 22, 1935.
18. Secretary of State to the Minister in the Dominican Republic, April 30, 1934, USNA, RG 59, 839.115.
19. Department of State to the U.S. Legation in the Dominican Republic, May 14, 1935, USFR, 1935, 4:494–95.

20. Vega, *Trujillo y el control financiero norteamericano*, 264; Crassweller, *Trujillo*, 109–10; Malek, "Rafael Leonidas Trujillo Molina," 46–248. For congratulations, see Blanco, *La era de Trujillo*, 8–59.

21. McClintock, report of December 12, 1938, USNA, RG 59, 839.20/82.

22. Trujillo Molina, conversation with Duggan, July 11, 1939, USFR, 1939, 5:579–81.

23. Atkins and Larman, *The Trujillo Regime*, 81.

24. *U.S. Military Intelligence Reports: Combat Estimates*, 4–5.

25. Dominican Republic, Combat Estimate, Record of the Joint Chiefs of Staff, Geographic File, 1942–1945, USNA, RG 218, HM, B36.22.

26. McGurk to the Secretary of State, October 10, 1945, USFR, 1945, 9:984–85.

27. Trujillo Molina, *Discursos, mensajes y proclamas*, 7:257.

28. Skjelsbaek, "Militarism, Its Dimensions and Corollaries," 94.

29. Kantor, *Patterns of Politics*, 318.

30. Ortiz, "El ejército nacional y su progresiva evolución"; Memorandum, Ciudad Trujillo to the Department of State, August 28, 1952, USNA, RG 59, 739.11, box 3387.

31. Moya Pons, "The Dominican Republic since 1930," 520. See also Gutteridge, *Armed Forces in the New States*, 31.

32. Ornes, *Little Caesar*, 138.

33. Vega, *Trujillo y las fuerzas armadas norteamericanas*, 445. For information on population by age group and sex, see Weil et al., *Dominican Republic*, 23.

34. *La Opinión*, January 30, 1934.

35. *U.S. Military Intelligence Reports: Combat Estimates*.

36. English, *Armed Forces in Latin America*, 29; Intelligence Memorandum, April 1, 1964, Office of Current Intelligence, Report no. 1063/64.

37. Ornes, *Little Caesar*, 132–33; Kantor, *Patterns of Politics*, 318.

38. Rodríguez, "La marina de guerra."

39. Atkins and Larman, *The Trujillo Regime*, 86.

40. "The Armed Forces," in *This Is the Dominican Republic* (Holland, 1958), 14.

41. Vega Pagán, *Historia de las fuerzas armadas*, 2:480–81.

42. Reyes, "Trujillo creador de la aviación militar," 66–67.

43. English, *Armed Forces in Latin America*, 231.

44. "The Armed Forces," 13.

45. Ornes, *Little Caesar*, 135.

46. Memorandum of conversation among Ramfis Trujillo, Major General Arturo Espaillat, and Francis L. Spalding, October 3, 1958, USNA, RG 59, 739.58.

47. As interpreted by Spalding, October 3, 1958, USNA, RG 59, 739.58.

48. Vega, *Trujillo y las fuerzas armadas norteamericanas*, 361; Atkins and Larman, *The Trujillo Regime*, 92.

49. Soto Jiménez, *Las fuerzas militares*, 231.

50. Soto Jiménez, *Las fuerzas militares*, 185–86.

51. See Cassá, *Capitalismo y dictadura*, 124–32, and his *Historia social y económica*, 2:124–28; Galíndez, *Era of Trujillo*, 238–42; Turits, "The Foundations of Despotism," 482–83.

52. Derby, "The Magic of Modernity," 210.

53. Ralph Ackerman to the Department of State, November 1, 1949, USNA, RG 59, 839.24/11/49; Vorshirm, *From Swastikas to Palm Trees*, 149–53.

54. Report, Richard Johnson to the Department of State, "Description of the Military Parade," August 28, 1952, USNA, RG 59, 739.11, box 3387.

55. The differences are featured in *El Caribe*, August 16, 1952, and in the report from Johnson to the Department of State.

56. Report, Johnson to the Department of State, "The Personality of Trujillo," August 28, 1952, USNA, RG 59, 739.11, box 3387.

57. Crassweller, *Trujillo*, 294.

58. Material drawn from reports from *La Nación*. Trujillo's press published and publicized the importance of la Feria in almost every publication in November 1955. The *Álbum de oro* also graphically recorded hundreds of the events that took place during the exhibit.

59. Ornes, *Little Caesar*, 132.

60. Crassweller, *Trujillo*, 263.

61. Confrontation between Perón and the military in Potash, *The Army and Politics in Argentina*, 1–47.

62. Millett, *Guardians of the Dynasty*, 207.

9. Citizens and Soldiers

1. For example, see his speech directed to the National Army, May 2, 1937, in *Discursos, mensajes y proclamas*, 3:129–31.

2. Espaillat, *Trujillo: The Last Caesar*, 27.

3. Arbaje Ramírez and Jourdain Heredia, *Gran desfile nacional*. For samples of photos showing the Dominican people who marched in honor of Trujillo, see pp. 165–71.

4. Ornes, *Little Caesar*, 4.

5. Tejada, "El folklore como mecanismo de control político en Heureaux y Trujillo," 32–37. Translations of the verses are mine.

6. Pacini, *Bachata*, 37–45.

7. Pacini, *Bachata*, 44.

8. Balaguer's idea in Nanita, *La era de Trujillo*, 61.

9. Johnson to the Department of State, "The Personality of Trujillo."

10. For figures, see Ornes, *Little Caesar*, 175.

11. Nanita, *Trujillo*, 290.

12. Cordero Michel, *Análisis de la era de Trujillo*, 81.

13. De los Santos, *La pintura en la sociedad dominicana*, 76–92.

14. Ornes, *Little Caesar*, 173.

15. Excerpts from *Cartilla cívica* in Balaguer, *El pensamiento vivo de Trujillo*, 273–81.

16. I heard the story from several people in the Dominican Republic.

17. Trujillo Molina, *Discursos, mensajes y proclamas*, 1:76.

18. "La Guardia Universitaria Presidente Trujillo," *Publicaciones del Partido Trujillista*, 2:11.

19. Galíndez, *Era of Trujillo*, 171.

20. Ornes, *Little Caesar*, 179.

21. "The Trujillo Regime," *Intelligence Report, No. 4190*.

22. Richard Johnson, "Personality and Current Policies of Trujillo," May 26, 1952, USNA, RG 59, 739.521, box 3387; Bustamante, *Una satrapía en el Caribe*, 164–67.

23. "The Trujillo Regime," *Intelligence Report, No. 4190*.

24. Galíndez, *Era of Trujillo*, 152–59; Pagán, *Por qué lucha el pueblo dominicano*, 245–57.

25. "Dominican Republic," *Hispanic American Report* 7 (March 1954): 20. See also Cassá, *Movimiento obrero*, 341–498.

26. Memorandum, W. F. Barber to Assistant Secretary of State Braden, "Uprising in Dominican Army," November 29, 1946, USNA, RG 59, 839.20/11–2946.

27. "Ex militar relata conspiración contra Trujillo en el año 1946"; "Ex miembro de FA dice dictadura no permitía ex militares fijar residencia en el extranjero"; Balaguer, *El pensamiento vivo de Trujillo*, 146.

28. Nolasco, "Gesta contra la tiranía," 2.

29. Crassweller, *Trujillo*, 170–71.

30. President's Secretary File in "The Caribbean Legion," the CIA's report about Latin America, 1946–1976, Papers of Harry Truman, Library of Congress 86/217.

31. See "The Caribbean Legion."

32. "La lucha contra Trujillo."

33. Johnson to the Department of State, "The Personality of Trujillo."

34. Captain Eurípides Peralta to the Dominican Minister of Defense, January 30, 1950, USNA, RG 59, 739.56. box 3387. Partial list of weapons collected by the government and sent to the OAS were: (a) 90 cartridges for 7 mm. caliber rifle, most of them model 1946; (b) 2,926 pistol cartridges, .45 caliber; (c) 3 "Mendoza" automatic rifles, 7 mm. caliber model C; (d) 26 rifles Spanish "Mauser," model 1893; (e) 25 submachine guns, Reising, .45 caliber, model 1950; (f) 3 submachine guns, New Hausen, 7.63 mm; (g) 1 submachine gun, Thompson, .45 caliber, model 1928.

35. Galíndez, *Era of Trujillo*, 166.

36. *Gaceta Oficial*, March 2, 1936.

37. Balcácer Vega, interview.

38. As presented by Agusto Ginebra in *Plan de instrucción general para los Alcaldes*

Pedáneos, 1940, a booklet that outlines the authority and the responsibility of the *alcaldes*. For a definition of the mission of the *alcaldes*, see pp. 1–2.

39. Many of the functions described by Ginebra in *Principales* were confirmed during my interviews in the Dominican Republic in 1990.

40. Inoa, *Estado y campesinos*, 189.

41. Ornes, *Little Caesar*, 93.

42. Report, Robert Mills McClintock, Third Secretary of the U.S. Legation in the Dominican Republic, December 12, 1938, USNA, RG 59, 839.20/82.

43. Vega Pagán, *Historia de las fuerzas armadas*, 2:349.

44. Plúyer Trujillo, "El servicio militar obligatorio."

45. Dominican Republic, Secretariado Técnico de la Presidencia, Oficina Nacional de Estadística, *República Dominicana en Cifras 1980* (Santo Domingo: Publicaciones de la Oficina Nacional de Estadística, 1980), 9:3.

46. Trujillo Molina, *Discursos, mensajes y proclamas*, 7:258.

47. Plúyer Trujillo, "El servicio militar obligatorio," 9.

48. "Social and Economic Legacy of Trujillo," *Intelligence Report, No. 8491*.

49. Several of Trujillo's schemes to eliminate Castro are recorded by Espaillat in *Trujillo: The Last Caesar*, 142–62.

50. "Gobierno Respalda Legión Extranjera," *El Caribe*, March 5, 1959.

51. General García's response to officers who previously sent a letter to him. *El Caribe*, March 5, 1959.

52. Crassweller, *Trujillo*, 347.

53. Vega, *Trujillo y las fuerzas armadas norteamericanas*, 429.

54. Harry M. Lofton to the Department of State, October 15, 1959, USNA, RG 59, 739.5/10.

55. Lofton's description of the physical appearance of the mercenaries in Lofton to Department of State.

56. Roberto Cassá, interview by the author, February 2, 1990, Santo Domingo.

57. See the Spalding and Lofton reports to the Department of State, USNA, RG 59, 739.5/6–659 and 739.5/10–1559.

58. Johnson to the Department of State, "The Personality of Trujillo."

59. Trujillo Molina, *Discursos, mensajes y proclamas*, 3:130.

60. García and Galán, "La Universidad de Santo Domingo," 112.

61. "La Guardia Universitaria Presidente Trujillo," 2:12; L. Mejía, *De Lilís a Trujillo*, 303.

62. "Guardia Universitaria Presidente Trujillo," *Anuario de la Universidad de Santo Domingo, 1944–1945*, 31:148–49; "La Guardia Universitaria Presidente Trujillo," 2:8.

63. Cornielle, *Proceso histórico domínico-haitiano*, 157.

64. "Guardia Universitaria Presidente Trujillo," 31:148.

65. Cornielle, *Proceso histórico domínico-haitiano*, 159–64.

66. Cornielle, *Proceso histórico domínico-haitiano*, 160.

67. See excerpt from Fabio de la Mota, *Prensa y tribuna de la guardia universitaria* in *Publicaciones del Partido Trujillista*, 2:8.
68. García and Galán, "La Universidad de Santo Domingo," 117; Cornielle, "El ejército y la guardia universitaria."

Epilogue

1. Zaglul, *Apuntes*, 16–18, 107–8.
2. "Dominican Republic," *Hispanic American Report* 12 (February 1959): 92.
3. Vega, *Kennedy y Trujillo*, 35–42; Diederich, *Trujillo*, 79–81.
4. "Dominican Republic," *Hispanic American Report* 12 (July 1959): 269.
5. Franco, *La era de Trujillo*, 154.
6. Constrasting stories about the church in Ross, *La obra cristiana del benefactor de la patria*, and "El silencio del clero."
7. See Organization of the American States, "Report of the Inter-American Peace Committee to the Fifth Meeting of Consultation of Ministers of Foreign Affairs," August 6, 1959.
8. "Dominican Republic," *Hispanic American Report* 12 (December 1959): 668.
9. Martin, *Overtaken by Events*, 53–64.
10. See Diederich, *The Death of the Goat*, 116–17; Guerrero, *Los últimos días de la era de Trujillo*, 9–23; Vargas, *Trujillo*, 43–47.
11. See "Sobre Trujillo hay mitos que hay que destruir," *Ultima Hora*, July 24, 2001.
12. Dr. Mejía, personal communication with the author, August 2, 2001, Stevens Point, Wisconsin.

SOURCES CONSULTED

Archival Sources

Archivo Ateneo Amantes de la Luz, Santiago
Archivo General de la Nación, Santo Domingo
Archivo Palacio Nacional, Santo Domingo
Biblioteca de las Fuerzas Armadas, Santo Domingo
Biblioteca Museo de Historia y Geografía, Santo Domingo
Private Collection of Fundación Cultural Dominicana
United States National Archives. Navy Department. Naval Records Collections of the Office of Naval Records and Library. Record Group 45.
———. Navy Department. Naval Records of the Military Government of Santo Domingo, 1916–1924. Record Group 38.
———. Records of the Department of State Relating to the Internal Affairs of the Dominican Republic, 1910–1960. Record Group 59.
———. Records of the Joint Chiefs of Staff. Geographic File. Record Group 165.

Dominican Government Documents

Álbum del centenario de la República. Ciudad Trujillo, 1944.
Álbum de oro de la Feria de la Paz y Confraternidad del Mundo Libre. Ciudad Trujillo, 1956.
Anuario estadístico. Dirección General de Estadística. Ciudad Trujillo, 1931–1954.
Anuario de la Universidad de Santo Domingo, 1944–1945. Ciudad Trujillo, 1946.
Boletín de la Cámara de Diputados, 1924–1938. Ciudad Trujillo: Imprenta La Provincia, 1924–1938.
Censo nacional de población, 1950. Ciudad Trujillo: Anuario Estadístico de la República Dominicana, 1950.
Censo de la República. Primer censo nacional, 1920. Santo Domingo: Secretaría de Estado de Interior y Policía, 1920.
Colección de leyes y decretos. Ciudad Trujillo: Archivo General de la Nación, 1945.

Cuarto censo nacional de población. Ciudad Trujillo: Dirección General de Estadística, 1960.

Gaceta Oficial, 1900–1960.

Ley orgánica de las fuerzas armadas. Ciudad Trujillo: Secretaría de Estado de las Fuerzas Armadas, 1957.

Memoria de la Secretaría de Estado de las fuerzas armadas. Ciudad Trujillo: Impresora Arte y Cine, 1956–1959.

Población de la República Dominicana, según el censo levantado el 13 de mayo de 1935. Ciudad Trujillo: Dirección General de Estadística, 1946.

Publicaciones del Partido Trujillista. Ciudad Trujillo: Impresora Cosmopolita, 1941.

La República Dominicana. Habana: Empresa Editorial Cubana, 1932.

La República Dominicana en Cifras, 1980. Santo Domingo: Publicaciones de la Oficina Nacional de Estadística, 1980.

U.S. Government Documents

Congressional Record. 85th Cong. 1st Sess. Vol. 103, pt. 8. June 21–July 10, 1957.

———. 85th Cong. 1st Sess. Vol. 103, pt. 9. July 11–25, 1957.

Department of State. *Papers Relating to the Foreign Relations of the United States: Records Relating to the Foreign Relations with the Dominican Republic.* Washington DC: GPO, 1900–1960.

Intelligence Report, No. 4190. December 31, 1946, Library of Congress 86/2100.

Intelligence Report, No. 8491. July 10, 1961, Library of Congress 86/2100.

Mutual Defense Assistance: Agreement between the United States and the Dominican Republic, U.S. Treaties and Other International Agreements. Vol. 4, pt. 1. Washington DC: GPO, 1953.

Office of Current Intelligence. Report no. 1063/64. Library of Congress 86/217.

Truman, Harry. Papers. President's Secretary File. CIA Research Reports. Latin America, 1946–1948.

U.S. Military Intelligence Reports. Combat Estimates: The Western Hemisphere, 1920–1943. Library of Congress 89/8815.

U.S. Treaties and Other International Agreements. Vol. 1, 1950. Washington DC: GPO, 1950.

Books and Articles

Academia Colombina. *Memorial de protesta contra la arbitraria ocupación militar de la República Dominicana por tropas de los Estados Unidos.* Santo Domingo: Imprenta del Listín Diario, 1916.

Acevedo, Agustín. "Lo que ví." *Clío* 28, no. 136 (January–February 1979): 61–172.

Álbum de oro de la Feria de la Paz y Confraternidad del Mundo Libre. Ciudad Trujillo, 1956.

Alexander, George. "Primary Groups, Organization and Military Performance." In *A Study of Organizational Leadership*, ed. Associate Office of Military Leadership of U.S. Military Academy, 255–73. Harrisburg PA: Stackpole Books, 1976.

Alfaro Reyes, Manuel, ed. *Álbum commemorativo del grandioso homenaje al General _1isimo Rafael Leonidas Trujillo Molina . . . 12 de mayo de 1934*. Santo Domingo, 1934.

Álvarez, Federico. *Ideología política del pueblo dominicano*. Santiago: La Información, 1929.

Álvarez, Julia. *In the Time of the Butterflies*. New York: Plume, 1995.

Álvarez Mainardi, Opinio. "El ejército nacional bajo la gloriosa inspiración del Generalísimo Trujillo." *Revista militar* 16 (March 1936): 40–41.

Andreski, Stanislaw. *Military Organization and Society*. Berkeley: University of California Press, 1968.

Aquino García, Miguel. *Tres heroínas y un tirano*. Santo Domingo: Editora Corripio, 1997.

Arbaje Ramírez, Elías, and Luis E. Jourdain Heredia. *Gran desfile nacional, 16 de Agosto, 1958*. Ciudad Trujillo: Editora del Caribe, 1958.

Arvelo González, Alberto. "Las fuerzas armadas dominicanas." *Unión Cívica*, November 8, 1961, pp. 1–3.

Atkins, George Pope. *Arms and Politics in the Dominican Republic*. Boulder CO: Westview, 1981.

———. "The United States and the Dominican Republic during the Era of Trujillo." Ph.D. diss., American University, Washington DC, 1966.

Atkins, George Pope, and Wilson Larman. *The United States and the Trujillo Regime*. New Brunswick: Rutgers University Press, 1972.

Austerlitz, Paul. "Dominican Merengue in Regional, National, and International Perspectives: Dominican Republic Dance Music." Ph.D. diss., Wesleyan University, 1993.

Aybar, Luis. "La revolución de febrero." *Listín diario*, March 2, 1935.

Ayuso, Juan José. *Todo por Trujillo: Fuerzas armadas y militares, un proceso político desde 1930*. Santo Domingo: Editorial AA, 1999.

Balaguer, Joaquín. *Dominican Reality: Biographical Sketch of a Country and a Regime*. Trans. M. Gilland. Mexico, 1949.

———. *El pensamiento vivo de Trujillo*. Ciudad Trujillo: Impresora Dominicana, 1955.

———. *La isla al revés: Haití y el destino dominicano*. Santo Domingo: Librería Dominicana, 1984.

———. *Memorias de un cortesano de la era de Trujillo*. Santo Domingo: Editora Corripio, 1988.

Balcácer Vega, Alfredo. "Las fuerzas armadas." Santo Domingo, 1988.

Barnes, Peter. *Pawns: The Plight of Citizen-Soldier*. New York: Knopf, 1972.

Betances, Emelio. *State and Society in the Dominican Republic.* Boulder CO: West-view, 1995.

Blanco, Pedro González. *La era de Trujillo.* Ciudad Trujillo: Editora El Caribe, 1955.

Blassingame, John. "The Press and American Intervention in Haiti and the Dominican Republic, 1904–1920." *Caribbean Studies* 9, no. 2 (July 1969): 27–43.

Boin, Jacqueline, and José Serrulle Ramia. *El proceso de desarrollo del capitalismo en la República Dominicana, 1844–1930.* 2 vols. Santo Domingo: Ediciones Gramil, 1981.

Bonetti, Arturo. "La aviación y el ejército dominicano." *La Revista,* October 1928, p. 36.

Bons, Paul. "An Organizational Approach to the Study of Leadership." In *A Study of Organizational Leadership,* ed. Associate Office of Military Leadership, United States Military Academy, 13–126. Harrisburg PA: Stackpole Books, 1976.

Booth, John, and Thomas Walker. *Understanding Central America.* Boulder CO: Westview, 1989.

Bosch, Juan. *Composición social dominicana.* Santo Domingo: Editora Tele-3, 1971.

———. *La fortuna de Trujillo.* Santo Domingo: Editora Alfa and Omega, 1985.

———. *Trujillo: Causas de una tiranía sin ejemplo.* Caracas: Librería Las Novedades, 1959.

"La brigada y el brigadier." Editorial. *La Revista,* August 1927.

Bustamante, Gregorio R. [pseud.]. *Una satrapía en el Caribe: Historia puntual de la mala vida del déspota Rafael L. Trujillo.* Guatemala: Ediciones del Caribe, 1946.

Calder, Bruce J. *The Impact of Intervention: The Dominican Republic during the U.S. Occupation of 1916–1924.* Austin: University of Texas Press, 1984.

Cambeira, Alan. *Quisqueya la Bella.* New York: M. E. Sharpe, 1996.

Campillo Pérez, Julio G. *El grillo y el ruiseñor: Elecciones presidenciales dominicanas. Contribución a su estudio.* Santo Domingo: Editora del Caribe, 1966.

Capdevila, Lauro. *La dictadure de Trujillo: Guide bibliographique.* Paris: Histoire des Antilles hispaniques, 1991.

Cassá, Roberto. *Capitalismo y dictadura.* Santo Domingo: Alfa y Omega, 1982.

———. *Historia social y económica de la República Dominicana.* 2 vols. Santo Domingo: Alfa y Omega, 1978.

———. "La isla al revés: Entre la cuestión nacional y la cuestión social." Supplement, *Hoy,* May 25, 1985, pp. 13–17.

———. *Movimiento obrero y lucha socialista en la República Dominicana.* Santo Domingo: Fundación Cultural Dominicana, 1990.

———. "El racismo en la ideología de la clase dominante dominicana." *Ciencia y Sociedad* 3, no. 1 (1975): 59–85.

Castillo de Aza, Zenón. *Trujillo: Benefactor de la iglesia*. Ciudad Trujillo: Editorial El Caribe, 1955.

Charles Dunlop, Clarence E. "El enganche." *Revista de las fuerzas armadas* 4, no. 35 (March 1954).

Cordero Michel, José. *Análisis de la era de Trujillo: Informe sobre la República Dominicana*. Santo Domingo: Publicaciones de la Universidad Autónoma de Santo Domingo, 1970.

Collin, Richard H. *Theodore Roosevelt's Caribbean: The Panama Canal, the Monroe Doctrine, and the Latin American Context*. Baton Rouge: Louisiana State University Press, 1990.

Cornielle, Carlos. "El ejército y la guardia universitaria." *Revista militar*, November–December 1938, p. 25.

———. *Proceso histórico dominico-haitiano*. Santo Domingo: Publicaciones América, 1980.

Crassweller, Robert D. *Trujillo: The Life and Times of a Caribbean Dictator*. New York: Macmillan, 1966.

Cuello, José Israel. *Documentos del conflicto dominico-haitiano de 1937*. Santo Domingo: Taller, 1985.

Cuello, Rafael. *El sisal: Esclavitud y muerte en la era de Trujillo*. Santo Domingo: Susaeta, 1998.

Cuevas Sena, Raymundo. "Gesta contra la tiranía: Complot de los sargentos técnicos A.M.D." *EL 1J4*, February 28, 1962, pp. 4, 9.

Danticat, Edwidge. *The Farming of Bones: A Novel*. New York: Soho Press, 1998.

De Besault, Lawrence. *President Trujillo: His Work and the Dominican Republic*. 2nd ed. Washington DC: Washington Publishing Company, 1936.

Dawes, General Charles G., James G. Harbord, Summer Welles, H. C. Smither, T. W. Robinson, J. C. Roop, R. T. Seidemann, and E. Ross Bartley. *Economic Commission Report of the Condition of the Dominican Economy*. Chicago: Lakeside Press, 1929.

De Castro, Rafael B. "Breves apuntes sobre las distintas fuerzas del ejército nacional de la República Dominicana." *Revista militar* 37 (August–September 1937): 31–34.

De la Rosa, Antonio [Alexander Pujols]. *Las finanzas de Santo Domingo y el control americano*. Santo Domingo: Sociedad Dominicana de Bibliófilos, 1987.

De la Rosa, Jesús. "El estado, la constitución, y las fuerzas del ejército nacional en la República Dominicana." *El nacional*, June 11, 1989, pp. 44–45.

De los Santos, Danilo. *La pintura en la sociedad dominicana*. Santo Domingo: Editora del Caribe, 1979.

Derby, Lauren Hutchinson. "The Magic of Modernity: Dictatorship and Civic Culture in the Dominican Republic, 1916–1962." Ph.D. diss., University of Chicago, 1998.

Despradel, Lil. "Las etapas del antihaitianismo en la República Dominicana: El papel de los historiadores." *Política y sociología en Haití y la República Dominicana*, ed. Gérard Pierre-Charles, 83–108. Mexico: Universidad Autónoma de Mexico, 1974.

Diederich, Bernard. *Trujillo: The Death of the Goat.* Princeton: Markus Wiener, 2000.

"Diez años de servicios." *La Revista* 3 (December 1928): 1–12.

"Dominican Republic." *Hispanic American Report* 12 (July 1959): 266–69.

Duff, Ernest A. *Leader and Party in Latin America.* Boulder CO: Westview, 1985.

Ducoudray, Félix Servio. *Los "gavilleros" del este: Una epopeya calumniada.* Santo Domingo: Editora de la Universidad Autónoma de Santo Domingo, 1976.

Dyer, Gwynne. "Dominican Republic." In *World Armies*, ed. John Keegan, 178–85. New York: Facts on File, 1976.

Eide, Asbjorn, and Marek Thee, eds. *Problems of Contemporary Militarism.* New York: St. Martin's Press, 1980.

"Ejercito Dominicano." *La Revista*, September 1928, p. 22.

"Ejercito nacional." *Los Quijotes*, San Juan, Puerto Rico. Reprinted in *La Revista*, September 1928, p. 23.

"El ejército dominicano." *La Revista*, May 1928, p. 1.

"El Generalísimo y el ejército." *Revista Militar* 4 (August 1938): 1.

"El Generalísimo Trujillo realiza extenso recorrido por distintas regiones de la República Dominicana." *Revista de las fuerzas armadas* 3, no. 18 (October 1952): 50–52.

El-Himani, Kassim. *Santo domingo de ayer y de hoy.* New York: L&S Printing, 1934.

"El presidente y el ejército. "*La Opinión*, April 1938. Reproduced in *Revista militar* 19 (March–April 1938): 24.

"El silencio del clero." *Tribuna Libre*, September 13, 1961.

English, Adrian. *Armed Forces in Latin America: Their History, Development, Present Strength and Military Potential.* London: Jane's, 1984.

Espaillat, Arturo R. *Trujillo: The Last Caesar.* Chicago: H. Regnery, 1963.

Espinal, Rosario Rafaelina. *Autoritarismo y democracia en la política dominicana.* San José: Centro Interamericano de Asesoría Electoral, 1987.

———. "Classes, Power, and Political Change in the Dominican Republic." Ph.D. diss., Washington University, 1985.

"Ex miembro de FA dice dictadura no permitía ex militares fijar residencia en el extranjero." *Unión Cívica*, April 25, 1962.

"Ex militar relata conspiración contra Trujillo en el año 1946." *Unión Cívica*, April 3, 1962.

Febles, Horacio. *El primero de abril y el ejército: Tres crónicas y un discurso.* Santiago: El Diario, 1941.

Fellowes, Eduard. "Training Native Troops in Santo Domingo." *Marine Corps Gazette* 8, no. 4 (December 1923): 215–33.

Fiallo, Fabio. *La comisión nacionalista dominicana en Washington, 1920–1921.* Ciudad Trujillo: Imprenta La Opinión, 1939.

Fontana, Gil. *Trujillo y su obra, 1930–1952.* La Romana: Impresora Romana, 1954.

Franco, Franklin J. *La era de Trujillo.* Santo Domingo: Fundación Cultural Dominicana, 1992.

———. *Los negros, los mulatos y la nación dominicana.* Santo Domingo: Editora Nacional, 1969.

Frómeta Nina, Joaquín. "El ejército nacional." *Revista militar,* March–April 1942, p. 27.

"Las fuerzas armadas de la República Dominicana." *El Exportador Español: Special Edition Dedicated to the Dominican Republic.* October 1956.

Fuller, Stephen M., and Graham A. Cosmas. *Marines in the Dominican Republic, 1916–1924.* Washington DC: Marine Corps, 1974.

Galíndez, Jesús de. *The Era of Trujillo.* Ed. Russell H. Fitzgibbon. Tucson: University of Arizona Press, 1973.

Gallegos, Gerardo. *Cara y cruz de una dictadura.* Madrid: Ediciones Iberoamericanas, 1968.

Gantenbein, James W., ed. *The Evolution of Our Latin American Policy: A Documentary Record.* New York: Columbia University Press, 1950.

García, Humberto. "Decolonization, Demilitarization and Denuclearization in the Caribbean." Occasional Paper Series 131. Miami: Florida International University, 1989.

García, José Gabriel. *Compendio de la historia de Santo Domingo.* 4 vols. Santo Domingo: Publicaciones Ahora, 1968.

García, Manuel Javier. *Mis 20 años en el palacio nacional junto a Trujillo y otros gobernantes dominicanos.* 2 vols. Santo Domingo: Taller, 1986.

García, Mary Rosa, and Tomás Modesto Galán. "La Universidad de Santo Domingo y su relación con el proyecto de dominación trujillista." Thesis, Universidad Autónoma de Santo Domingo, 1987.

Gardiner, Harvey. *La política de inmigración del dictador Trujillo.* Santo Domingo: Universidad Nacional Pedro Henríquez Ureña, 1979.

Gilbert, Greogorio Urbano. *Mi lucha contra el invasor yanqui de 1916.* Santo Domingo: Universidad Autónoma de Santo Domingo, 1975.

Ginebra, Augusto. *Principales deberes de un alcalde pedáneo en la era de Trujillo.* Puerto Plata, 1940.

Goldwert, Marvin. *The Constabulary in the Dominican Republic and Nicaragua: Progency and Legacy of the United States Intervention.* Gainesville: University of Florida Press, 1962.

González Blanco, Pedro. *La era de Trujillo*. Ciudad Trujillo: Editora del Caribe, 1955.

Gordon, Martin, ed. *Pendleton Papers*. Folder no. 18. In *Joseph Henry Pendleton, 1860–1942: Register of His Personal Papers*. Washington DC: U.S. Marine Corps, 1975.

Grant, Frances R. "Hemisphere Repudiates Trujillo." *Hemispherica* 9 (October 1960): 1–2.

Greestein, Fred, and Nelson W. Polsby, eds. *Handbook of Political Science*. Vol. 3: *Macropolitical Theory*. Reading MA: Addison-Wesley, 1975.

Guerrero, Miguel. *Los últimos días de la era de Trujillo*. Santo Domingo: Editora Corripio, 1991.

Guerrero Pou, Eugenio. *Yo maté a su hijo: Testimonio de un cadete de la era de Trujillo*. Santo Domingo: Taller, 1996.

Gutteridge, William. *Armed Forces in the New States*. London: Oxford University Press, 1962.

Harries-Jekins, Gwyn. "Armed Forces and Society." In *Brassey's Encyclopedia of Military History and Biography*, ed. Franklin D. Margiotta, 77–90. Washington: Brassey's, 1994.

Hartlin, Jonathan. *The Struggle for Democratic Politics in the Dominican Republic*. Chapel Hill: University of North Carolina Press, 1998.

Hazard, Samuel. *Santo Domingo: Su pasado y presente*. Santo Domingo: Editora de Santo Domingo, 1974.

Henríquez, Enrique Apolinar. *Episodios imperialistas*. Ciudad Trujillo: Editora Montalvo, 1958.

Henríquez Ureña, Max. *Los yanquis en Santo Domingo*. Santo Domingo: Editora de Santo Domingo, 1977.

Hernández Flores, Ismael. *Lecciones de trujillismo y balaguerismo para el discipulado*. Santo Domingo: Símbolo, 1996.

Hernández Franco, Tomás. *La más bella revolución de América*. Santo Domingo: Amberes, 1930.

Hicks, Albert D. *Blood in the Streets: The Life and Rule of Trujillo*. New York: Creative Age Press, 1946.

Hillman, Richard, and Thomas J. D'Agostino. *Distant Neighbors in the Caribbean: The Dominican Republic and Jamaica in Perspective*. New York: Praeger, 1992.

Hoepelman, Rafael. "Se organiza en el país el movimiento 14 de junio." *La Nación*, July 8, 1961.

Hoepelman, Virgilio. *Nuestra vida exterior: Notas sobre historia diplomática dominicana, 1844–1950*. Ciudad Trujillo: Arte y Cine, 1951.

Hoetink, Harmannus. "The Dominican Republic." In *Race and Class in Latin America*, ed. Magnus Morner, 96–121. New York: Columbia University Press, 1970.

————. *El pueblo dominicano, 1850–1900*. Santiago: Universidad Católica Madre y Maestra, 1972.

————. *The Two Variants of Race Relations in Caribbean Race Relations: A Contribution to the Sociology of Segmented Society*. Trans. Eva M. Hooykaas. London: Oxford University Press, 1967.

"Homenaje en Conmemoración de la investidura del Generalísimo Rafael Leonidas Trujillo Molina como Doctor Honoris Causa en Leyes de la Universidad de Pittsburgh." *Publicaciones de la Universidad de Santo Domingo* 22 (1942): 13–14.

Huertas, J. "Trujillo es el ejército." *Revista militar* 14 (September–October 1935): 26.

Hunt, Alfred. *Haiti's Influence on Antebellum America: Slumbering Volcano in the Caribbean*. Baton Rouge: Louisiana State University Press, 1988.

Huntington, Samuel P. *The Soldier and the State: The Theory and Politics of Civil-Military Relations*. New York: Vintage Books, 1964.

Incháustegui, Arístides. "Cronología de gobiernos y gobernantes de la República Dominicana." *Eme Eme* 1, no. 36 (May–June 1978): 3–14.

Inoa, Orlando. *Bibliografía haitiana en la República Dominicana*. Río Piedras: Editorial de la Universidad de Puerto Rico, Serie Bibliográfica, 1994.

————. *Estado y campesinos al inicio de la era de Trujillo*. Santo Domingo: Librería La Trinitaria, 1994.

Jimenes Grullón, Juan Isidro. "Desarrollo histórico de las fuerzas armadas." *Ahora*, January 16, 1965, pp. 40–48.

————. *La República Dominicana: Análisis de su pasado y su presente*. 3rd ed. Santo Domingo: Editora Cosmos, 1974.

————. *Sociología política dominicana, 1844–1966*. 3 vols. Santo Domingo: Editora Alfa y Omega, 1980.

Jiménez, Élida y Ana Marina Méndez. "Antecedentes: Instrucción, educación y evolución de la enseñanza en las instituciones castrenses dominicanas." Photocopy, Santo Domingo, 1988.

Jiménez, Ramón Emilio. "La fábrica de armas y la suspicacia de nuestros enemigos." *La Nación*, August 27, 1949.

Johnson, John J. *The Military and Society in Latin America*. Stanford: Stanford University Press, 1967.

Kantor, Harry. *Patterns of Politics and Political Systems in Latin America*. Chicago: Rand McNally, 1969.

Karsten, Peter, ed. *The Military-State-Society Symbiosis*. New York: Garland, 1998.

Keegan, John, ed. *World Armies*. New York: Facts on File, 1976.

Kelsey, Carl. "The American Intervention in Haiti and the Dominican Republic." *Annals of the American Academy of Political and Social Sciences* 100, no. 189 (1922): 110–202.

Klein, Alan. *Sugarball: The American Game, the Dominican Dream.* New Haven: Yale University Press, 1991.

Klein, Herbert. "David del Toro and the Establishment of 'Military Socialism' in Bolivia." *Hispanic American Historical Review* 45, no. 1 (February 1965): 25–52.

Knight, Melvin M. *Los americanos en Santo Domingo: Episodios de imperialismo americano.* Santo Domingo: Editora de Santo Domingo, 1980.

Kucuk, Ejub. "The Socio-Class Determinants of Militarism." In *Problems of Contemporary Militarism*, ed. Asbjorn Eide and Marek Thee, 148–72. New York: St. Martin's Press, 1980.

Labourt, José. *Trujillo: Seguiré a caballo.* Santo Domingo: Taller, 1984.

Lane, Rufus. "Civil Government in Santo Domingo in the Early Days of the Military Occupation." *Marine Corps Gazette* 7, no. 2 (June 1922): 127–46.

Langley, Lester. *The United States and the Caribbean in the Twentieth Century.* Athens: University of Georgia Press, 1989.

Laguerre, Michael S. *The Military and Society in Haiti.* Knoxville: University of Tennessee Press, 1993.

Latorre, Eduardo. *Política dominicana contemporánea.* Santo Domingo: Ediciones INTEC, 1975.

León Estévez, Luis José. *Yo, Ramfis Trujillo.* Santo Domingo: Editorial Letra Gráfica, 2002.

Lieuwen, Edwin. *Arms and Politics in Latin America.* New York: Praeger, 1960.

———. *Generals versus Presidents.* New York: Praeger, 1964.

———. "The Problem of Military Government." In *New Military Politics in Latin America*, ed. Robert Wesson, 1–16. New York: Praeger, 1982.

Linz, Juan. "Totalitarian and Authoritarian Regimes." In *Handbook of Political Science.* Vol. 3: *Macropolitical Theory*, ed. Fred I. Greestein and Nelson W. Polsby, 175–411. Reading MA: Addison-Wesley, 1975.

Logan, Rayford. *Haiti and the Dominican Republic.* New York: Oxford University Press, 1968.

López de Santa Anna, Antonio. *Misión Fronteriza: Apuntes Históricos, 1936–1967.* Dajabón, 1957.

Loveman, Brian, and Thomas M. Davies, Jr., eds. *The Politics and Anti Politics: The Military in Latin America.* Wilmington: Scholarly Resources, 1997.

Lozoya, Alberto. *El ejército mexicano, 1911–1965.* Mexico: El Colegio de México, 1970.

"La lucha contra Trujillo: La invasión de Luperón, un episodio de valor y patriotismo." *Ahora* 606 (June 1975).

Luperón, Gregorio. *Notas autobiográficas y apuntes históricos.* 2nd ed. 3 vols. Santo Domingo: Editora de Santo Domingo, 1974.

Malek, Michael. "Rafael Leonidas Trujillo Molina: The Rise of a Caribbean Dictator." Ph.D. diss., University of California, Santa Barbara, 1971.

MacMichael, David. "The United States and the Dominican Republic, 1871–1940: A Cycle in Caribbean Diplomacy." Ph.D. diss., University of Oregon, 1964.

Marine Corps Gazette 8, no. 4 (December 1923): 215–33.

Maríñez, Pablo. "Las fuerzas armadas en la República Dominicana: Profesionalización y politización." *Revista de Ciencias Sociales* 25, nos. 3–4 (July–December 1986): 601–02.

———. "Relaciones dominico-haitianas y raíces histórico culturales africanas en la República Dominicana. Bibliografía básica." *Historia y sociedad* 70 (1986): 9–42.

Martin, John B. *Overtaken by Events: The Dominican Crisis from the Fall of Trujillo to the Civil War.* Garden City NY: Doubleday, 1966.

Martínez, Rufino. *Diccionario biográfico-histórico dominicano, 1821–1930.* Santo Domingo: Universidad Autónoma de Santo Domingo, 1971.

———. *Hombres Dominicanos: Deschamps, Heureaux y Luperón. Santana y Báez.* Santo Domingo: Editora Corripio, 1985.

Mateo, Andrés L. *Mito y cultura en la era de Trujillo.* Santo Domingo: Editora de Colores, 1993.

Matos González, Ramiro y José Soto Jiménez. *Historia militar dominicana.* 2 vols. Santo Domingo: Edita Libros, 1984.

Medina Benet, Víctor. *Los responsables del fracaso de la tercera república.* Santo Domingo: Amigo del Hogar, 1976.

Medina Peña Ramos, Viterbo. "El ejército nacional en la era de Trujillo." *Revista de las fuerzas armadas,* March–April 1951, p. 19.

Medina, Sonia, Yocasta Méndez, and Alejandro Paulino. "Análisis socio-histórico y premisas de la ascendencia de Trujillo al poder, 1924–1930." Thesis, Universidad Autónoma de Santo Domingo, 1980.

Mejía, Félix E. *Alrededor y en contra del plan Hughes-Peynado.* Santo Domingo: Imprenta de Gran Librería Selecta, 1922.

———. *Vía crucis de un pueblo: Relato sinóptico de la tragedia dominicana bajo la férula de Trujillo.* Mexico, 1951.

Mejía, Luis F. *De Lilís a Trujillo: Historia contemporánea de la República Dominicana.* Santo Domingo: Editora de Santo Domingo, 1976.

Mejía Ricart, Marcio Antonio. *Las clases sociales en Santo Domingo.* Ciudad Trujillo: Librería Dominicana, 1953.

Metcalf, Clyde J. *History of the United States Marine Corps.* New York: G. F. Putnam and Sons, 1939.

Millett, Richard. *Guardians of the Dynasty: A History of the U.S.–Created Guardia Nacional de Nicaragua and the Somoza Family.* Maryknoll NY: Orbis Books, 1977.

Millett, Richard, and Marvin Soloman. "The Court Martial of Lieutenant Rafael L. Trujillo." *Revista/Review Interamericana* 2 (fall 1972): 396–404.

Monclús, Miguel Angel. *El caudillismo en la República Dominicana*. Ciudad Trujillo: Editora Montalvo, 1948.

Montás Guerrero, Salvador. "El desenvolvimiento militar de la frontera." *Revista de las fuerzas armadas* 4 no. 31 (November 1953): 11.

Morner, Magnus. *Race and Class in Latin America*. New York: Columbia University, 1970.

Morrison, DeLesseps S. *Latin American Mission: An Adventure in Hemisphere Diplomacy*. New York: Simon and Schuster, 1965.

Moscoso Puello, Francisco. *Cartas a Evelina*. Ciudad Trujillo: Editora Montalvo, 1941.

Moya Pons, Frank. *La dominación haitiana*. Santiago: Publicaciones UCMM, 1972.

———. "The Dominican Republic since 1930." In *The Cambridge History of Latin America* 7, ed. Leslie Bethell, 509–43. Cambridge: Cambridge University Press, 1990.

Nanita, Abelardo R. *Trujillo*. 5th ed. Ciudad Trujillo: Editora del Caribe, 1954.

———. *La era de Trujillo*. Ciudad Trujillo: Impresora Dominicana, 1955.

Nolasco, Carlos M. "Gesta contra la tiranía: Complot de los sargentos técnicos AMD." *El 1J4*, March 7, 1962, p. 2.

Nunn, Frederick. "On the Role of the Military in Twentieth-century Latin America: The Mexican Case." In *The Modern Mexican Military: A Reassessment*, ed. David F. Ronfeldt, 33–49. La Jolla: Center for U.S.–Mexican Studies, University of California, 1984.

———. *The Time of the Generals: Latin American Professional Militarism in World Perspective*. Lincoln: University of Nebraska Press, 1992.

Ornes Goiscou, Germán. *Trujillo: Little Caesar of the Caribbean*. New York: Nelson and Sons, 1958.

Ortiz, Vicente. "El ejército nacional y su progresiva evolución." *Revista militar,* January–February 1939, pp. 8–9.

Osorio Lizarazo, José Antonio. *Germen y proceso del antitrujillismo en América*. Santiago de Chile: Imprenta Colombia, 1956.

———. *Portrait of Trujillo*. Ciudad Trujillo, 1958.

Otley, C. B. "Militarism and Militarization in the Public Schools, 1900–1972." In *The Military-State-Society Symbiosis*, ed. Peter Karsten, 219–37. New York: Garland, 1998.

Padilla D'Onís, Luis. *Anecdotario de Trujillo*. Ciudad Trujillo: Editorial Padilla, 1960.

Pagán Perdomo, Dato. *Por qué lucha el pueblo dominicano? Análisis del fenómeno dictatorial en América Latina*. Caracas: Los Talleres de Impresos Caribe, 1959.

Paret, Peter. "Military Power." *Journal of Military History* 53 (July 1989): 239–56.

Pacini Hernández, Deborah. *Bachata: A Social History of the Dominican Popular Music*. Philadelphia: Temple University Press, 1995.

Peguero, Valentina. "Participación de la mujer en la historia dominicana." *Eme-Eme*, January–February 1982, pp. 21–49.

Peguero, Valentina, and Danilo de los Santos. *Visión general de la historia dominicana*. Santo Domingo: Taller, 1978.

Peña, Ángela. *Así era Duarte*. 3rd ed. Santo Domingo: Ediciones Lozano, 1996.

Penson, José E. *Una gestión histórica*. Ciudad Trujillo, 1953.

———. *El Partido Dominicano*. Ciudad Trujillo: Imprenta Arte y Cine, 1957.

Pepín, Ercilia. *Feminismo*. Santiago: Tipografía El Diario, 1930.

Pichardo, José M., ed. *Gallos y galleros*. Santo Domingo: Editora Corripio, 1985.

Pierre-Charles, Gérard, ed. *Problemas dominico-haitianos y del Caribe*. México: UNAM, 1973.

———. *Política y sociología en Haití y la República Dominicana*. Mexico: Universidad Autónoma de Mexico, 1974.

Plúyer Trujillo, Agustín R. "El servicio militar obligatorio." *Revista de las fuerzas armadas* 5, no. 40 (August 1954): 9.

Potash, Robert A. *The Army and Politics in Argentina, 1945–1962*. Stanford: Stanford University Press, 1969.

Prestol Castillo, Freddy. *El masacre se pasa a pie*. Santo Domingo: Ediciones Taller, 1973.

Publicaciones del Partido Trujillista. *La Guardia Universitaria Presidente Trujillo*. 2 vols. Ciudad Trujillo: Imprenta Cosmopólita, 1941.

Quezada, Teresita. "El ejército nacional y Trujillo en los primeros quince años de su dictadura." *Eme-Eme*, January–February 1974, pp. 105–17.

Regehr, Ernie. "What Is Militarism?" In *Problems of Contemporary Militarism*, ed. Asbjorn Eide and Marek Thee, 127–39. New York: St. Martin's Press, 1980.

Renda, Mary A. *Taking Haiti: Military Occupation and the Culture of U.S. Imperialism*. Chapel Hill: University of North Carolina Press, 2001.

Reyes, Rafael Antonio Jorge. "Trujillo creador de la aviación militar." *Revista de las fuerzas armadas*, November–December 1958, pp. 66–67.

Rippy, Fred. "The Initiation of the Custom Receivership in the Dominican Republic." *Hispanic American Historical Review* 17 (November 1937): 419–57.

Rivera Cuesta, Marcos. *Las fuerzas armadas y la política dominicana*. Santo Domingo: Talleres de Artes Graficas, 1986.

Rodríguez, Domingo A. "La marina de guerra y su ilustre creador Generalísimo Trujillo" *Revista de las fuerzas armadas* 1 (March–April 1956): 2.

Rodríguez Beruff, Jorge. *Los militares y el poder*. Lima: Mosca Azul Editores, 1983.

Rodríguez Demorizi, Emilio. *Cronología de Trujillo*. 2 vols. Ciudad Trujillo: Impresora Dominicana, 1955.

———, ed. *Hostos en Santo Domingo*. 2 vols. Ciudad Trujillo: Imprenta J. R. Vda. García, 1939.

———. *Papeles de Santana*. Roma: Stab. Tipografico G. Managlia, 1952.

Ronfeldt, David F. "The Mexican Army and the Political Order since 1940." In *The Modern Mexican Military: A Reassessment*, ed. David F. Ronfeldt, 63–86. La Jolla: Center for U.S.–Mexican Studies, University of California, 1984.

Roorda, Eric Paul. *The Dictator Next Door: The Good Neighbor Policy and the Trujillo Regime in the Dominican Republic*. Durham: Duke University Press, 1998.

Ross, Eduardo. *La obra cristiana del benefactor de la patria*. Ciudad Trujillo: Editora del Caribe, 1959.

Rossi, Ernest, and Jack Plano. *The Latin American Political Dictionary*. Santa Barbara CA: ABC-Clio, 1980.

Rouquie, Alan. *The Military and the State in Latin America*. Trans. Paul Sigmund. Berkeley: University of California Press, 1987.

Sáez, José Luis. *Loyola, Dajabón: Cincuenta años de educación agrícola en la frontera, 1946–1996*. Santo Domingo: Editora Corripio, 1995.

Sagás, Ernesto. "The Case of Mistaken Identity: Antihaitianismo in Dominican Culture." *Latinamericanist*, December 1993, pp. 1–5.

———. *Race and Politics in the Dominican Republic*. Gainesville: University Press of Florida, 2000.

San Miguel, Pedro L. "La paradoja de la democracia dominicana. Un libro para romper el silencio: *Estado y campesinos al inicio de la era de Trujillo*, de Orlando Inoa." *Estudios Sociales*, October–December 1994, pp. 83–91.

San Miguel, Pedro. "The Dominican Peasantry and the Market Economy: The Peasants of the Cibao, 1800–1960." Ph.D. diss., Columbia University, 1987.

Schoenrich, Otto. *Santo Domingo: Un país con futuro*. Santo Domingo: Editora de Santo Domingo, 1977.

Selden, Roman. *Quisqueya: A History of the Dominican Republic*. Seattle: University of Washington Press, 1964.

Silié, Rubén. "Prejuicio racial y el antihaitianaismo en la identidad dominicana." Facultad Latino Americana de Ciencias Sociales (FLASCO), n.d.

Sinks, Alfred H. "Trujillo, Caribbean Dictator." *American Mercury* 60, no. 202 (October 1940): 164–71.

Skjelsbaek, Kjell. "Militarism, Its Dimensions and Corollaries: An Attempt at Conceptual Clarification." In *Problems of Contemporary Militarism*, ed. Asbjorn Eide and Marek Thee, 77–106. New York: St. Martin's Press, 1980.

Skelton, William. *An American Profession of Arms: The Officer Corps, 1784–1861*. Lawrence: University Press of Kansas, 1992.

"Sortean 50 casas entre alistados de fuerzas armadas." *Revista de las fuerzas armadas*, October 1954, p. 44.

Soto Jiménez, José Miguel. *Temas sobre la profesionalización militar en la República Dominicana*. Santo Domingo: Editora Corripio, 1988.

———. *Las fuerzas militares en la República Dominicana*. Santo Domingo: Ediciones Grupo 5, 1996.

Stepan, Alfred. *The Military in Politics: Changing Patterns in Brazil*. Princeton: Princeton University Press, 1974.

Swilley III, Monroe F. "The Haitian-Dominican Republic Incident of 1937: Press Reaction." *Caribbean Archives, Archivos del Caribe* 8 (1978): 6–23.

Tejada, Adriano Miguel. "El folklore como mecanismo de control político en Heureaux y Trujillo." *Eme-Eme*, January–February 1978, pp. 19–39.

Thee, Marek. "Militarism and Militarisation in Contemporary International Relations." In *Problems of Contemporary Militarism*, ed. Asbjorn Eide and Marek Thee, 15–35. New York: St. Martin's Press, 1980.

Tolentino Dipp, Hugo. "El prejuicio racial en Haití y en la República Dominicana." In *Problemas domínico-haitianos y del Caribe*, ed. Gérard Pierre-Charles, 111–44. México: UNAM, 1973.

Tolentino Rojas, Vicente. *This Is the Dominican Republic*. New York: Consulate General of the Dominican Republic, 1954.

Torres-Saillant, Silvio. "The Tribulations of Blackness: Stages in Dominican Racial Identity." *Latin American Perspectives* 25, no. 3 (1998): 126–46.

Troncoso Sánchez, Pedro. *Ramón Cáceres*. Santo Domingo: Editorial Stella, 1964.

Trujillo, Flor de Oro. "My Tormented Life as Trujillo's Daughter." *Look* 29 (June 15, 1965): 44–66.

Trujillo Molina, Rafael Leonidas. *Cartilla cívica para el pueblo dominicano*. San José de las Matas: Imprenta La Información, 1932.

———. *Discursos, mensajes y proclamas*. 11 vols. Ciudad Trujillo: Publicación Oficial, 1938.

———. *Discursos, mensajes y proclamas: Selecciones, 1952–1957*. Madrid: Ediciones Acies, 1957.

———. "The Evolution of Democracy in Santo Domingo." In *Dictatorship in Spanish America*, ed. Hugh M. Hamil, 155–73. New York: Knopf, 1966.

———. *Fundamentos y política de un régimen*. Ciudad Trujillo: Editora del Caribe, 1960.

———. *La nueva patria dominicana: Recopilación de discursos, mensajes y memorias del Generalísimo Rafael Trujillo Molina, Presidente de la República Dominicana, Benefactor de la Patria, durante el cuatrienio de 1930 a 1934*. Santo Domingo: Publicación Oficial, 1934.

———. *Obras*. Ciudad Trujillo: Editora Montalvo, 1956.

———. *El pensamiento político de un estadista: Discursos, mensajes, y proclamas del Hon. Dr. Rafael L. Trujillo*. 11 vols. Santiago: El Diario, 1946.

Tumin, Melvin M., and Arnold Feldman. *Social Class and Social Change in Puerto Rico*. Princeton: Princeton University Press, 1961.

Turits, Richard Lee. "The Foundations of Despotism: Peasants, Property, and the Trujillo Regime, 1930–1961." Ph.D. diss., University of Chicago, 1997.

United Nations. *Yearbook 1946–1947: Resolutions Adopted by the General Assembly during the Second Part of Its First Session, from 23 October to 15 December 1946.* New York: United Nations, Department of Public Information, 1947.

Vagts, Alfred. *A History of Militarism.* New York: Meridian Books, 1959.

Vargas, José Rafael. *Trujillo: El final de una tiranía.* 2nd ed. Santo Domingo: Editora Universitaria, 1993.

Vargas Llosa, Mario. *The Feast of the Goat.* New York: Farrar, Straus and Giroux, 2001.

Vega, Bernardo. *Control y represión en la dictadura trujillista.* Santo Domingo: Fundación Cultural Dominicana, 1986.

———. *Eisenhower y Trujillo.* Santo Domingo: Fundación Cultural Dominicana, 1991.

———. *Kennedy y Trujillo.* Santo Domingo: Fundación Cultural Dominicana, 1991.

———. *Nazismo, fascismo y falangismo en la República Dominicana.* Santo Domingo: Fundación Cultural Dominicana, 1985.

———. *Trujillo y el control financiero norteamericano.* Santo Domingo: Fundación Cultural Dominicana, 1990.

———. *Trujillo y las fuerzas armadas norteamericanas.* Santo Domingo: Fundación Cultural Dominicana, 1992.

———. *Trujillo y Haití, 1930–1937.* 2 vols. Santo Domingo: Fundación Cultural Dominicana, 1988.

———. *Trujillo y los Estados Unidos, 1930.* Santo Domingo: Fundación Cultural Dominicana, 1982.

———. *Trujillo y los Estados Unidos, 1945.* Santo Domingo: Fundación Cultural Dominicana, 1988.

———. *La vida cotidiana dominicana: A través del archivo particular del generalísimo.* Santo Domingo: Fundación Cultural Dominicana, 1986.

Vega Pagán, Ernesto. *Historia de las fuerzas armadas.* 2 vols. Ciudad Trujillo: Impresora Dominicana, 1955.

———. *Military Biography of Generalissimo Rafael L. Trujillo Molina: Commander in Chief of the Armed Forces.* Ciudad Trujillo: Editorial Atenas, 1956.

———. *Síntesis histórica de la guardia dominicana.* Ciudad Trujillo: Editorial Atenas, 1953.

Véliz, Claudio. *The Centralist Tradition of Latin America.* Princeton: Princeton University Press, 1980.

Vidal, Rafael. "La República Dominicana debe organizar un pequeño ejército." *Revista de la Secretaría de Estado de lo Interior, Policía, Guerra y Marina* (1927): 67–70.

Vorshirm, Alfredo F. *From Swastikas to Palm Trees.* Lauderdale-By-The-Sea: Phantom Books, 1991.

Weil, Thomas E., Jan Knippers Black, Howard I. Blutstein, Kathryn T. Johnston, David S. McNorris, and Frederick P. Munson. *Dominican Republic: A Country Study*. Washington DC: GPO, 1982.

Welles, Sumner. *Naboth's Vineyard: The Dominican Republic, 1844–1924*. 2 vols. New York: Payson and Clark, 1928.

Wesson, Robert, ed. *New Military Politics in Latin America*. New York: Praeger, 1986.

Wiarda, Howard J. "The Aftermath of the Trujillo Dictatorship: The Emergence of a Pluralist System in the Dominican Republic." Ph.D. diss., University of Florida, Gainesville, 1965.

————. *Dictatorship and Development: The Methods of Control in Trujillo's Dominican Republic*. Gainesville: University of Florida Press, 1968.

————. *The Dominican Republic: A Nation in Transition*. New York: Frederic A. Praeger, 1969.

Wiarda, Howard J., and Michael Kryzanek. "Dominican Dictatorship Revisited: The Caudillo Tradition and the Regimes of Trujillo and Balaguer." *Revista/Review Interamericana* 7, no. 3 (fall 1977): 417–45.

————. *The Dominican Republic: A Caribbean Crucible*. Boulder CO: Westview, 1982.

Wucker, Michelle. *Why the Cocks Fight: Dominicans, Haitians, and the Struggle for Hispaniola*. New York: Hill and Wang, 1999.

Yates, Lawrence. *Power Pack: U.S. Intervention in the Dominican Republic, 1965–1966*. Combat Studies Institute. Fort Leavenworth KS: U.S. Army Command and General Staff College, 1988.

Yunén, Rafael Emilio. *La isla como es: Hipótesis para su comprobación*. Santo Domingo: Amigo del Hogar, 1985.

Zaglul, Antonio. *Apuntes*. Santo Domingo: Taller, 1974.

Zakrzewski Brown, Isabel. *Culture and Customs of the Dominican Republic*. Westport: Greenwood, 1999.

INDEX

In *Studies in War, Society, and the Military*

Military Migration and State Formation
The British Military Community in
Seventeenth-Century Sweden
Mary Elizabeth Ailes

The Rise of the National Guard
The Evolution of the American Militia,
1865–1920
Jerry Cooper

In the Service of the Emperor
Essays on the Imperial Japanese Army
Edward J. Drea

You Can't Fight Tanks with Bayonets
Psychological Warfare against the Japanese
Army in the Southwest Pacific
Allison B. Gilmore

Civilians in the Path of War
Edited by Mark Grimsley and
Clifford J. Rogers

Soldiers as Citizens
Former German Officers in the Federal
Republic of Germany, 1945–1955
Jay Lockenour

The Militarization of Culture in the
Dominican Republic, from the Captains
General to General Trujillo
Valentina Peguero

Arabs at War
Military Effectiveness, 1948–1991
Kenneth M. Pollack

The Grand Illusion
The Prussianization of the Chilean Army
William F. Sater and
Holger H. Herwig

The Paraguayan War: Volume 1, Causes
and Early Conduct
Thomas L. Whigham

The Challenge of Change
Military Institutions and New Realities,
1918–1941
Edited by Harold R. Winton and
David R. Mets